THE BEST INTEREST
A NOVEL

BY
ERIC L. TERLIZZI

© 2021 by Eric L. Terlizzi. All rights reserved.

Words Matter Publishing
P.O. Box 531
Salem, Il 62881
www.wordsmatterpublishing.com

ISBN: 978-1-953912-15-2

Library of Congress Catalog Card Number: 2021939608

The Court shall determine custody in accordance with the best interest of the child.

750 Illinois Compiled Statutes 5/602.

Rarely do great beauty and great virtue dwell together.
Petrarch, De Remediis

Dedication

To the bench and bar of Marion County, Illinois. It has been my great good fortune and privilege to have practiced law for all these years amongst you.

Acknowledgements

Thanks to Shannon, Steven and Tammy at Words Matter Publishing for having faith in a previously unpublished author. Special thanks to my secretary, Karen Tinsley who somehow was able to read my chicken scratches and managed to find the time to type my manuscript. Thanks to my clients over the past 40 plus years who entrusted me with helping them in a time of need. I hope I never let you down. Special thanks to my partner, David Garner, the brother I never had, who taught me what it is to be a lawyer. And, finally and foremost thanks to my wife Vicki and my entire family for giving me a reason to try.

Hashtags

#divorce

#custodybattle

#doingwhatisbestforthechild

#legalthriller

#thebestinterest

#ericterlizzi

CHAPTER 1

Nick Barnett of the law firm of Ford, Ford, Osgood, Barnett and Thomas had experienced better days. It wasn't just that he had lost the case. Any lawyer who had been in practice sixteen years got used to losing. Maybe you didn't grow to like it, but, eventually, you got used to it. As Winthrop "Old Man" Ford had told Nick the day he had hired him sixteen years earlier: *if you aren't losing some, you aren't trying the tough ones.*

Nick knew that any halfway competent lawyer could win every case he tried. Just settle or dump the tough ones and try the dead-bang winners. If it didn't piss him off so much he would almost be amused by the peacocks that strutted around crowing about how many straight trials they had won. One of Nick's own partners, Larry Osgood, had a bit of that peacock bullshit in him.

No, it wasn't losing the Metcalf trial that had him in such a foul mood. It was the way he had lost and the stakes that were involved. Metcalf was a custody case and the future of two young children was at stake. Nick could be as cynical as the next guy when it came to fighting over money or land. But when you were arguing over the future and well-being of kids...well, that was a whole other ball game.

Being a father, if only every other weekend, Friday at 6:00 to Sunday at 6:00, and alternate holidays and two weeks in the summer, had cured him of any incipient cynicism when it came to custody cases. And there was not a shred of doubt in Nick's mind that his client, Louis Metcalf, was the better parent. But Judge Westbrook had assumed the bench back in the days when mothers invariably got custody, especially if the kids were young. *Tender years* doctrine the law used to call it. *Bullshit*, Nick called it. And then there was that damn psychologist, Miranda Cox. Metcalf had been Nick's fourth trial with Dr. Cox as either the other side's expert witness or the court-appointed expert and it was becoming increasingly obvious that the woman had never met a man she would consider psychologically competent to change a dirty diaper.

And Mrs. Brenda Metcalf. What a piece of work that woman was. Manipulative, lying, scheming. Her life's goal was to make those two little boys hate their daddy as much as she did and Nick was sure that by losing the case he had enabled her to do just that. Maybe Louis Metcalf wasn't the brightest bulb in the lamp. His judgment certainly wasn't the best. Selma was a small town. Did he really expect that he, a 33 year old high school science teacher could carry on an affair with a twenty-year-old waitress at Pizza Hut for six months and not get caught? But, my God, to get caught, flashbulbs popping, in the back seat of his Buick on the high school parking lot! That was not good, especially since his paramour, Melissa, had been his student only three years earlier.

So Brenda Metcalf had good reason to bear a grudge and to think in less than glowing terms of her now ex-husband. But there hadn't been a shred of evidence that Louis Metcalf had been anything other than an exemplary father. By all accounts, he had been the primary caretaker. He had been the one bandaging the bloody knees, giving baths, reading the boys their bedtime stories, making supper while Brenda was occupied going to meetings of every club, organization and group within three counties. Anything to be out of the house and away from the kids. No wonder, Nick rationalized, Louis had succumbed to Melissa's more than ample charms.

It was so painfully obvious to Nick that Brenda's sole object in life was to punish Louis for his indiscretions by making his boys hate him. Why couldn't the judge see it? Why couldn't Dr. Cox, a trained professional, see it? Anyone could see it on the boys' faces. How they'd look away when their father entered the room and glance nervously at their mother, clearly aware of what fate awaited them behind closed doors if they demonstrated the slightest affection.

It's my fault, Nick berated himself. *I should have recused Westbrook. I should have found a better expert to counter Dr. Cox.* He had little doubt that within a few years there would be no further contact between Louis and the boys. Brenda would see to that. She'd do anything she could to obstruct and interfere with visitation. After a couple of years of Brenda's brainwashing, the boys would actually grow to hate their father. He'd seen it too many times to figure it would turn out any different this time. For the first year or two, Louis would fight to force visitation, to hold Brenda in contempt. But eventually, he knew, Louis would tire of the games, of the expense, of forcing his two boys to continue to see him when they genuinely hated him. Eventually, Louis would drop it and pray that someday when the boys were older, they'd understand what had happened and how hard he had tried. Maybe someday, if he could put his bitterness and pain behind him, he'd start a second family. Nick could only hope for Louis' sake that, if he did, love would be lovelier the second time around.

He completed the drive back from the courthouse in neighboring Butler, parked, and went straight to his partner, Rosa Thomas', door. He could have talked to Stu or Larry, his other partners, but Stu would only be interested in how big a fee he had gotten out of Louis Metcalf. Larry would simply tell him everything he had done wrong...hell, he already knew that...and how he would have kicked Dr. Miranda Cox's ass all over the courtroom. And Nick was in no mood for Stu's lectures or Larry's bullshit.

Winthrop Ford's son, Stuart, joined the firm four years before Nick did, and became senior partner upon his father's death. Less than a year after Nick joined the firm, Winthrop Ford had keeled over dead right in the middle of a trial in the Martin County Courthouse. *At least,* Nick thought, *he died with his boots on.* To Nick's eternal dismay, Stu became self-designated "Financial Management Partner" upon his father's untimely demise. Nick hardly considered himself an idealist. He acknowledged that he liked a buck as much as the next guy. But for Stuart Ford, the practice of law was a business, pure and simple. Stuart would be willing to bear any burden, fight any foe, tilt at any windmill, take up any cause so long as, and only for so long as, the client was willing to pay him two hundred fifty dollars an hour to do so. Most lawyers hated the two words *you lose* more than any others. For Stuart Ford, the hated words were *pro bono.*

Larry Osgood, Nick's other partner, was sought out by Stuart and joined the firm two years before Nick had. Larry, in his brief tenure before joining Ford, Ford, and Osgood, had developed a well-deserved reputation as a pit bull. Let Larry sink his teeth into a case and you knew he wasn't going to let go until the other side was dead and buried. Stuart and Larry were a good fit. Larry couldn't balance his own checkbook. He knew nothing about money except how to spend it. Nor did he seem to care all that much. He would have spent two dollars for every dollar he made whether he made twenty grand or two hundred grand. Stuart and Larry each cared about one thing. Stuart...money, and Larry...winning. Larry Osgood lived to kick ass. Only instead of doing it in a barroom or back alley, Larry did it in a courtroom.

Nick had watched in open-mouthed amazement once as Larry had brutally cross-examined a seventy-five-year-old grandmother to the point where Nick was fearful the old lady was going to meet the same fate as Winthrop Ford had in that very same courtroom. Mercifully, the Judge had finally declared a TKO and put a stop to the mauling. It had never even occurred to Larry that the jury, looking on in horror, might not appreciate him brutalizing an old defenseless woman right in front of them. What had amazed Nick even more was how Larry had bragged about it afterward. Nick could remember it like it was yesterday. "Did you see how I kicked that lying bitch's ass? She was begging the damn judge for mercy by the time I was done with her. Damn, that felt good."

Nick was surprised that Larry had not yet been disbarred or shot. In fact, there were times Nick would have volunteered to do the latter. But Larry was effective in his own way. His reputation as a no-holds-barred street fighter grew by leaps and bounds after he joined forces with Stu Ford. He now had someone to look after the financial end and could concentrate all his efforts on what he loved most about the practice of law: destroying people. It was getting tougher and tougher for Larry to try cases. His reputation preceded him and most of the attorneys within the adjoining ten counties would rather have gone on a date with Lizzie Borden than litigate against Larry. Larry's cases settled, early and often. And thus, despite Larry's best intentions, he made money by the bucketful. He didn't have a single friend in the bar and that's just how he wanted it. Lawyers, insurance adjusters, judges all detested trying a case involving Larry...so usually, they didn't. Nick had heard Larry complain more than once recently, "These sons of bitches 'round here are so afraid of me, I can't try a God damn case to save my life."

But as much as his partners, Stu and Larry, got on his nerves, he had to admit, however grudgingly, that they were each effective in their own way. Stuart, more due to his last name and his father's fifty years of practice than due to his professional skills or personality, was a rainmaker. He brought in clients by the drove. And you could take it to the bank that if Stu signed up a client he or she was a well-paying client. He also somehow managed to be an effective restraint on Larry's profligate ways. Larry was always wanting to buy new computers, hire more secretaries, get the latest new expensive technology. But the firm checking account required Stu's signature as Financial Management Partner. And if Stu had had his way the secretaries would still be using Royal typewriters and carbon paper.

So Stu brought the clients in, gave Larry the tough and the big cases and distributed the rest to Nick and Rosa. Consequently, the two of them were left doing the divorces, the real estate, representing Selma First National Bank and doing all the other grunt work that was too genteel for Larry's taste and not lucrative enough for Stu's.

But Rosa...Rosa he could talk to. Rosa would listen. Rosa would understand. She would offer empathy, not pity, and as low as Nick felt today, probably a hug too. Rosa Thomas, 30, five years out of law school, was the brand new junior partner at Ford, Ford, Osgood, Barnett and Thomas, and, of course, the only woman. A woman could never have been hired as an attorney, so long as Winthrop Ford had been alive. But Old Man Ford, the firm's founder, had died not long after Nick had joined the firm. Nick had been second chairing the Old Man in a trial over whether a veterinarian had killed their client's prize bull when Winthrop Ford had suddenly stopped cross-examining the vet, turned around, looked Nick straight in the eye with an oddly quizzical expression, turned red in the face, clutched his chest, shit his pants and keeled over dead. The vet jumped down from the witness stand and tried CPR on him but his lifesaving efforts were no more successful with the old man than they had been with the prize bull.

Nick had to threaten to break up the partnership to get Stu and Larry to agree to hire Rosa. The two considered Nick's ultimatum and knew that neither of them had the time or the inclination to do the work Nick was doing. They eventually capitulated and Rosa had been hired as an associate fresh from Southern

Illinois University Law School.

Nick knew it was a gamble to force his partners to hire a kid straight out of law school. If law school hadn't changed since he graduated, she wouldn't know shit about actually being a lawyer. Stu had reminded him several times that his father would roll over in his grave if he knew a *girl* lawyer had been hired at the firm that bore his name. It was lucky, Stu added, that his father had passed before too many *girl* lawyers had started practicing in Martin County. Larry had also been forthcoming with his skepticism. She just didn't seem tough enough to Larry. Didn't have enough balls to survive in this business. When Nick pointed out that she, in fact, had no balls, Larry replied, "My point exactly, Nick. The girl's got no balls."

But when they were convinced that Nick's threats to leave were real and when faced with the prospect of having his divorces, custody battles, real estate closings, and foreclosures dumped on their laps, they relented. Five years later it had taken the threat of both Nick and Rosa leaving to get them to admit Rosa to the partnership.

Naturally, Nick had ended up being Rosa's mentor. Neither Stu nor Larry gave her the time of day. Nick and Rosa were handling the same types of cases, even working together on some of their bigger files. Nick liked being Rosa's mentor. She was intelligent, eager to learn, could cuss like a drunken sailor on shore leave, and had a wicked sense of humor that she would repeatedly ambush Nick with when he least expected it. He had felt big brotherly towards her. At least until they both became single. When the firm had hired Rosa, she had been engaged. She and her fiancé were planning on getting married the following summer. But Stan, an unemployed wannabe writer, had found that the bucolic life in the small town of Selma, Illinois wasn't as Faulkneresque as he had imagined it would be. According to Rosa, it was, in Stan's succinct analysis, "too fucking boring." Jobless, laying around the house drinking beer by the case, Stan had insisted, as the titular head of their as of yet unformed family, that they move and that Rosa get a job in Chicago where he would have more excitement and more opportunities. "Opportunities for what?" Rosa had countered, "to drink more beer?" Their engagement, mercifully, was terminated.

Rosa had occasionally mentioned some casual dates here and there. But decent, educated, single men who didn't drink beer by the case were in short supply in Martin County and Nick had not heard her mention anything about any boyfriends or relationships in quite some time.

Nick's divorce followed less than six months after Rosa's broken engagement. It had come as a complete shock to Nick. Looking back, he realized that was only because he hadn't been looking around. The signs had been everywhere, but, consciously or subconsciously, he had chosen to ignore them. That is, until Sheila had packed Natalie off to grandma's and Nick had come home to meet Roger who would be moving in next week, and could Nick please not make a scene and make all of this any more difficult than it already was. Nick did not make a scene. He politely declined Larry's offer to "sue the cocksucker for alienation of affections and to rip him a new asshole." Nick had gathered his things, kissed Natalie goodbye, and found himself a bachelor apartment within walking distance of the office. Four long years ago and somehow, though he doubted he ever would, he had adjusted. He had adjusted to being a weekend dad, to writing child support checks to *Sheila Davis*, to seeing Roger, Sheila, Natalie and their new addition, baby brother Jason, drive through town in their maroon mini-van.

Both Nick and Rosa had realized that their nearly simultaneous introduction to single life was rife with potential for danger. Stu had also recognized it, taking Nick aside and cautioning him, "Look Nick, now that you and Rosa are both single, don't be getting any ideas. You keep it in your pants, buddy. I'm not having this firm sued for sexual harassment. Million-dollar verdict against a Chicago firm last month...got it?" "Thanks for your concern, Stu," Nick had replied.

There arose a palpable tension between Nick and Rosa. They enjoyed each other's company and made each other laugh. And Rosa was, to Nick's mind, an attractive woman. Certainly not attractive in the beauty pageant or movie star sense of the word. Stu had once, in a private moment with Nick, described her as "funny looking." "Damn," he had commented to Nick, "legs and a figure to die for. Too bad she's got a funny-looking face." Nick had become almost personally offended and had forced Stu to retract his slander and offer an apology. But, if he had been honest with himself, he would have had to acknowledge that Stu's opinion would probably have represented a majority one. Perhaps *funny* was a poor choice of words; maybe *different* was better. There was something just slightly different about her face. Something yes, but not something Nick could pinpoint. The longer he knew Rosa, however, the more the different nature of her appearance struck him as attractive. Maybe even exotic.

As Stu had pointed out, though, whatever deficiencies Rosa had in facial beauty, she more than made up for with a stunning figure and wonderfully shapely legs all perfectly proportioned on a tiny five-foot one-inch frame. Her trademark short skirts and sky-high heels had scandalized a few of the older secretaries and Stu's wife but they had all eventually accepted it as something they had no control over. Larry simply ignored her, appearing as if he couldn't have cared less whether Rosa paraded around the office naked. On the other hand, Nick had caught Stu ogling Rosa on several occasions when she had been wearing a particularly short skirt. But the ever-present fear of a dreaded lawsuit kept Stu from so much as acknowledging that Rosa was a different gender. He treated her exactly as he treated Nick; which is to say as a means to make money; a cog in the profit-making machine he so carefully oversaw.

Several years ago, Nick and Rosa had been working late. It was hot, they were tired and Rosa was tilted back in her office chair, her feet propped up on her desk crossed at the ankles, her heels long since discarded, her short skirt made even shorter by her slouched posture in her chair when Nick suddenly realized in the middle of discussing strategy on how to cross-examine the defendant's expert that he would like nothing more at that exact moment than to sweep Rosa's desk clean, place her on it and ravage her. When his subconscious thoughts suddenly and uncontrollably became conscious ones, he muttered an excuse about having a headache and beat a hasty retreat. He glanced over his shoulder as he left her office and thought he noted an expression of disappointment, perhaps of rejection, in her eyes.

Ever since he had been the perfect gentleman around Rosa. But there were times when he had to wonder, *was I right? Did she want me that night?* Those thoughts had been on his mind more and more of late, as loneliness had begun taking a toll on Nick's psyche. Four years since the divorce. A few flings here and there. Even a very regrettable encounter with a professional for the first and only time in his life when he had been in New Orleans on a business trip. That encounter had left him even lonelier. *Maybe, just maybe,* Nick thought, *I made a mistake that night with Rosa. Maybe I should find out if there is any attraction on her part. Then to hell with Stu and his fear of lawsuits. If she wants me, she can have me. Life's too short to wait forever. I'm forty-one. She's thirty. She's going to meet someone someday. Then it will be too late.* He decided that, as subtly as he possibly could, he would probe and see if she was interested. Maybe a dinner invitation. Ostensibly to talk about cases, of course. But who knows where it might lead? He tried to erase the frown from his face and the nervousness from his demeanor and knocked on Rosa's door.

"Come in," came the unseen answer. Nick opened the door and stepped in, briefcase in hand. Rosa was seated at her desk. An eclectic menagerie of manila file folders, papers, pens, paper clips, staplers, sticky notes, phone messages, a framed photo of her and her parents, a bottle of Evian and a half-eaten, half brown apple covered its walnut top. Rosa took one look at Nick and said, "Oh, Christ, we lost Metcalf?"

"Is it that obvious?" Nick replied.

"Well, last week when you won the Johnson trial, you ran in here with a grin like a kid in a candy store, so it didn't take Miss Cleo to figure out this one didn't go quite so well."

"Shit, Rosa," Nick replied, "it was my fault. I should've recused Westbrook. I should've found a better expert to rebut Dr. Cox. I should've..."

Rosa rudely interrupted his self-flagellation. "Stop. You're one of the best divorce lawyers in the circuit. You know that. How many straight custody trials did you win before Metcalf? Seven? You didn't know Westbrook would try it 'til you walked in the courtroom Monday morning. A recusal would've meant a couple of months' delay. And as far as Cox is concerned, you'd think the judges would have figured out her agenda by now. It's not your fault Nick. It's the nature of the beast. Forget it."

Nick sat down across the desk from Rosa. "This one's going to be tough to forget. Sure, Louis screwed up, but you wouldn't believe that woman. She's already got those little boys afraid to even smile at their own dad. And she gets up on the stand and cries and carries on like she's June Cleaver and that damn Westbrook falls for it. He didn't even take it under advisement. Ruled right from the bench. And that bitch Cox...how the hell can she sleep at night...?"

Nick didn't get the hug he was relishing but Rosa smiled at him, reached across the desk and gently squeezed his hand. "Why don't you take the rest of the day off? I'll provide cover for you if Stu asks where you're at. You look like you need it."

Nick looked up and their eyes met. She continued to lightly squeeze his hand. *Well if I'm going to do it, it's now or never,* Nick thought. *Just ask her if she's free for dinner tonight and if she looks embarrassed or declines, tell her it was to discuss some files and I'll catch her at the office tomorrow...*

Nick swallowed hard and plunged ahead, "Thanks. Maybe you're right...Say I was wondering, maybe if you're not..." Rosa suddenly took her hand back and interrupted him again, "Oh, hey, before I forget it, let me tell you my good news...I'm so excited...."

"What?" Nick inquired.

"I've got an honest to goodness, real live date tonight," she said with a big smile.

Nick forced himself to smile back. "Really?" he said. "With who?"

"Guy named Mike Sellers," she replied. "Just started work at Farmer's Bank. Met him at the health club. He was working out. Abs to die for. I was practically drooling...."

Nick laughed, trying desperately to conceal his disappointment and his jealousy. He knew there was no chance any woman would ever drool over his abs. Sneer maybe, belch possibly, but drool? No way.

"Only one problem..." Rosa continued.

"What?"

"He's only twenty-six. I'm gonna feel like a cradle robber."

Nick wanted to say, *yeah, you're right Rosa, he's much too young,* but instead answered, "Oh come on, what's four years? Go for it, girl."

Rosa took a sip from her Evian, raised her eyebrows, gave a lecherous look and replied, "Believe me, I intend to. He's not going to be on the market long. I can guarantee that. By the way, you haven't filled me in forever. What's going on with your love life?"

"What love life?" he frowned.

"Come on. You're just not trying. A divorced lawyer. A nice guy. All those divorced gals out there. Get with the program!"

"I don't know. I don't think they want *nice guys* anymore. Maybe I should be an asshole. They'd probably be beating my door down then."

Rosa laughed. "Want me to check around the health club,

see if I can find any available women that seem like your type?"

Nick demurred. *I'm looking at my type right now,* he thought. *Why did it take me so long…too long…to realize it?* "No. I appreciate the offer, but I'd rather make my own mistakes…"

"Boy, the glass is really half empty, isn't it?" Rosa interjected.

"Hey, it's been a long week."

"Jeez," Rosa said, "I really hate to ask you for a favor in the mood you're in."

"Go ahead, ask away," he replied. "Anything to distract me."

"I've got a client scheduled tomorrow afternoon…" she paused, glanced at her desk calendar and continued, "Livinia Taylor. Married to a pathologist who practices in Mt. Vernon. Going to be contested custody. Lots of assets. Family money. Probably good for a twenty-five thousand dollar retainer. Anyway, she was in a huge hurry. Asked to see you, but Pat figured you'd still be in trial on Metcalf so she put her on my book. But Judge Swanson just scheduled an emergency T.R.O. for tomorrow and I hate to put this gal off. Pat said she was really antsy to get in. Can you see her and take the case?"

"Oh, God…I'm not sure I'm up to another contested custody. I've got four pending right now. Things just aren't going all that great right now…"

"Look, you fall off the horse, you get back on. You said you needed a distraction."

"I do."

"Well, this one sounds nasty. Plus, a twenty-five thousand dollar retainer! Stu will give you his *Partner of the Month* award. Maybe even his parking spot."

Nick chuckled. "Okay. All right. I'll see her. But I'm not even promising I'll take the case. Damn it, Rosa, you could talk me into representing a serial killer."

Rosa smiled, batted her eyes, and assumed a wholly contrived southern belle accent and demeanor, "Well, I do declare, it just must be my innate charm, Mr. Barnett, I surely do." Nick laughed, rose and against his better judgment added, "Have fun tonight," as he left her office.

"Believe me, Mr. Barnett," he heard her say, still the southern belle, "I do declare I most certainly will."

CHAPTER 2

Nick took Rosa's advice and played hooky the rest of the day. In the mental state he was in, he knew he would have been worthless at the office anyway. He got quite drunk. At home. Alone. Not a good sign, he knew. The alcohol merely fueled his depression which alternated between lamenting that he blew the Metcalf case and lamenting that he blew any chance with Rosa. He inflicted further torture upon himself by fantasizing all night about precisely what activity Rosa and Mr. Six Pack Abs were engaged in at any given moment.

By his second six-pack, he had convinced himself that he hadn't blown it with Rosa at all. He'd never even had a chance in the first place. *What was I thinking?* he scolded himself. *Rosa's thirty, smart, and sexy as hell. What would make her look twice at me?* Middle age paunch, some gray starting to sprout at the temples. Those same temples rapidly receding despite his heroic effort to stem their retreat. *What in the hell was I thinking?* he thought again, as mercifully exhaustion, depression and alcohol finally conspired to end his masochistic ruminations and sleep overcame him.

He decided to do penance for playing hooky by getting to the office by seven a.m., a good half hour before even Stu arrived. His head finally quit pounding after lunch and he was at least able to consider the prospect of facing the balance of his day when he remembered the favor he had promised Rosa and that Mrs. Livinia Taylor was coming in at one-thirty. *Oh great,* he thought, *I am at absolute rock bottom and I'm taking on another hotly contested custody battle. I barely have the energy or motivation to do a small claims today.* He took two more Excedrin then answered his buzzing phone.

"Mrs. Taylor's here, Nick," Pat, his secretary, told him.

"Okay," he replied, "be right there."

Nick had no court scheduled that day so he was wearing Dockers and a polo shirt. He walked out to the firm's waiting room. There were two women seated there, aimlessly flipping through magazines. One was wearing jeans and a tee-shirt, no makeup and was packing a good thirty pounds she didn't need. The other woman took his breath away. He couldn't help but stare. There, seated in his waiting room, was...Audrey Hepburn... incarnate. His mother had worshiped Audrey Hepburn and apparently, in his impressionable youth, a mental image of Audrey Hepburn as the perfect woman had been hard-wired into his brain. And now...here she was...seated in his waiting room. She was immaculately dressed in a cream-colored suit covering a pumpkin-colored silk blouse. A single, elegant string of what undoubtedly were real pearls circled her neck. She wore a matching pearl bracelet on her left wrist. Pumps and a bag, which clearly were not purchased at any store in Martin County, Illinois, matching the cream color of her suit, completed the ensemble. Her shoulder-length brunette hair and her makeup were perfectly and subtly done so as to appear not to have been done at all. And the piēce de rēsistance; gloves. Cream-colored of course to match the suit, shoes and bag. Gloves! Nick thought the last time he had seen gloves on a woman when the temperature was above thirty degrees was...well...never. He recognized that he lacked the most rudimentary knowledge concerning fine ladies' apparel, but he mentally guessed that, head to toe, the woman was a ten thousand dollar walking fashion show. He swallowed hard and inquired, "Mrs. Taylor?" not knowing which of the two women would respond.

The fashion show uncrossed her legs, demurely smiled, rose, extended her gloved hand, then said in a voice that was at once utterly feminine, yet utterly powerful, "Mr. Barnett, I presume?" Nick approached her. She smelled wonderful. For an instant, Nick didn't know whether to be excited or disappointed that the fashion show was his prospective client. On the one hand, it would be a sensual delight...visually, olfactory and auditory... to have Ms. Fashion Show for a client. But Nick also knew that he, like so many men...and women...was intimidated by a stunningly beautiful woman and that despite his best efforts, his professional judgment would be slightly off-kilter representing Mrs. Livinia Taylor. That he would try maybe a little harder than he should. That he, subconsciously, would be trying to please her. That he would be subtly intimidated from reading her the riot act if it became necessary...as it so often was with clients. And even though he knew he would try to be vigilant to guard against these things, he knew just as surely, that they would happen. On the other hand, Miss Jeans and Tee Shirt sitting in his waiting room would be a pop fly. He could treat her just like a male client. Yell at her if he had to...tell her this is the way it's going to be or you get a new lawyer...be in total complete charge of the case and the client. Just as it should be and had to be when your professional reputation was on the line.

But with Ms. Fashion Show he had ceded the high ground before he had spoken his first complete sentence to her. He knew, especially in their first meeting, he would have to assume control, let her know that if she desired the benefit of his professional skills that he would have to call the shots. He also feared that there could come a time when he might simply be unable to say *no* to Mrs. Livinia Taylor. Nick suddenly realized it had been several seconds since she had offered him her hand and he was simply standing there, attempting to take her in, nearly catatonic. Finally, he took her hand. "Yes...yes...please call me Nick...my office is this way. Care for anything? Coffee? Water?"

"Bottled water, please," she replied as she retrieved her gloved hand back from his grip before adding "...Mr. Barnett."

She followed Nick back to his office, seated herself in one of the client chairs facing Nick's huge desk, set her purse on the floor and crossed her legs at the ankle. Nick returned with her bottled water, handed it to her and she began before he uttered a word, "Mr. Barnett, I wish to get a few things clear before we go any further. Is that all right?"

Nick leaned back in his office chair. He had already retrieved his *Dissolution Client Questionnaire* from his desk drawer and had been about to start going through the checklist of questions and information with her. *So much for being in control,* Nick thought. *She's already put me in my place for being too familiar now she's going to take charge of our initial conference.* "Okay, Mrs. Taylor, but..."

"Fine then," she interrupted, "first, my husband is a doctor. A pathologist. He makes a lot of money and he comes from a rather moneyed family. They have virtually unlimited resources to fight me..."

"Mrs. Taylor, I'm not concerned about..."

"Well I am," she again interrupted with a sharp edge to her voice. She then smiled. "I apologize Mr. Barnett. Please just let me voice my concerns and then I'll be quiet and let you speak your piece...."

"Fine," Nick replied, realizing that Mrs. Livinia Taylor was likely going to do whatever Mrs. Livinia Taylor decided to do irrespective of what he said.

"Thank you. The Taylors...especially the other Mrs. Taylor, my mother-in-law, are...how shall I put it...let's just say they're rather different. I met my husband Daniel in college at Northwestern. Daniel was not exactly a scholar but certain contributions from the Taylor family trust to certain endowment funds at Northwestern assured that Daniel would graduate and then get into med school. We dated, and after several months got engaged, but, for personal reasons, I broke the engagement a short time later. My future mother-in-law was not particularly upset when I did so. No woman, believe me, no woman will ever be good enough for her little Danny Boy. You know, she actually still calls him that.

Anyway, you're a busy man, I'm sure, and you don't need the entire history, but we went our separate ways. Four years ago we met at a medical conference in Chicago. I was working in pharmaceutical sales, doing quite well, actually. I had been briefly married and divorced. Daniel was still single. Well, we decided to catch up on old times and one thing led to another and if you can believe this...me, a thirty-five-year-old drug rep...became pregnant after one...indiscretion. Like a pimply-faced teenager on prom night.

He had established his practice in Mt. Vernon and it seemed as if he had matured and cut the apron strings and I...I was thirty-five...I wasn't getting any younger...I wanted children. So we got married. I quit work. We certainly didn't need the money. I moved here and we built a house outside of Selma and our daughter, Jessica, was born. Unfortunately, I was quite wrong about my husband's maturity level and I was wrong about the apron strings, too." She paused momentarily, sipped her water and continued. "Mr. Barnett, our marriage is a sham. It's already over in every sense but legally. And he and that mother of his have made my life and my daughter's life a living hell..."

"I'm so sorry," Nick interjected.

"...and I've finally come to the conclusion that I have two choices. Live like this forever, be miserable and allow my daughter to be miserable, or end this marriage and save my life and my daughter's."

"Sounds like an easy choice," Nick commented.

"Well, it's not. You'll think I'm being dramatic, but these people...this family...are evil. She's told me that if we ever divorce, she'll guarantee that Daniel will get custody of Jessica if it's the last thing she does..."

"Mrs. Taylor, please, let me..."

She reached over, unsnapped her bag and removed some tissue. She looked up at Nick, tears in her eyes.

"I CANNOT, WILL NOT, let that happen Mr. Barnett."

"Please..."

"No...let me finish," as she spoke, she reached back into her bag and pulled out a checkbook. She began writing as she continued to speak. "I've seen the handwriting on the wall for some time. It hardly took a genius. I had quite a bit of money saved up before we married. Daniel's not aware of it, but I cashed in my 401(k) and I've been putting substantial sums away for the last two and a half years from the 'allowance' he pays me just preparing for this day." She tore off the check she had been writing and held it in her gloved hand. "I've just written a check to your firm for a hundred thousand dollars..."

"Please," Nick protested, "Mrs. Taylor..."

"I've done a good deal of research," she continued, ignoring his protest, "you and your firm come highly recommended. These people will stop at nothing. Believe me. I need to know when I hire an attorney that I have his undivided attention. I don't want my calls returned two days later. I don't want to call for an appointment and be told you're tied up but maybe you could squeeze me in next week. I expect for this check..." she waved it around with a dramatic flourish "...that I will be buying you, lock, stock and barrel. I want the best. The best experts, the best attorneys. If you need more help, you tell me and you'll have it. There's more where this came from," she added, again waving the check. "I am not some stupid housewife. I have been planning for this moment for some time. I will not lose my daughter to those people. Now, do you understand my position?"

Nick leaned back further in his chair and thought for several silent moments. His gut told him to tell Mrs. Livinia Taylor that he appreciated her coming in but that he had many other clients and all of their cases were important. That he could not promise favored treatment to one client over another no matter the size of her check. That he couldn't guarantee results, particularly in a custody case, no one could. And that, overall, he thought it would be best if she took her business elsewhere. But he could almost hear Stu now, "you turned down a hundred thousand dollar retainer in a God damn divorce? That's coming out of your partnership share, buddy. If you think Larry and I are eating that because you're getting lazy, you're nuts."

Of course, it will take time and effort, he rationalized, *but the bottom line is it's just another divorce like hundreds of others I've done. Hundreds of others at five, ten, twenty thousand maybe. But certainly none at a hundred thousand dollars. Hell, with a hundred grand in the bank, I can coast a little the next few months, take fewer cases, have more time for the demanding Mrs. Livinia Taylor.* He looked at her. A tear was meandering down her cheek. If possible, it made her even more beautiful. Nick sat upright in his chair. He grabbed the *Dissolution Client Questionnaire.* "Spelling of your full legal name, including maiden name?" he asked as he read question No. 1.

CHAPTER 3

Nick rarely spent more than an hour in the initial client in-
terview. He spent nearly three hours with Livinia Taylor.
When they were done, Nick looked at the yellow legal pad he
had been writing notes on and saw that he had filled seventeen
pages. They finished and he escorted her to the front office door.
They passed Stu in the hall on the way out and Nick could see
Stu do a double-take, his eyes practically bugging out of his head.
Nick made an appointment for her to return the next day at four.
He knew he would be at the office until midnight, drafting the
Petition for Dissolution, the Petition for Emergency Temporary
Relief, the Petition for Exclusive Possession of the Marital Home,
the Financial Affidavit, the Notice of Intended Child Custody
Dispute, the Attorney Fees Contract, a half dozen other docu-
ments that he would normally dawdle over for a week. But he
had a hundred thousand dollars of Livinia Taylor's money in his
pocket. He intended to start earning it.

After escorting her out the door, Nick turned and was surprised to see Stu still standing in the hallway. Nick hoped desperately that he could walk by Stu and return to his office and get back
to work without some inane comment from Stu. No such luck.

"JESUS H. CHRIST, Nick," Stu said, then whistled. "Are
you paying her to be a client or is she paying you?" he asked

through his chuckle.

"She's paying," Nick replied.

"Well God damn, I don't know what her case is about but I'll trade you three foreclosures and a condo conversion for her."

"You don't want it, Stu. Nasty divorce and custody fight."

"Shit," Stu answered, then returning to his favorite subject added, "you got a decent retainer I hope?"

"How's this," Nick replied taking Mrs. Taylor's check from his front shirt pocket and holding it in front of Stu's face. Stu's eyes bulged out even further than when he had first set eyes upon Livinia Taylor. Feminine beauty was one thing, but a hundred grand, that was another. "Jesus H. Christ! A hundred grand! Are you kidding me? Well Nick, my boy, as of this moment you are Partner of the Month!" Stu slapped him on the back.

Nick smiled, "Thanks. I've got a feeling I'm going to earn it though. And I better start earning it right now." Nick started down the hall towards his office. Stu grabbed him by the elbow and stopped him. Nick turned to face Stu.

"One other thing, partner."

"What?"

"That is one nice piece of ass there..."

"For God's sake..."

"Hear me out. You just watch yourself. You're divorced, not been real successful with the ladies lately..."

"Fuck you, Stu."

"She'll be vulnerable. Just be careful is all I'm saying. Hell, she could tempt Larry..."

"Are you done?"

"Yeah. I'm done. I just don't want this firm to get its tit in the ringer because your dick's not in your pants."

Nick turned back around and stomped to his office. When he reached his door he stopped and turned. Stu was still standing in the hall. "Have I ever told you that you're a complete and total asshole?" Nick said.

"Many times, partner. Many times," came the reply.

***

Nick retreated to his office and closed the door. He leaned back in his chair, propped his feet on the desk and devoted some thought to his newest file: Taylor v. Taylor. His opponent, Dr. Daniel Taylor was a pathologist with a thriving practice. According to Livinia, his family had made a fortune in Southern Illinois coal decades before the pollution laws had shut down virtually all the mines. His grandfather and father had apparently invested it prudently. Dr. Taylor had only one sibling, an older sister, and rumor was that the two of them were in line to share over thirty million dollars when the family matriarch, Mrs. Martha Taylor, passed on. There was no question that his opponents had the resources to fight a long tough battle. No doubt that they could outspend Nick and his client a hundred to one. But as Nick had tried to point out to Livinia, Dr. Taylor and his mother had two and a half strikes against them before the first pleading was even filed.

First, Dr. Taylor was a man. Jessica was a three-year-old little girl. No amount of money, not the best expert in the world, could change that unalterable fact. Second, Dr. Taylor was not only a man, he was a doctor. A busy doctor, who, besides running a medical practice, spent dozens of hours per week helping his mother manage the family trust fund. If he got custody, he'd have to leave Jessica in the care of nannies and babysitters 24/7. Third, Livinia was, and had been since the day Jessica was born, a stay at home mom. As best he could tell she appeared to be neither a drug addict nor a child abuser.

Nick had played the game long enough to know money talked. But, for Christ's sake, a stay at home mom versus a busy, overworked doctor who would dump the kid on babysitters? We were talking about the custody of a three-year-old girl. He'd take those odds any day. He had tried to assure Livinia that unless she had some deep dark secret she was not revealing to him, her chances of winning the custody battle were excellent. Of course, he wouldn't take it lightly. He'd prepare for war. Hire experts, psychologists so as to leave no chance that they could possibly lose. But the bottom line was he'd much rather have his dog in this fight than the other guy's.

There would be plenty to fight over besides custody. Livinia had not been boasting when she had told Nick that she had been preparing for this day for two and a half years. She told him that she had gotten ahold of financial records, tax returns, trust accountings, that gave a detailed and highly revealing picture of the Taylor financial empire. She even chuckled as she told Nick how she would get up late at night and rifle through her husband's briefcase while he slept, scanning documents into her laptop. "Just like a bad spy movie!" she had laughed. If the documents contained information anywhere close to what she had promised, they would be a gold mine.

Livinia Lawrence had been told in no uncertain terms that if she expected to become Livinia Taylor she would have to sign a prenuptial agreement, prepared by the Taylor family law firm, Farnsworth, Livingston, Sedgeworth & Jagger. And she would sign it "as is." No negotiations, no modifications. As her future mother-in-law, Martha Taylor, had told her, "Dear, I would prefer that my grandchild, if in fact it is my grandchild, not be a bastard. On the other hand, I am not about to let some little trollop who couldn't keep her legs crossed get her hands on this family's hard-earned resources. You can sign it and I will endeavor to put my feelings aside and welcome you and your child into this family. Or you can refuse to sign it and it will be a cold day in hell before Danny Boy marries you. And then you and your little bastard child can fight until hell freezes over for every nickel you can scrounge. Do I make myself clear, dear?"

Livinia had replied that *yes* she was quite clear but that it was Livinia's recollection that Martha's precious little Danny Boy had played some significant part in the creation of her grandchild to be and perhaps she should have this same conversation with him. Livinia held out for a week after that conversation before facing reality and signing the prenup. Two weeks later a hastily arranged wedding, modest by Taylor family standards, was celebrated at Our Lady of Hope in Mt. Vernon. Seven months later, Jessica Erin Taylor came into the world.

The documents that Livinia had promised to produce for Nick would be crucial. If they demonstrated anything close to what Livinia had represented, they would show that Daniel Taylor had been worth at least twice, perhaps three times, what he had disclosed on the prenup. A failure to fully and honestly disclose one's assets was a solid basis to throw out a prenup as invalid. Nick was convinced that between the misstated assets, the fact that Livinia had been pregnant, and had been threatened by her future mother-in-law, and finally, that the lawyer who had reviewed the prenup for Livinia had been handpicked by and paid by Martha Taylor, the prenup wasn't worth the paper it was printed on.

Nick, as he had feared, had worked on the Taylor divorce until after midnight. He knew in a case like this you had to strike first: hard and fast, shock and awe. He would hit them with a Petition for Emergency Temporary Exclusive Possession of the Home. He leaned back in his chair and smiled just imagining the look on Dr. Daniel Taylor's face if he got evicted from his own home before he even knew what hit him. A Petition for Emergency Temporary Custody would also be filed as well as one for Temporary Alimony and Child Support. When Dr. Taylor's lawyers answered and cited the prenup as a defense to payment of alimony and loss of the house, Nick would have a Petition to Set Aside the prenup ready to file with all the documents attached which demonstrated that Dr. Taylor had grossly understated his assets.

If things went according to plan he would hit them so hard and so fast in the first two weeks of the litigation that maybe, just maybe, they'd sue for peace and negotiate a fair settlement for his client. And then Nick could pocket the hundred thousand dollar retainer he'd been paid with maybe thirty hours in the case. Not a bad hourly rate, he chuckled to himself. Of course, he had been doing divorce law long enough to know that the exact opposite response was as likely, if not more so. If Martha Taylor was half the bitch Livinia had described, there would be no easy settlement. It would be war. Long, nasty, bloody and expensive.

There was one other opening volley they could fire. He had questioned Livinia briefly to see if there had been any hint of domestic violence. "Now, has Dr. Taylor ever been physically violent with you?" he asked.

She laughed in reply, "I'm sorry to laugh at your question. But Daniel?...violent?...if you knew him you'd know how ridiculous that question is. Violence assumes a certain amount of passion...a loss of self-control. Believe me, Daniel is capable neither of passion nor is he capable of losing control. Mustn't make a scene, you know."

"Well, fine," Nick replied, "it's just that, the petitions and motions we've been discussing, they all require notice to your husband. They give him time to obtain an attorney, to prepare a defense against our petition, but if, and I repeat if, he is physically abusive or even threatening we could get an emergency order of protection...giving you the house, evicting him, giving you custody of Jessica, without even notifying him or his attorney..."

"I see..." Livinia interjected.

"But please, understand they'd still be entitled to a hearing within ten days. It's just, usually, in practice, they're not ready for a hearing in that short time. They ask for a brief continuance. Then we ask for one, ask for a psychological evaluation. It can stretch out for months. And all that time you've got custody of Jessica and possession of the house. The longer it goes on, the less likely the judge is to change things. Do you follow my point?"

Livinia appeared contemplative for a few moments before replying. "Yes, I believe I do."

Nick sat in his office playing with a paperclip, bending and unbending it until it finally heated and broke, recalling the conversation from yesterday. *Shit,* he thought, *it's already happened. I was trying to impress her, trying to show her how damn clever I was, how tough, how "win at all costs" and I virtually suggest she provoke her husband into threatening her so we can use it against him. Have I sunk that low?* he asked himself.

He glanced at his watch. Three forty-five. Mrs. Taylor would be in shortly. He prayed that she hadn't acted on his less than subtle suggestion. He would straighten things out as soon as she came in, make sure she understood he was in no way suggesting that she should provoke or initiate a fight, that that would be unethical conduct and he would not countenance it. As he was preparing his speech for her, there was a soft knock on his door. "Come in," he said.

Rosa entered and took a seat across the desk from Nick.

"So," Nick inquired, "how was the hot date with Mr. Six Pack Abs?"

Rosa looked at him, grimaced, and replied, "A train wreck. A fucking train wreck."

Nick could not suppress a slight smile and chuckle.

"It's not funny," Rosa snapped. "My first real date in six months and it's a disaster."

"Sorry," Nick apologized. "What happened?"

"God, I don't know if I should even be telling you this stuff. You're a guy..."

"Thanks for noticing," he interjected.

"You know what I mean. Jesus, Nick, if you tell anyone this stuff, I'll hunt you down and..."

"Okay, I get the picture," Nick replied. "Just tell me what happened."

"I should've known that a guy with a perfect body would make for a perfectly bad date. First, he doesn't even pick me up. I have to drive to his place. Then we go to dinner, a lousy burger joint, and all he talked about all night long was himself...and working out...and what he could bench press or jerk or squat... and how I could improve my body if I did this or that exercise. I didn't realize my body needed so much improvement. Then... we go Dutch on dinner and we catch a movie, Dutch again, of course, and this prick has his hand up my skirt before I can even take a bite of popcorn."

"That does sound like a lousy date," Nick said. "Sorry."

"That's not the best part...you swear this is between us...I mean it, I'll..."

"Jesus, want it in blood? Yes, my lips are sealed. What could be worse than a Dutch date with an obsessed, egocentric exercise nut with wandering hands?" Nick replied.

"Well, I'm thinking, this is one of my all-time worst dates. I also can't help but wonder if...you know...the rest of his body... you know...matches what I'd already seen at the health club..."

"You didn't!" Nick interjected.

Rosa blushed, "Of course not. But I'm thinking, *damn I've had to listen to this asshole all night. I had to pay for my own dinner and movie. I had to wrestle with him the whole movie. I need some revenge.*"

"So, what did you do?"

"Well, we have to go back to his place to get my car. So, of course, Mr. Stud Muffin invites me in. So I decide to play along... bat my eyes, hang all over him, a real femme fatale. We go into his place and it's like a God damn dorm room...Britney posters on the walls...a beer can pyramid in the living room. I swear this guy had the maturity level of a frat pledge boy. So I tell him I'm just going to excuse myself to the powder room for a minute and freshen up and *get ready* and I start to unbutton my blouse and I ask him if he'd like it if I kept my high heels on. And, of course, he starts drooling and grinning like the cat that ate the canary. I'm in there like five minutes trying not to laugh. Then I come out...still fully dressed of course...and he's standing with his back to me, in front of a full-length mirror, stark naked, doing this

Hans and Franz *pump you up* thing and I broke down, laughing hysterically, and he turns around, and he's already got his pump primed and he looks at me still dressed and gives me this *what gives baby?* look. And I just look him up and down for a good ten seconds then say, 'No thanks, I've seen better' and walk out the door."

"Rosa, I can't believe you did that!" Nick said, barely getting the words out over his laughter.

"Oh, God, it was priceless. By the way, the rest of his body definitely did NOT match his abs." She held up her thumb and index finger three inches apart.

Nick wiped his tears of laughter and waited a moment before replying " Oh Jesus, that's funny. But I'm sorry your date was so bad...I guess."

"What do you mean, *I guess?*" she asked, looking perplexed. Nick realizing the implications of what he said, stammered, "Oh...nothing...I'm sorry. I didn't mean that."

"I swear I'm about ready to give up," she sighed. "Okay, enough about me and my love life, and remember..." She zippered her mouth.

"How could I forget?"

"So, did you see Mrs. Taylor?" she asked, changing the subject.

"Yeah."

"Take the case?"

"Yeah."

"How's it seem?"

"Tough."

"Boy, you're in a talkative mood. What's wrong?"

"It's just...you ever have a case that when you take it, your gut's telling you not to, but you do anyway?"

"Every day," she responded.

"Well, my gut was telling me loud and clear to send Mrs. Livinia Taylor elsewhere."

"But you didn't?"

"No."

"Why not?"

"A hundred thousand dollars."

"JESUS CHRIST, Nick! That's the retainer?"

"Yeah."

"How'd you talk her into one that size?"

"She volunteered it. I never even asked. She also told me there's more where that came from."

"Holy shit. Did you tell Stu?"

"Yeah. I'm officially Partner of the Month."

"I'll bet. So what's the problem that this Mrs. Taylor causes your gut?"

"I've got two."

"And they are?"

"One. She's rich, or at least her husband and his family are."

"Well, last time I checked, that's a good thing in a divorce..."

"I know, but the rich clients are high maintenance. You know that."

"Yeah, but they pay for the privilege. What's number two?"

"She's beautiful."

"So she's rich and she's beautiful."

"Yeah."

"And that's your problem?"

"Yeah."

"Nick, you need a vacation."

"She's not just beautiful. She's...she's striking. And she was dressed like...well...like Audrey Hepburn. She had gloves on, for Christ's sake."

"Do you hear yourself? You're wanting to turn down the biggest divorce fee you'll ever get because your client wore gloves? What's wrong, really?"

"God, I don't know. I just feel...intimidated dealing with her." He hesitated to continue, but she had just confided in him and he thought he'd return the favor. "I haven't been a whole lot luckier with the opposite sex lately than you have, and well, it's just tough...".

"Good Lord, she's a client, you'd get disbarred, you'd get us all sued."

"Give me some credit. I know that. I'm not going to do anything. But, as you so astutely pointed out...I'm a guy...I can't help...looking."

Rosa crossed her legs and played briefly with Nick's pen holder on his desk. "Look, you want me to take it? I'll give you credit for the fee, or I could just sit in on the conferences?"

"No. Thanks, but I don't want it to look like I need a chaperone. You were honest with me. I was just being honest with you. That's all. I'm okay. Really."

"Okay. But if things start getting...weird...you let me know. Got it?"

"Yeah, sure."

Nick's phone buzzed and he picked it up. "Yeah?...okay, thanks," he said into the phone. He hung the phone up and smiled at Rosa. "Speak of the devil. Mrs. Livinia Taylor is in our waiting room as we speak."

CHAPTER 4

Nick walked out to the waiting room to greet Livinia. He had been sure to wear one of his best suits, a charcoal gray, muted pinstripe with a gray and maroon patterned tie, even though he only had a few small claims cases in court. Normally he saved his premium suits for important trials but he had felt self-conscious wearing his Dockers and polo shirt in his first meeting with the immaculately dressed and coifed Mrs. Taylor. He thought, or hoped, his best suit might level the playing field some. He rarely wore his suitcoat while in the office but he made sure to put it on before greeting Livinia. He even had Rosa check him out and straighten his tie before she left his office. "Jesus, Nick," she teased, "are you getting married or just meeting with a client? Sure you don't need a chaperone?"

Although Nick was prepared this time, Livinia Taylor nevertheless again took his breath away. She was sitting impatiently, legs crossed at the ankles. Today she was attired in a navy blue suit. A beige blouse, pumps and bag and blue gloves and hose complimented perfectly the blue of the jacket and skirt. A few pieces of understated gold jewelry, a broach, bracelet and watch, worn over her gloves, and today's surprise du jour, a small navy blue pillbox hat, completed the ensemble. Nick swallowed hard and tried mightily to conceal his apprehension. *It's just another client,* he scolded himself. *Get a grip.* He knew he needed to start taking charge before their relationship went much further.

"Good afternoon, Mrs. Taylor," Nick said as he extended his hand.

She did not rise, but extended and lightly shook his hand, "Yes, it is," she replied "Nick, would you mind? I have a box of documents, tax returns and so on, in the trunk of my car in your lot. It's the white Lexus. I'll wait in your office." With that, she rose, handed him her keys and began walking down the hall to Nick's office. She then stopped, turned and added, "Oh, a bot- tled water would be nice too." *God damn it,* Nick thought, *this is too much. I'll get her God damn box and her God damn water and then she and I are having a God damn talk before this thing goes any further.* Nick went out to the parking lot and retrieved the box and deposited it by his desk. He handed her the bottle of water and sat down.

"Mrs. Taylor..." he began.

"Please, Livie is acceptable," she interrupted.

Nick smiled briefly, then continued, "Mrs. Taylor, you were very up-front with me yesterday, I want to return the favor before this goes any further..."

"Certainly."

"You are no doubt aware that the stakes in your divorce and the amount of money involved are rather extraordinary...as was the size of the retainer you paid me yesterday..."

"I'm sure you'll earn it," she commented.

"I am too," he replied. "You are also aware, I'm sure, that you are..." he hesitated a moment then decided to plunge ahead. The air definitely needed some clearing, "...an extremely attractive woman."

"Yes," she replied nonchalantly, as if his observation was self-evident, which, of course, it was.

"Well, I want to be clear on some things up-front. First, while you are paying me, handsomely, I might add, I am the professional here and I am in charge as long as my name is associated with this case..."

"Well, certainly. I hope nothing I've said makes you think otherwise."

"Fine. Because otherwise, I'll be pleased to refund your retainer to you right now. And in the future, you come back to my office when I escort you back here. In the future, I will be pleased to help you bring documents in...if I am asked, not told, to do so..."

"Nick, please...may I call you Nick?" she looked contrite and Nick felt he had made his point. "I apologize. You can't imagine the strain I've been under. I'm aware that sometimes I can get a bit...overbearing. My mother-in-law uses another term to describe me. So please, I do want you to be my lawyer and if I get presumptuous again, don't hesitate to tell me. All right?"

"Yes fine...and I assume from this point on first names are appropriate, Livinia?"

"Yes, Nick, they are. Only it's *Livie,* please."

"Good. Should we tackle the documents in the box before we go over the paperwork I've prepared?" he inquired.

"First, can I inform you of something that happened last night?"

"Sure."

"As you know, Daniel knows nothing about my plans, about my seeing an attorney. A couple we know, the Richardsons, are divorcing and I casually brought the subject of their divorce up and said I thought it was ridiculous that Chris...the husband... was going for custody since Shelly stayed home and the kids are only five and seven.

Well, Daniel just exploded. He never loses his temper as I told you yesterday. But he was in my face, literally. Yelling, saying men have a right to custody too and women can be such... excuse my language...cunts, and what makes them think they're the only ones who know how to raise kids and that if I ever tried anything like that he'd guarantee that I'd regret it and have the fight of my life on my hands."

"Did he hit you?"

"No."

"Grab you?"

"No, but he was right in my face screaming. At one point, he did bump into me. I was shocked. I told him to stop screaming at me, I had a right to my opinions and then I went to the bedroom."

"Did Jessica see or hear this?"

"No. She was asleep already."

"What you've just described may be sufficient basis for an Emergency Order of Protection giving you the house and temporary custody of Jessica. In large part, it will depend on the judge. If Judge Westbrook hears it he'll give it to us in a minute. Judge Swanson may be a tougher sell. But, I have to know that you're being truthful with me, that what you've just described actually happened exactly as you've just described it. I need to know that nothing I said yesterday precipitated this. Do I have your assurance of that?"

"Yes, of course. I swear to God. I won't ever lie to you."

"Thank you. Okay. Here's the plan. We'll use the rest of today to go over the pleadings I've already prepared. Friday, tomorrow, I'll have Pat prepare a Petition for Emergency Order of Protection and an affidavit describing the confrontation. We'll ask for possession of the house and temporary custody of Jessica. You come back in, we'll get everything signed and ready. What will his schedule be Monday?"

"He'll be at the office by seven-thirty."

"Okay, the judge usually takes Emergency OP's at eight-thirty before court starts. Can you meet me at the courthouse in Butler Monday morning at eight-twenty?"

"Yes. I'll have to get someone to watch Jessica...but I can do that."

"Great. If we can get the order entered, we'll have him served with it before he heads home. The poor bastard won't know what hit him."

"Oh, God, that sounds perfect. It will be such a relief to get him out of the house. I don't think I could last another week. What about his mother, can I keep her away?'

"Sure. She's not on the title. She'd be a trespasser. Call the cops if she shows up and won't leave."

Livie laughed and reached across the desk and squeezed Nick's hand. "Oh my God! I can just see it. Mrs. Martha Taylor, matriarch of the Taylor empire arrested. Oh God, I'd give up everything in the divorce to see that."

"Livie, remember, it's important that you get through until Monday without him knowing about this. We have to have the element of surprise."

"Don't worry about that. He'll be surprised," she said with a smile.

"Understand that this is all just temporary. The first volley in what will likely be a very long and costly war."

"I understand."

"Good. Now let's start going through this paperwork."

"Okay," Livie replied as Nick got out the stack of pleadings Pat had spent the entire morning typing.

"Nick?" she added.

"Yes."

"I'm glad I chose you as my lawyer," she said with a smile.

"Well," he replied, "I hope you feel that way a year from now."

"I have no doubt that I will," she answered. "No doubt at all."

CHAPTER 5

"I don't like it," Rosa said with a frown.

"What's not to like? We get her the house and the kid before he even knows what hit him." Nick countered. He was speaking with a false bravado to cover up his own self-doubts about his proposed actions.

"Yeah, but it stinks," she replied. "It's one step above being totally unethical. These damn OP's are so abused. They're supposed to protect women from violence and instead they're used just like you're using it, to get a leg up in the divorce. It's like a damn race to the courthouse. First one to the courthouse gets the O.P. and wins. It sucks."

"That's our job, to win. We're getting paid a hundred grand to win. I have to use every tool at my disposal. If the legislature wanted to restrict OP's to situations involving physical violence they could have said so."

"Look," she replied, "it's just that you, me, this firm, well... excluding Larry, have never practiced law like that before. Why are you doing it for Livinia Taylor all of a sudden? Is it because of the money? Or is it something else?"

"What something else?" Nick snapped, knowing full well what something else Rosa was referring to.

Rosa could not help but notice the edge in his voice and

backed down. "I'm sorry. I didn't mean anything. I'm just wondering if it was a mistake to ask you to take the file."

"She asked for me initially. You told me that."

"I know. I know. I'm sorry. I didn't mean anything. It's just...I don't know. Maybe I'm still in a pissy mood because of that date the other night. I guess I'm just trying to tell you that you got where you are by practicing law in a certain manner; tough but fair. You've earned the reputation you have with the judges and other lawyers. This firm doesn't need another Larry. Don't change the way you practice law just for Livinia Taylor. No matter how much she pays you, no matter how good she looks."

Nick looked directly into Rosa's eyes and could see her concern. "If I didn't know better," he replied, "I'd think you were jealous."

"Maybe," she said almost too quietly for Nick to hear as she turned and retreated to her office, "you don't know better."

***

Nick went back to his office, sat down and leaned back in his chair. He tuned his Sirius to the smooth jazz station. "Shit," he muttered to himself. He knew it was too late to turn back now. He had already promised that come Monday morning they would be proceeding on the O.P. They would be declaring war and would be getting as many shots off as possible before Daniel Taylor even knew what hit him. *And what in the hell did Rosa mean by that last comment? Was she telling me she was jealous of Livie Taylor? That she's interested in me? Or was it just concern for me as a partner and a friend?*

Nick ran his hand through his thinning hair and muttered *shit* again. He attacked the stack of files on his desk with a vigor intended to distract him. At four-fifteen, he happened to glance at the clock in his office. *That's funny*, he thought, *Livie was sup-*

posed to be here at four to sign the O.P. paperwork. He picked up his phone and buzzed his secretary Pat.

"Pat?"

"Yes."

"Where's Mrs. Taylor?"

"No idea. Not here.

"Did she call?"

"No."

At five, just before Pat left for the day, he walked out to her desk. "Still no word?" he asked.

"No. Nothing. Want me to call?"

"No. No. We can't take a chance her husband would be home or see our number on the caller I.D. I'll try her cell from my office."

"Okay, Nick. See you Monday."

Nick smiled back, "Have a good weekend."

He walked back to his office muttering under his breath. "God damn clients." *I bust my balls,* he thought, *getting all this shit prepared and she doesn't show up, doesn't call. So now what happens Monday morning? Will she show up at the courthouse?*

He pulled out the file and found her cell phone number. She had warned him repeatedly about not calling unless it was a dire emergency, fearful that her husband might find out that a lawyer was calling her and put two and two together. *Well,* Nick thought, *this qualifies as an emergency in my book.* He dialed *67 then dialed her number. It rang five times, then the unmistakable voice of Livie Taylor began. "This is Livie. I'm sorry I'm away from the phone. Leave a message." Nick hesitated for a moment then proceeded. "Mrs. Taylor. Please call Mr. Barnett at your earliest convenience." He then thought he'd better create a cover in case somehow her husband got the message. "Umm...that couch you were interested in has come in." He hung up the phone and ran his hand through his hair again. *What the hell is going on?* he wondered. *The woman waltzes in here, plops a hundred grand on* *my desk, I drop everything I'm doing, we plan our sneak attack and then...she doesn't show. Well, she better have a damn good excuse.*

He quickly glanced through the stack of files on his desk and grabbed four or five that urgently needed his attention. He stuffed them in his briefcase. He planned, theoretically, to work on them over the weekend, but lately, theory and practice had become more divergent in his life. Although he felt guilty, he was almost glad it wasn't his weekend to have custody of Natalie. He wanted some alone time, some thinking time.

He went through the process of disconnecting his computer from the network and shutting it down then grabbed his brief-case. He saw Rosa's light still on in her office as he was leaving. He knocked on her half-opened door and entered. She was furiously multitasking; writing on her yellow legal pad, attacking the remnants of an apple, taking huge gulps from her ever-present Evian bottle and moving subtly and rhythmically to the music emanating from her stereo.

"Hey, Nick," she said as she quickly munched and swallowed some apple, "heading home?"

"Yeah."

"Big weekend?"

"No, nothing. Natalie's with her mom."

"Oh, sorry."

"It's okay. I need some time anyway," he said as he raised his briefcase to show her he was taking work home.

"All work and no play," she said, "not a good thing."

"Yeah, you're right. I guess I'm not in much of a playful mood though."

"What's wrong now?" she asked.

"Oh, you know...fucking clients, it's nothing. I'm okay." He tried, but did not look very convincing.

"Who?"

"Shit. You want a list?"

"No. Just public enemy number one."

"Okay. Livinia Taylor."

"I told you...things get weird, let me know. Maybe it's just not the right time for you to be representing her."

"No, it's not that. I drop everything, bust my balls...do things I probably shouldn't have for this woman...you know the whole O.P. thing...and then today she doesn't show up. Doesn't call. I call her cell, leave a message. Nothing. She's probably made up with hubby and is screwing his brains out as we speak. Maybe she'll get around next week to calling me and filling me in on what's going on and asking for her money back.

I called Judge Westbrook today to make sure he'll be there early Monday morning for an O.P. Now I have no idea whether she's going to show up in court or what. If it wasn't for the damn clients, this job would be easy."

Rosa chuckled slightly but could see he was greatly perturbed. She rose and walked over to him, sat in front of him on the edge of her desk and crossed her legs. She smiled and Nick smiled back. Neither spoke. He could sense the feelings deep within him surging forth like a tidal wave. *I better get the hell out of here before I say or do something I regret,* he thought. He smiled again and said, "See you Monday," and turned to leave. He was halfway out the door when he heard her say, "Nick?"

He turned and looked at her. She was still sitting on her desk, legs crossed. She was dangling a high heel off her upper foot and rapidly moving it up and down.

"Yeah?"

"Since you don't have Natalie...and...no plans...maybe... if..." she hesitated, looked at him, smiled, then plunged ahead, "want to maybe come over Saturday, say seven, and grill a steak and have a few beers and cuss about clients?"

"Gosh," he stammered like a nervous teenager, "...why sure... thanks, Rosa. I'll bring the beer."

"Okay, great," she smiled. "But one condition".

"What's that?" he asked.
"You say one word about working out and you're history."
"Deal," he said as he smiled, turned and left.

CHAPTER 6

Nick showered and then primped as he hadn't primped in years. He was uncasually focused like a laser beam on achieving a casual look. He was still wholly uncertain of Rosa's intentions. They could be entirely innocent. Perhaps she was just feeling sorry for Nick, and also perhaps, for herself. Just lonely and dreading the thought of another Saturday night alone. Perhaps they'd spend the whole night talking about clients and judges and cases and telling Stu and Larry stories. But, maybe, just maybe, Nick thought, there was more to it.

Nick realized he was terrible at reading women. He had been a late bloomer in high school, a bad case of acne and a skinny little one hundred fifty pound body draped over a six-foot-three frame doing little to boost his innate lack of self-esteem and sophistication. Then, following his father's wishes, or more honestly, his demands, he went to college at Rose-Hulman in Terre Haute to become, like his father, a mechanical engineer. The guys outnumbered the girls by a good ten to one and his college career did little to increase his experience or success with the opposite sex. He, like the rest of the nerds at Rose, had to get lucky to get lucky. Senior year his body finally blossomed and fulfilled its potential, his acne miraculously cleared and, lo and behold, he got noticed. He decided after three and a half years that mechanical engineering held almost as much interest for him as Japanese origami. He told his father, breaking his heart, took the law school admission test, did well and the following August enrolled as a first-year law student at the University of Illinois in Urbana. Within a month he had met Sheila, a senior in interior design, while washing dishes at her sorority. Six months later they were married. He had never asked himself why he was getting married at twenty-two, and with such a small amount of *experience* with women. At the time, it just seemed like the thing to do. Sheila wanted to. Half the guys in law school were already married and it sounded like an awfully grown-up thing to do. So they did.

Sheila graduated the following May and managed to get a job at the cosmetics counter at Famous Barr in the mall. Nick finished his last two years of law school while clerking part-time for a law firm in Urbana. Nick couldn't help but smile as he thought back to those years. They didn't have two nickels to rub together but he could not have cared less. As long as they had enough money to go out on Friday night to Deluxe Diner for the world's best fried cod sandwiches and some cold drafts, life was perfect. And they screwed as if the world was about to end. Mornings before school, noon rendezvous in the cramped back seat of their rusted old Chevy in the mall parking lot, before supper, or after, or even, at times, during. *Jesus,* Nick asked himself, *what happened?*

The firm he clerked for offered him a job when he graduated, but Sheila was the youngest of six kids. Her parents, three brothers, two sisters, their husbands and wives and thirteen nieces and nephews all lived in or near Selma. Sheila wanted to go home and have lots of babies. Her father, president of Selma First National, a client of Ford, Ford & Osgood, had heard that Winthrop Ford was looking to hire an associate. A few good words from Sheila's dad had iced the deal. Nick passed the bar in August and started at Ford, Ford & Osgood in September. In October, Sheila got pregnant and in December she quit work. The following July Natalie was born. They still didn't have two nickels to rub together, only now it wasn't so much fun. Sheila was wanting to get pregnant again immediately. She had, after all, two sisters and three sisters-in-law to compete with and they all had a substantial head start.

It didn't take Nick long to weary of their constant discussions about the issue. He tried to explain that it took time, years, to establish yourself in this business. That there would be many more lean years ahead before he would start to reap the benefits of his education and hard work. But patience was not a virtue Sheila held in high regard. Their discussions gradually morphed into arguments. The arguments morphed into sullen silence made all the more intolerable by the continued fecundity of Sheila's sisters and sisters-in-law.

When they separated and divorced, they still had only one child, Natalie, but the niece and nephew count had risen to nineteen. Nick was not surprised that Sheila was pregnant with Roger's child less than a month after their own divorce.

***

He looked in the mirror and marveled at the irony of the fact that while hair no longer grew on his head, it had begun to sprout prodigiously on his ears and nose. *What was that about?* he wondered. *Some kind of divine practical joke?* Despite his less than devout religious convictions, he could almost picture God, chuckling in heaven, as Nick struggled to shave his ears without slicing them off. He finished shaving, splashed a moderate amount of Nautica on his face...the Brut was for everyday use. Too much would ruin the casualness he was so ardently striving for.

He found as he drove his Acura to Rosa's house, that he was nervous. *Why?* he asked himself. *Why not?* came the answer. It dawned on him that Rosa had, unnoticed, become his best friend. The first one he went to when he needed to unload. The one he could confide in and who confided in him. The one who could, invariably, make him laugh, irrespective of his mood. And the one person, tellingly, he wanted to be with more than any other. He thought back and realized that Sheila had never been his best friend. He had loved her, yes. He had lusted for her, yes. But their personalities, their moods, their aspirations were so totally different. They had made love hundreds of times and had produced the love of his life...his daughter Natalie. But he realized as he passed a slow-moving hog truck on Route 161 that they had never shared the ultimate intimacy, friendship.

Was it possible, he wondered, *for friendship and sexual intimacy to coexist?* He had a few, very few, friends who described their spouses as their best friends. And he had wondered: *Did they say that just for public consumption? Or was it true? Did they really think of their spouse as their best friend? If so, how incredible. How absolutely wonderful that one could share one's life, one's body, one's children, with your best friend.*

He pulled into Rosa's driveway, immediately realizing that he had never been to her house before. It was a small, restored Victorian on the south side of Selma in an older neighborhood where the lawns were carefully manicured and the children notable only by their absence. It appeared that most of the homes were owned by older retired couples. Rosa's home was cheerfully painted in contrasting tones of green and gold giving it a gingerbread look. There was the obligatory front porch and Victorian tower. A striking menagerie of flowers, which Rosa constantly, and which Nick could now see, rightfully, bragged about, surrounded the foundation. A porch swing moved rhythmically with the gentle evening breeze, its chains squeaking at the apogee of each arc.

Nick sat in his Acura for a few moments and took in the view. It told him a lot about Rosa and he liked everything it said. Begrudgingly he shut off the ignition, silencing James Taylor singing "You've got a Friend" from the car's stereo.

He grabbed the two cold six-packs of Rhinelander Lager off the front seat. He had saved them from his fishing trip to Eagle

River last summer but could not think of a better occasion to break them out. He doubted, but still hoped, that Rosa would recognize that sharing his last two six-packs of Rhinelander's with her was only one small step short of pledging his undying fidelity.

It was April and the weather was expressing its feminine side, changing moods in an instant. Thunderstorms had rumbled through in the morning and again in the early afternoon, but it had since cleared. The sun had broken through just as he had pulled into Rosa's driveway, creating a glorious evening. The ozone was heavy in the air as he set one of the six-packs down and knocked on the front screen door.

"Coming," he heard Rosa yell with a voice that seemed to come from the far end of the house. Nick picked up the six-pack he had set down and waited for Rosa to come to the door. He pressed his nose to the screen and tried to peer through the screen door and reconnoiter, but it was rusted over and there were no lights on in the front room. He startled as a light suddenly went on in the living room. He instinctively moved his head back from the screen and saw Rosa trotting to the door. She was wearing a pale blue tee shirt and jeans and was barefoot. Her jet black hair was pulled back into a ponytail, but curled tendrils told Nick she had been as focused on achieving a casual look as he had.

She opened the door. "Come in, Nick. Glad those storms stopped. It would have been a crime to have to fry those steaks I bought on the stove." She glanced down at the six-packs he was holding. "The kitchen's this way," she said, gesturing. "Rhinelander Lager? Never heard of it. German?"

"You could say that," Nick replied. "I go fishing with some old law school buddies in northern Wisconsin every year. When we're in northern Wisconsin, we drink Rhinelander, period. I always bring a stash back with me. These are my last two from last year's trip," he added, hoping to impress her.

"Wow. I'm honored. Figured you'd save something that precious for a hot date," she replied. Nick smiled, trying to hide his disappointment over the fact that Rosa apparently did not consider their dinner engagement a hot date.

They killed the first six-pack sitting in lawn chairs while Rosa grilled the steaks and what proved to be a delicious green pepper, onion and mushroom medley on the Weber. By the time they were done cooking, darkness had descended and they retreated to a tiny table in the dining room where they began on the second six-pack and ravenously consumed the steak and vegetables. They kept each other in stitches most of the evening with war stories about clients and judges and other attorneys. The amusement of their stories increased in direct proportion to the amount of beer consumed.

Rosa topped off the steak dinner with a homemade cheesecake and coffee. The cheesecake was wonderful. Better even that the authentic Chicago cheesecakes a lawyer friend occasionally sent to Nick. He savored the sensual delight of the cheesecake on his palate and, after five beers, began to hope, as he gazed at Rosa, that there would be more sensual delights before the night was over.

As they nibbled at the remnants of their cheesecake, their conversation dwindled. They occasionally glanced up and smiled at each other, each wondering if the other would first broach the subject that was obviously on both their minds. The living room stereo was playing softly, the music drifting quietly into the dining room where they were still seated. A James Taylor song had apparently been in the cloud awaiting its turn and was now playing. Nick perked his ears when he discerned the beginning of "You've Got a Friend."

"Funny," he said.

"What?" Rosa asked.

"James Taylor was singing 'You've Got A Friend' on my car radio when I pulled into your driveway...and it just made me think that...you know...that I'm thankful that I have a friend." He looked up from his plate and smiled.

She returned the smile, "Me?"

"Yeah, Rosa, you. Of course."

She took a last sip from her coffee. "God, I love James Taylor."

"Yeah?" he replied. "Me too. We should see him if he comes to Riverport."

"Yeah, we should," she answered, then asked, "would that be a date?"

"Is this?" he answered with a question of his own.

She rose, grabbed his hand and lead him silently through the living room, down a short hall and to the bedroom. She pushed open the door and turned and faced him.

"Yeah, Nick," she said, "I think it is."

***

They started slowly, but soon the combination of lust and alcohol overpowered their self-restraint. Arms, legs, clothes and sheets intertwined in a frenzy of passion. Rosa was on top, kneeling over the prone Nick methodically moving up and down. The phone rang. "Oh Jesus," Nick moaned, "do you have to answer it?"

Rosa stopped moving and swept her hair back off her sweaty brow. "It could be my mom, my dad's not been well." She pointed to the phone.

Together they scooted to the edge of the bed and Nick half rolled over with Rosa still over him and grabbed the phone off the nightstand. He handed it to her.

"Hello," she said, still straddling him. "...Oh yeah. Look, Mr. Cole, can I call you back later...no...I know it's important to you...." She stopped talking for a moment and rolled her eyes to Nick. "No, she doesn't have to let the kids go if you haven't called first...I've told you that..."

Great, thought Nick, *a damn client.* He decided to have some fun and without warning thrusted into her. Rosa moaned involuntarily. She put her hand over the phone and laughed. "Jesus, Nick," she scolded, "cut it out, it's a fucking client."

"No," he said laughing harder than her, "it's two fucking lawyers," and thrusted again.

She put the phone back to her ear, "Mr. Cole...sorry, it's just the TV...Look it's really not a good time...I know..." She tried to dismount from Nick but he wasn't done playing. She attempted to rise and as she did he grabbed her hips and pulled her back down onto him. As he pulled her down, her left knee missed the edge of the bed. She started to fall off the bed, Nick held on tighter and desperately tried to keep her from tumbling off. But gravity had already trumped Nick's overmatched efforts to restore equilibrium and the two of them, still fused together, tumbled off the bed. They crashed to the soft carpet. The phone went flying. The fall broke them apart and for an instant, they lay on the floor next to each other.

They could barely hear, "Miss Thomas...Miss Thomas..." coming from the cordless before they both burst out into uncontrolled laughter. Nick stretched for the phone, grabbed it, and disconnected.

"You okay?" he asked her when he finally regained some degree of control.

"Yeah. You?"

Nick got up off the floor, looked up and down at himself for a second, and said, "Yeah, all parts accounted for."

"Okay," Rosa said as she too stood up, "you better think of something good I can tell Mr. Cole."

"Tell him," Nick replied, "that it was your fucking partner's fault," and they both dissolved into laughter again.

CHAPTER 7

Nick spent a good part of Sunday wondering what to do. He had an overpowering urge to call Rosa. His parting words to her on Saturday night had been, "I'll call you." They should talk like adults, figure out what it all meant, where they were headed, and especially how to handle things at the office. On the other hand, he was terrified that today Rosa would wake up with a hangover, mortified at what she had done and, especially, who she had done it with.

He tried to remember the last time he had laughed so hard and so long and had had so much fun. *Damn,* he thought, *two people who can have that much fun together, deserve to be together.* He spent half the day Sunday at the office trying to make a dent in the growing mountain of files on his desk and preparing for a brief divorce trial he had scheduled for Monday. His divorce client, Joe Martin, was a nervous little hypochondriac who always seemed to be suffering from some new ailment. Nick prayed the poor guy could make it through the trial without having a heart attack, stroke or nervous breakdown.

He was relieved that Rosa didn't show up at the office on Sunday. He didn't know what he would say to her and wanted more time to think about it. Sitting at his desk, he noticed the Taylor file. He still had received no word from Livinia Taylor and had no idea what was going on. His best guess was that she had reconciled with her husband and would be in next week for a refund. *She'll get her money back, alright,* he thought, *less ten grand for my trouble, but she'll also get a lecture from me about common courtesy.* He double-checked the pleadings Pat had prepared for Livinia Taylor's signature on the odd chance that she would show up in court Monday morning as they had planned. He made one more attempt to reach her cell phone but got her voice mail again and disconnected before leaving a message.

***

Nick arrived at the office early Monday and then left for court in Butler before Rosa arrived. She was generally one of the first to arrive at the office, usually before him, and he couldn't help but wonder if her lateness today was intentional. *Shit,* he thought, *I should've called her yesterday. I should've gone over there. We should've talked. But I didn't want to act like I was coming on too strong...like I was assuming Saturday night meant we were in a relationship. By the time I figure out how to deal with women,* he mused, *I'll be too old to enjoy them.*

Even though he was early, he drove the Acura at breakneck speed, knowing he was immune from tickets on the way to court. Besides, after sixteen years of practice, he knew all the cops in the county and had represented a good number of them. He found a parking spot and bounded up the three flights of stairs to the third floor. He had not noticed Livinia Taylor's white Lexus parked anywhere near the courthouse but nevertheless was nervously anticipating her presence. As he bounded up the last of the few steps, he glanced at the Monday morning crowd. At first glance, he did not see her, but Nick wanted to search more carefully. He did see Joe Martin sitting in one of the chairs, sweating profusely and chugging his bottled water. Joe saw Nick and jumped up out of his chair as if assisted by a bolt of lightning.

"Nick, I gotta talk to you," Joe blurted between gulps of water.

Nick smiled back and replied, "Sure thing, Joe," while he continued to peruse the crowd. He knew Livinia Taylor would stand out like a sore thumb in the sea of blue jeans and tee-shirts of the Monday morning crowd but he still continued to look.

"What's up?" Nick inquired.

"I've got...this problem..." Joe started to explain.

"What problem?"

"Well it's just...my kidneys...and I went to the doctor and he said it was a urinal infection. I have to drink all this damn water and this medicine he gave me...well, I have to piss like a racehorse, every couple of minutes."

"So," Nick replied, unimpressed.

"So, what am I gonna do on the witness stand? This medicine makes my mouth so dry and I have to have my water, and I'll need a break every few minutes and..."

Nick was angry. Angry at himself for not having the balls to call Rosa yesterday. Angry at Livinia Taylor for not calling him or letting him know what was going on. And angry at Joe Martin and his God damn hypochondria. They had spent half of each conference and telephone call talking about Joe's various medical problems, real and imagined, and he had little interest this morning in conducting an extended discussion on the condition of Joe's urinary tract.

"I'll tell the judge about your problem. Give me a signal... bat your eyes...if you need to pee," Nick replied brusquely before turning and walking away. He briefly reconnoitered the rest of the third floor but knew it was not likely that he could have overlooked Livinia Taylor. *That bitch! That rich bitch!* With false bravado fueled by anger he thought; *no way I'll represent her now if she plops another hundred grand on my desk.*

He chatted with some other lawyers in the Judge's Chambers and, in his anger, forgot to tell Judge Swanson about Joe's problem. Joe and Nick sat in the spectator benches for fifteen minutes waiting for Joe's case to be called. True to his word, Joe had left the courtroom twice during that span.

"Did you talk to her about, you know...?" Joe whispered to Nick.

"Yeah, I told Judge Swanson," Nick lied. Joe was sweating even more profusely and Nick could see his shirt palpating as Joe's heart beat like a rabbit's.

"Don't forget our signal," Joe whispered and batted his eyes.

Nick had to turn his head to avoid laughing at the absurdity of it. Judge Swanson called Joe's case and he was sworn in and took the witness stand. Joe's soon to be ex-wife and her lawyer sat at the other counsel table. They had settled ninety-five percent of the case and Nick figured Joe's testimony would only take ten or fifteen minutes. Nick's mood robbed him of his natural empathy and he unilaterally decided that Joe could just damn well make it through ten minutes of testimony without taking a piss.

By the time Nick rose and asked, "State your name," Joe was already furiously batting his eyes. Nick suppressed a smirk and repeated, "State your name."

Joe looked up at the Judge and batted his eyes at her too and said, "Joseph Martin."

Judge Swanson looked quizzically at Nick.

"Age?" Nick asked.

Joe crossed his legs and leaned forward. He was now manically batting his eyes, nodding his head towards the courtroom exit and turning red in the face.

"Forty-seven," he groaned.

"Occupation?"

Joe was frantically squirming and crossing and uncrossing and recrossing his legs at a furious pace.

"Contractor," he finally grunted.

The judge could take it no more. "Mr. Martin," she inquired, "are you alright?"

"It's...you know...my problem," he said, assuming the judge

knew what he was talking about.

"No, Mr. Martin," she replied, "I do not know. But you look as if you are about to explode right there on the witness stand. Do you need five minutes to compose yourself?"

"Oh Jesus, YES!" Joe screamed and was off the witness stand and out the door in a flash.

Judge Swanson leaned forward and glared at Nick over her reading glasses. "Counsel, do you know what's wrong with your client?"

Nick rose and assumed a sheepish demeanor. "I'm sorry your Honor. He did mention something about a urinary tract infection. But I guess I didn't realize it was so urgent. I apologize on his behalf."

"Well, for God's sake, Mr. Barnett," she scolded, "go out there and tell him to raise his hand if he needs a break. I don't want to have to call the janitor in here to clean up a mess."

"Yes, your Honor," Nick replied.

***

Joe managed to get through the rest of the testimony with two more breaks. When they were done, they retreated to the hall and he asked Nick. "What happened? God, didn't you see me batting my eyes?" He paused and once again demonstrated his very proficient eye batting technique. "I thought I was going to piss my pants."

"Sorry," Nick replied, "I forgot. I thought you said you were going to raise your hand if you had to go."

On the drive back to Selma, Nick berated himself. *That was mean, cruel even. That wasn't the real me. Or at least I hope it wasn't. I was being a bully. Livinia Taylor shit on me, so I shit on poor Joe. Isn't that how it always works? The predators higher up the food chain feeding on the weaker ones?* For penance, he decided he'd knock a hundred dollars off Joe's bill.

***

He pulled into the office parking lot and immediately noticed Rosa's Grand Cherokee in its spot. He had teased her incessantly about why she, a single gal, drove a mommy mobile but she had defended her choice of vehicle by noting that she felt safe in it and it was good in the infrequent snows of Southern Illinois.

He retrieved his briefcase from the back seat, entered the office, grabbed his phone messages, chatted with Pat for a few moments then went to his office. He debated with himself. *Should I go straight to Rosa's office?* he wondered, *or wait for her to come see me?* He settled the debate when he realized he would not be able to get a lick of work done until he talked to her. He checked himself in the mirror, squirted breath spray in his mouth, walked the few steps down the hall to her office and asked her secretary, Betty, if she had anyone in with her.

When Betty told him, "No," he knocked softly.

"Come in," came the reply.

Nick entered. Rosa was seated in her high back tufted desk chair with several files spread out in front of her. She glanced up and smiled briefly and added casually, "Oh, hi Nick, what's up?"

"Hi," Nick replied as he took a seat across the desk from her. "Um..." he began haltingly, "...I thought...maybe...we should talk."

Rosa had directed her attention back to her files. "What about?" she said without looking up.

"Come on, you know what about," he pleaded.

She put her pen down and looked up at him. "I don't know what you think happened Saturday night. Maybe you think that's something I do all the time..."

"No, please, I don't think that..."

"Well, anyway, I thought Saturday was rather...special...and it made me rethink a lot of things and...well, I guess I just expected that you might want to call or talk to me about it before now, especially since you said you would."

"I'm sorry...."

"Look. I'm a big girl. We're both partners here. It's not like you're my boss. So you made a mistake. We can still work together fine. You and Stu have nothing to worry about..."

"Please, give me a chance to explain," he begged.

"You don't owe me an explanation. We had a little too much to drink and had some fun Saturday. Now it's Monday. Time to get back to work." She picked up her pen and started writing again.

Nick stood up, leaned over and grabbed her hand, stopping her from writing further. "Rosa," he said firmly, "I didn't call because I was afraid."

She retrieved her hand from his grip and leaned back in her chair. "Afraid? Of me?" she asked.

"No...yes...not of you," he paused and tried to explain. "I was afraid that, maybe, you know, it was no big deal for you..."

"No big deal!" she exclaimed.

"Yes, I didn't know. The truth is I've had...feelings...for you for years, and I guess I just never really thought you felt likewise."

"Even after Saturday night?" she asked.

"Yes, even then. Look, I'm considerably older than you. I have a mirror. I know what I look like. I just didn't want to be one of those pathetic old bald guys chasing a younger woman. I didn't want to seem like I was coming on too strong."

Rosa laughed.

"What's so funny?" he asked.

"Oh God, Nick. You don't know a whole lot about women, do you?"

"I guess not."

"You make me laugh."

"So does Jay Leno."

"Yeah, but how good is he in the sack?" she added, laughing again. "Besides, I don't like big hair on guys."

"Lucky for me," Nick said as he ran his hand through his thinning hair.

"Yeah," she agreed, "lucky for you."

***

They spent another twenty minutes discussing ground rules. Rules they both knew would ultimately prove to be utterly unenforceable. They discussed rules even though they both knew that in relationships, like knife fights, there were no rules. Nevertheless, they covered the obligatory points. There would be no exclusivity; they were both free to commence other relationships. However, no new sexual relationship would be commenced without advance notice to the other side. The office was off-limits. While they would not attempt to hide their relationship, they would not go out of their way to advertise it either. And finally, and most crucially, either party could terminate the relationship at any time without reason or cause and, and, most lawyerly and least realistically, without recrimination, repercussion, or hurt feelings. If it ended, they would continue to be business partners and friends. When they were done discussing the rules, they smiled and shook hands. Two lawyers had just contractually agreed upon an *at-will* love affair; terminable at will.

"Okay great," Nick said, " that was all very adult."

"Yes, very adult," Rosa agreed.

"Very professional," he added.

"Oh yes," she commented, "very business-like."

"Certainly," Nick concurred, "very lawyer-like."

"Yes. Definitely".

Nick nodded his head in agreement. After a few seconds, Nick broke the silence with a mischievous grin, "Rosa?"

"Yes?"

"Wanna do it tonight?"

"Sure," she said through her smile as Nick turned and left her office.

CHAPTER 8

They did in fact make love that evening. But this time Rosa turned the ringer off the phone. She didn't want to risk a repeat of Saturday night's performance. It would be difficult, even for lawyers, to explain how they simultaneously broke bones the same evening.

By Tuesday, Nick found it increasingly difficult to focus on the mounting stack of files perched on his desk. His thoughts alternated between Rosa and Livie Taylor. The situation with Rosa was fraught with danger.

What if things didn't work out? What if she wanted to end it? Or even though he couldn't imagine it now, what if he did? Despite the *rules* they had agreed upon, things were already different between them at work. *How could I have thought that they wouldn't be?* he asked himself. He knew several lawyers who used their wives as their secretaries and he had always wondered, how the hell they did it. How did they keep from bringing home problems to the office and vice versa when they were one and the same? He then berated himself for engaging in his principal vice; thinking too much; worrying about the future too much. *Just take it a day at a time,* he told himself. *Enjoy today and let tomorrow take care of itself. Easier said than done. Where was Dr. Phil when a guy really needed him?*

He turned his thoughts to Livie Taylor again. He had last

seen and talked to her the prior Thursday. She was to come back on Friday and then be in court Monday morning. Yet here it was Tuesday...he glanced at his watch...at four-thirty...and not a damn word from her. What should he do? What about the hundred thousand dollars she had paid him? Should he just mail it back to her (less ten grand for his time and aggravation) with a note saying he assumed she no longer desired his services?

As he was debating what to do, his phone buzzed. He picked it up, "Yeah Pat, who is it?" he asked.

"Mrs. Livinia Taylor," came the reply.

"Are you serious?" Nick asked as his blood pressure went up fifty points.

"It's her," Pat replied.

He had half a mind to get revenge by leaving her to sit on hold until she tired of it and hung up. But on the other hand, he was genuinely curious as to what had happened. Curiosity prevailed over spite and he punched line two and connected. "What can I do for you Mrs. Taylor?" he asked with an unmistakable edge to his voice.

"Nick..." she began falteringly "...God. I'm so sorry. I'll explain when I come in. Something's happened. I'd like to see you this evening."

"Mrs. Taylor," he answered, refusing to concede that whatever the *something* was it excused her failure to at least call him over the last four days. "I went to court on Monday morning with a briefcase full of paperwork with your name on it. And you didn't show up. You didn't call. I was just getting ready to mail a portion of your retainer back to you. I simply cannot represent a client who fails to communicate with me."

"Nick..." her voice was faltering even worse and Nick thought it sounded as if she was crying. "Please...you'll understand when I tell you what's happened."

"Mrs. Taylor..."

"Call me Livie...please, for God's sake, don't punish me. I

have to see you tonight."

His instincts told him to tell her that her retainer, less ten grand, was in the mail and to hang up. But he already knew he would not follow his instincts in this case. "Okay...Livie...be here at eight...but I am in no way assuring you that I will continue as your attorney. Do you understand that?"

"Yes, I understand. Thank you. And you'll understand after I explain."

Nick hung up the phone and leaned back in his chair. *This had better be a good one,* he thought. *I'll make her beg, grovel even, for forgiveness and for me to continue as her attorney. Then I'll have the upper hand throughout the rest of this relationship.* As he was relishing thinking about how he was going to make Livie Taylor grovel, there was a soft knock on the door. The door opened and Rosa poked her head in and smiled.

"Hey," she said.

"Hey."

"Long day?"

"Aren't they all?"

"Yeah. There's gotta be an easier way to make a living."

Nick sensed that she wanted to ask him about his plans for tonight but didn't want to seem too pushy. They had been together last night. He rescued her. "Gotta work late tonight," he said then added, "you'd never believe it."

"What?"

"Livie Taylor just called."

"You're kidding? So are she and her hubby back together?"

"No...at least she didn't say so. She's coming in tonight at eight. Says she'll explain everything. Can't wait to hear this one."

Rosa had been standing by the door but now walked the few steps to his desk. "You're meeting with Livie Taylor here, tonight, at eight?" She looked perturbed.

"Yeah. Why?"

"Do you think that's a good idea?"

"What do you mean? Why not?"

"Well...it's just that...you know...you told me yourself how attractive you find her...and I'm just not sure it's wise..."

"Rosa! For God's sake...she's a client...a very well paying client I might add. I don't want to have to send a hundred grand back if I don't have to. She said she absolutely had to see me tonight; it was very important. So I said *okay*. Case closed."

"Case closed?" Rosa snapped.

"Yes, case closed," Nick replied.

"Don't you talk to me like I'm some jealous little girlfriend. I am speaking to you as a partner in this firm who does not wish this firm...or one of its partners...to get in trouble. That's all."

"Oh, so you're speaking to me as a law partner, huh?"

"Yes."

"It has nothing to do with what's happened between us?"

Rosa started to speak, then closed her mouth. He could see her face redden. She rose from her chair. "Fuck you, Nick. Do whatever you want. Obviously, you don't think it's any of my business anyway." With that, she spun on her heels and stormed out ignoring his pleas of, "Rosa! Please!"

Great, he thought, *just great. Boy, I really handled that well. We managed to maintain our professional relationship for three whole days after jumping into the sack. Jesus,* he scolded himself, *I should have known better.*

***

Nick went home, drank a couple glasses of Chablis to unwind and microwaved some leftover hamburger helper. He showered again, dressed in khaki's, a tee shirt and loafers and got back to the office by seven-thirty. At precisely eight he heard the front office door chime, announcing that someone had entered. A woman wearing a blue denim skirt and a pink sweatshirt was standing in the waiting room facing away from him.

Not believing the Livie Taylor he knew could be dressed so casually, he asked himself silently *Who the hell is this?* As the thought formulated in his head, the woman turned around and he was shocked to see it was in fact Livie Taylor. Tears were running down her face, streaking her mascara.

Nick was stunned, "Livie...what?..."

"Please," she interrupted, "let's go to your office...and could I have some water?"

"Certainly," Nick replied as he escorted her back to his office, then retrieved some water for her. He sat down in his office chair, "What's happened? What's going on?"

She took some tissue out of her bag and dabbed her eyes, "Please excuse my appearance..."

"No...you look fine. Really."

She glanced down at herself disbelievingly and continued, "They're on to us...I'm certain of it."

"What do you mean?" Nick asked.

"I mean they know I've been to a lawyer, that we're going to file."

"What makes you think that?"

"Do you want to know why I didn't show up Friday? Why I wasn't in court?"

"Yes, I certainly do."

"Because Daniel stayed home Friday, all weekend and Monday. He wouldn't let me out of his sight. He never, never misses work. Never takes a day off. Friday afternoon when I was supposed to come here I told him I had to go to the grocery store. He said 'Fine. I'll go with you.' He went with me and Jessica to the damn IGA. He's never set foot in a grocery store in his life. Then my cell phone and laptop mysteriously disappear. Of course, he denied knowing anything about it. I was afraid to call from home. That bastard probably had the phone tapped, and finally, as he walked out the door this morning to go to work, she walks in."

"Who?"

"His mother. My God, she never comes over. I said, 'Martha what are you doing here?' and she says, 'Oh I wanted to spend some time with my granddaughter, dear'. What bullshit! I doubt she knows Jessica's middle name. She stayed all day. Then I call Daniel's office this afternoon and I'm told 'he's out.' I'm sure he was seeing a lawyer. The second his mother left today I left with Jessica. I was driving in circles to make sure I wasn't being followed. I went and got a TracFone to call you for God's sake. I'm so scared."

"Calm down," Nick interjected. "Even if he did see a lawyer today we still have a big head start. It'll take them a few days to get the paperwork ready." He patted his hand on her file. "We're ready to file tomorrow. All you have to do is sign and show up in court tomorrow morning."

"We can do that?"

"Sure, I have some appointments but I can move them. We may have to wait a while for a judge to be available. But emergency O.P.'s are a priority by law."

"What if the judge denies the order of protection?"

"I won't lie to you. That's a risk. It depends solely on the judge. Quite honestly, yelling at you, even being in your face and bumping into you, it's pretty thin..."

"What about the threats?"

"What threats?"

"You know, that if I ever filed for divorce he'd fight me for custody."

"That's not a threat. He's Jessica's parent too. He has a right to seek custody."

"What right?" she exclaimed. "He's either at the office, or the hospital, or with his precious Momma. I doubt he changed two dirty diapers..."

"That goes to the merits of who should win, not to whether he has the right to ask for custody."

"What if I told you he pushed me the other day and I fell? Would that help?"

Nick sat upright in his chair and set the pen he had been taking notes with down. For some unexplainable reason, he liked Livie Taylor. She was rich. She was demanding. She was spoiled. She, no doubt, had a good deal of bitch in her. He had already learned, so early in their relationship, that he was capable of doing things for her that were pushing the envelope of acceptable conduct, but this, this was too much. Here was a client, sitting across the desk from him, virtually suggesting that he countenance perjury to gain an advantage in a case. He looked her straight in the eye and spoke "I'm going to try to forget I heard that…"

"Please, I didn't…"

"No, let me finish. We have a good case here. It's solid. You're a stay at home mom. He's a busy doctor. You've been the primary caretaker. And let's face it, he's a man and Jessica's a little girl. All big factors in our favor. But the key, the absolute key, will be credibility. If you lose your credibility, if you give the judge reason to doubt your credibility on anything, on the tiniest little issue, he'll doubt your veracity on everything you say. The surest way to guarantee you'll lose this case is to be less than totally honest and forthright."

"Nick, I wasn't suggesting…"

"Yes. I think you were, and if I ever suspect you're lying to me or the court, as of that moment I'm no longer your lawyer. Am I clear?"

"Please, I'm sorry. I swear I won't. It's just…you can't understand what's at stake here…"

Nick interrupted her again, his voice intense and angry. "I do understand. I'm divorced. I've had to watch another man raise my daughter for the last four years. If I'm lucky, I get to see her every other weekend. Even then, she's fifteen now, she's got so many activities I barely get to see her. I barely know what's going on in my own daughter's life. So don't sit there and tell me I don't understand the stakes involved here."

Livie looked away, avoiding eye contact with him, "I'm sorry. Truly." She looked back at him, a tear trickling down each cheek. "I didn't know you were divorced. I didn't know about your situation. It's just...I have to get him out of the house. I'm afraid I'm going crazy. I can't sleep, I can't eat..." She was barely able to get the words out as she broke down and the tears came forth in droves. She buried her head in her lap and continued to cry. Nick pushed his box of tissues to the edge of the desk in front of her and remained silent.

Finally, she raised her head, grabbed a couple of tissues, dabbed her eyes, and spoke "I'm sorry. I promise I'll be completely honest with you. It's just, on Sunday, we were in the kitchen and he was walking past me and he grabbed my shoulders and kind of moved me out of his way and I kind of stumbled over the dog dish. So it's not like I was making it up."

"Did he do that intentionally, with anger?"

"Well, no, I don't really think so," she responded.

"Then we go with what we have and take our chances. If the O.P.'s not granted, we proceed on the Petition for Temporary Relief. You have to understand, the litigation process is like a war. You cannot win every battle, every skirmish. We have to keep our focus on winning the war, getting you permanent custody of Jessica and a fair financial settlement. I have to know you're in this for the long run."

"I am. I promise."

"Good. How can I contact you now that your cell is gone?"

"This is my TracFone number." She handed it to him and he wrote it down.

"Fine. You said your laptop is missing too?"

"Yes."

"Does that mean we've lost the documents you scanned in?"

"No," she said as she grabbed her purse off the floor and dug through it. She pulled out a flash drive and handed it to Nick

"I made a backup."

"You were prepared, weren't you?"

She smiled, "I used to be a girl scout."

"Okay," Nick replied, "meet me at the courthouse in Butler tomorrow at eight-fifteen, third floor, we'll try to grab a judge before the regular call starts at nine."

"But what happens if the judge denies it?"

"Then we get a date on our temporary petitions and he gets served with the paperwork."

"But then what do I do when he comes home tomorrow after he's been served with the papers?"

"Nothing."

"Nothing?"

"Yes, nothing. You tell him you will not, under any circumstances, discuss it with him. Tell him to have his lawyer contact me."

"What if he makes me?"

"Livie," Nick replied, "you're not listening. I said you DO NOT discuss it with him. Period. End of discussion. If he becomes coercive or violent, you call the police first and me second. Do you understand?"

"Yes," she said hesitantly.

"Okay," Nick replied as he pushed her file across the desk to her, the pages marked with little red *Sign Here* tabs, "Let's get the paperwork signed."

She finished signing and pushed the file back to him. "Done," she said.

"Okay. Now I want to ask you one more time. You're sure this is what you want? After tomorrow morning, there's likely no turning back. You understand that?"

"Yes, I understand. There's no turning back."

"Fine," Nick said as he rose to escort her to the door.

As he exited his office she turned and without warning gave him a hug. Without her heels, she was more than a head shorter than Nick, the top of her head just coming to his chest. She smelled wonderful. As she pressed herself tightly against him, he could hear her begin to sob gently again. "Thank you. Thank you so much," she repeated, then added, "I'm sorry about what I said."

Compassion overcame common sense and Nick raised an arm and lightly returned her embrace. "It's okay," he said. At that moment, the door to Rosa's office opened and she stepped out. Livie and Nick broke their hug and Livie took a step backward from him. The two women stared at each other for a moment.

Nick broke the silence, "Oh...Livie. This is my partner... Rosa Thomas. She'll probably be helping me with your case. Rosa, Livinia Taylor." Rosa stepped forward and extended her hand. Livie reciprocated.

"Well," Rosa said, "I doubt Nick's going to need any help. You've got yourself a very fine attorney, Mrs. Taylor."

"I know, Nick's been so great," Livie replied. "Nice to meet you, Mrs. Thomas."

Rosa smiled and said, "It's Ms."

Livie returned the smile. "I'm sure it is." She grabbed Nick's left hand in both of hers, squeezed it, smiled and added, "Nick, see you tomorrow morning." With that, she turned and left.

When she was out the door, Nick turned to Rosa. "What are you doing here, Rosa?"

"What am I doing here?" she snapped. "I'm a partner here. I work here. Do you think you're the only one who comes in at night?"

"Please," Nick said in a pleading tone, "I don't want things to be like this between us. Let's talk about it."

"Talk about what?" she responded. "You've already made it quite clear that you don't want my interference in your decisions."

"I never said that. You're twisting my words."

"Am I?" she retorted. She looked as if she was wanting to tear into him, but paused, took a few deep breaths then proceeded in a calm voice while looking downwards. "Look, maybe this...

us...wasn't such a good idea after all. I don't know. I'm just very confused right now." She looked back up directly into his eyes. "And, by the way, just when did you start getting touchy-feely with clients in the office?"

"She hugged me. I didn't expect it. I didn't ask for it. For God's sake, I saw...what's his name...Mr. Parker give you a hug last week."

"He's eighty," she replied in a disgusted tone of voice. "Look, I better go before I say something I regret."

She turned and headed towards the back door of the office.

"Rosa!" he called as she stormed away. But she didn't turn or respond and went out the door. A moment later Nick heard a car start, and tires squeal. "Shit," Nick said to himself, "shit."

CHAPTER 9

Nick circled the block surrounding the Martin County Court-house a second time, compulsively rubbernecking searching for a parking spot. He noted Livie Taylor's white Lexus already parked. He acknowledged his profound ambivalence about her presence; glad that she wasn't standing him up in court again and glad that he wouldn't be having to write a ninety thousand dollar refund check, but deeply uncertain as to whether her appearance in his professional life was worth the apparent cost in his personal life.

As he circled the block a third time, his thoughts turned to Rosa. It was obvious that if he wanted a romantic relationship with Rosa...and how could he not? Things were going to have to change. It was also obvious that the long discussion they had had about the ground rules of their relationship was out the window. *So much for contracts between lawyers,* he mused.

But no matter how long they talked, whatever consensus they came to, was it workable in practice? Could they actually continue to be business partners? And in this particular business. After all, they weren't manufacturing widgets. Their jobs involved intensely personal relationships with clients over the most intensely personal issues; their marriages, their children, their health, their lives. It wasn't possible to do this job without becoming personally, emotionally involved with your clients. Not that you ever actually crossed the line. Cross that line, just one time, and there would be no crossing back.

When Nick had been married, thoughts about crossing lines with clients had been nonexistent. Sure, he occasionally had very attractive female clients. But he had neither the desire nor the inclination to do anything other than appreciate their beauty from an almost academic point of view. Occasionally he would even have a brief discussion with Stu about whether the blonde or the brunette was better looking. But their discussions were all purely theoretical. They could just as easily have been discussing whether Corvettes or Vipers were sexier.

About six months after he and Sheila divorced, he had been surprised when one day it had suddenly dawned on him that his abstract thoughts about his attractive clients had become more corporeal. Not that he crossed the line, but the flirtations had become more overt, the fantasies more prevalent and more prurient. And now he had taken on as a client Livie Taylor, the mother of all male fantasies. Smart, educated, cultured, drop-dead gorgeous and sexy beyond words and soon to be, if he did his job right, very single, and very, very rich. *How come it has to be virtually simultaneous with jumping into bed with Rosa?* he wondered.

He tried to think about how he would feel if Rosa was representing a GQ cover boy. If he had walked out of his office to see Mr. G.Q. hugging Rosa. *Would I be jealous? Upset?* he asked himself. *You bet,* came the surprisingly honest answer.

Nick concluded his ruminations with the acknowledgment that it was decision time. Not his forte, he knew. He had generally found, in his personal life at least, that procrastination was his preferred coping mechanism. Put off dealing with a problem long enough and sometimes it died a natural death. *Yeah,* he scolded himself, *just like my marriage did.* No, procrastination would not solve this problem. He knew he didn't want to lose Rosa. He would not only be losing a woman he had lusted after but his best friend too.

As he gave up on finding a parking spot, he recalled Frank

Bernard's standing offer to park in his office lot only a block away from the courthouse. Frank was a sole practitioner in Butler and they had graduated the same year from law school at the University of Illinois. They had not really known each other well in law school and were surprised to run into each other in the Martin County Courthouse after they had begun their practices in Selma and Butler respectively. They had become professional, and casual social friends. As he pulled into Frank's lot and exited his car, Frank pulled in.

"Hey Frank, mind if I park here?" Nick said as Frank got out of his Miata. "Thought I'd take you up on your offer. They must be having a sale at the courthouse. Two years for the price of one. Not a parking space in sight."

"No problem. Any time. Same goes for anyone in your firm," Frank replied.

"Even Larry?" Nick asked with a laugh.

"Yeah," Frank chuckled in reply, "even Larry. Hasn't he started to mellow out yet?"

"Larry?" Nick answered, "Larry will start to mellow about the same time as Stu gets Philanthropist of the Year award."

Frank smiled in response.

"How's Marty?" Nick inquired.

"Great. Just great. Motherhood agrees with her," Frank replied.

"That's great. That's wonderful. Enjoy. They grow up so quick. My baby's fifteen."

"Yeah, they sure do," Frank answered wistfully.

"Yeah," Nick responded shaking his head in agreement, "better get to the courthouse. Emergency O.P. Gotta try and grab a judge."

"See ya," Frank answered as he walked to his office. "Say hi to Rosa and the guys."

"Will do," Nick said as he turned and walked in the April morning's coolness to the courthouse.

***

It didn't take long for Nick to locate Livie Taylor seated in one of the hardback wooden chairs lining the perimeter of the third floor of the Martin County Courthouse. She stood out as conspicuously as Queen Elizabeth would have at Woodstock. She was once again, immaculately dressed, this time in a tan silk blouse and a conservative brown pantsuit that looked as if it had been custom-tailored, which, no doubt, it was. She was hatless and gloveless but clearly projected an abundance of money, class, and refinement.

To her immediate left sat a very huge older woman whose ass clearly overmatched the struggling chair she was seated on, spilling out prodigiously on both sides. Nick would have been willing to wager that when she rose, the chair would be along for the ride. She was wearing a house dress that appeared older than her and knee-high's rolled down to her ankles. She was holding a worn bible and was muttering incoherently to herself about Jesus and redemption.

To Livie's right sat a man who, though he looked forty-five, was probably only twenty-five. He was dressed in grease-covered blue jeans and a muscle tee shirt that allowed for the display of a collection of tattoos on each arm from wrist to shoulder. The tattoos ranged the entire gamut from tasteless to obscene. He had bad teeth, a bad complexion, a bad mustache and bad manners. He was enthusiastically pointing out a particularly obscene tattoo on his left arm to Livie and apparently trying to explain to her its deep personal significance. Nick walked up to Livie. She turned her attention away from the tattoo tutorial and looked up at Nick, a look of intense relief and salvation on her face.

"Mrs. Taylor. Let's see if we can find a judge, shall we?" he said.

"Oh yes, please," Livie replied as she stood.

The tattooed man stood too. "You a lawyer?" he asked Nick.

"Yes."

"Fuckin' cops busted me for D.U.I. and meth but didn't read me no fuckin' rights. Can you beat it?" he asked.

"I'm sorry," Nick replied, "I don't do criminal work." Nick grabbed Livie's arm and lead her away. He heard Tattoo Man say "fuckin' lawyers" as the man took a seat next to Knee-Hi Lady and began showing her his tattoo collection. She appeared to take little interest however and continued muttering about her imminent salvation.

"Thank you," Livie whispered to him.

"Sure," he said as he directed her to the jury room. It was empty. "Wait here. Hopefully, no one will bother you. I'm going to see if I can get a judge. Usually, they do O.P.'s in chambers. You ready?"

"Yes," she replied, "certainly."

Nick walked through the door leading to the judge's chambers. Court reporters, lawyers, clerks and judges were milling about, drinking coffee, gossiping, flirting and generally pretending that the day they were about to embark upon had significance in the grand scheme of things, despite overwhelming evidence that it rarely did. Nick saw Judge Leslie Jones-Swanson grabbing a cup of coffee. He noted no other judges. He grabbed the elbow of one of the court reporters. "Helen," he asked," who's sitting today?"

"The Ice Queen on civil, Hanson on criminal," she replied.

"Shit," Nick replied.

"You got civil?" Helen asked knowingly.

"Yeah an emergency O.P. Swanson makes such a production out of them. Damn, I wish Westbrook was here. He'd sign a death warrant if you put it under his nose."

"Good luck," Helen replied as she returned to the young public defender she had been flirting with.

Nick walked up to Judge Swanson, "Morning, Judge."

"Morning, Nick. What can I do for you?"

"Any chance of hearing an emergency O.P. before the regular call?" he inquired. She sipped her coffee and glanced at her watch before replying, "Perp still in the home?"

"Yeah."

"Violent?"

"Well, he kind of bumped into her."

"He...bumped...into her?"

"Yes."

"When did it happen?"

Nick swallowed hard, "Last Wednesday."

"Well bumping into someone a week ago hardly seems like an emergency then, does it? File a Petition for Exclusive Possession and set it for hearing. Come back on an emergency O.P. if she has a black eye." Nick was determined to push it, though he recognized that an argument with a judge lacked an essential element that made it worthwhile to engage in: the ability to win.

"But Judge," he pleaded, "this is an unusual situation. Her husband's a doctor, a pathologist, there's a young child involved, psychological abuse..."

"Nick," she interrupted, "don't try your case in chambers before your opponent even knows there's a case. Is she in actual, real physical danger from this man?"

Nick knew that the absolute worst crime he could commit as a lawyer was to make representations to a judge and not deliver. "No," he conceded.

"Then file your petitions and notice them up," she said as she retreated, a cup of coffee in hand, to her private office and closed the door.

The last thing Nick wanted to do was to go out to Livie Taylor and tell her he had failed, that he had been unable to get the O.P. Of course, they would still file the Petition for Dissolution this morning, along with the Petitions for Temporary Relief. But those all required notice to Dr. Taylor and an evidentiary hearing. That could take weeks.

Inspiration struck as he stalled for time thinking of what to do next. He tapped Helen on the shoulder. She was paying close attention to a story the young public defender was telling her, laughing with a verve out of all proportion to the amusement of the story. She ignored the tap on her shoulder. Nick tapped harder and said, "Helen, excuse me."

She smiled rapturously at the P.D., then turned to face Nick "What?" she said with an undisguised air of contempt. The young P.D., Alex Hixenbaugh, who had been hired only a short time ago, was apparently considered quite the catch, and the single girls at the courthouse had all been staking their claim.

"Did you say Judge Hanson was doing the criminal docket?" Nick asked.

"Yeah, but I thought you had civil," she snapped.

"I do. Do you know where he is?"

"Yeah," she said and nodded towards the restroom just as the door opened and Judge Hanson exited. She turned her attention back to Alex.

Nick walked directly over to Judge Hanson all the while keeping one eye on Judge Swanson's office door making sure it remained closed.

"Judge Hanson?" he asked as he extended his free hand, "Nick Barnett, with Ford, Ford, Osgood, Barnett & Thomas in Selma."

Michael Hanson was a newly appointed Associate Judge from Shelby County, about as far as you could get from Butler and still be in the Fourth Judicial Circuit. He had been on the bench only a few months and to Nick's knowledge, it was his first appearance in Martin County. The thought crossed Nick's mind that, perhaps for the first time in this life he was dealing with a judge younger than himself.

"Mike Hanson," the judge replied as he smiled and returned Nick's handshake. "What can I do for you, Nick?"

Nick smiled back. *Great,* he thought, *a genuinely nice guy. First names. No pretension. Things are looking up.* "Well," Nick began hesitantly, "it was just before you got tied up on your call, I wondered if you might consider reviewing an emergency O.P. Petition?"

"Judge Swanson's doing civil," he said as he walked to his office, Nick in tow.

"I know," he replied "but..." Nick certainly did not want to lie to a judge...ever...but he wanted that O.P. and what the hell difference did it make who issued it "...um...she couldn't issue it."

"Conflict?" Hanson asked.

Nick smiled back without replying.

The judge took that for an affirmative reply and glanced at his watch. "Okay," he answered, "let's do it in chambers. Find Helen and get your client back here while I read this."

"Fine. Thanks, Judge," Nick replied as he exited the office.

He retrieved Livie first and then Helen who was mightily perturbed to have her tete a tete with Alex interrupted a second time. Helen set up her reporting machine and took a chair facing the judge's desk. Livie sat in the other chair. Nick stood.

"All right. Let the record show this is D-83, Taylor v. Taylor. Present in Chambers is Petitioner Livinia Taylor and her counsel Nicholas Barnett."

"Ma'am?" the judge said looking at Livie after he administered the oath.

"Yes."

"I've read your Petition for Emergency Order of Protection. Is everything in it factually correct and truthful?"

"Yes, your Honor."

"And when this incident occurred did you feel as if your personal liberty was interfered with and/or you were harassed?" the judge asked.

Livie glanced quickly up at Nick.

He subtly nodded his head.

"Yes," she responded.

"Let the record show order entered this day," he said as he

signed the order Nick had prepared and slid the file back across the desk to Nick.

"Good luck to you Mrs. Taylor."

"Thank you, Judge," she replied. "Is that it?"

"Yes," Nick said as he grabbed her under the arm hoping to get her out of chambers before Judge Swanson reappeared. "Thank you, Judge," he added as they left. They threaded their way through the crowded judge's chambers and Nick was amused to see that Carla, a deputy clerk, had already taken Helen's place with Alex. As soon as they were outside the chambers door they stopped.

"It's done?" Livie asked.

Nick hoisted the file in his hand, smiled and said, "Yep. Now we have to serve him with copies."

"Oh my God," she said as she spontaneously hugged him. Nick, with the court file in one hand and his briefcase in the other, was helpless to protest her hug.

"Oh my God," she repeated as she finally relented, broke her hug and took a step back. "Thank you, Nick. Thank you so much."

"Livie," Nick replied, still reeling from the intensity of the hug, "right after I get back to the office I have to get these papers to my process server so your husband can be served today. But as of this moment, the house is yours and Jessica is yours. Just please understand this is all very temporary. Let me walk you to your car."

He transferred the court file to his briefcase hand, grabbed her elbow and led her to the elevator past Tattoo Man, still feverishly discoursing about the artwork on his arms with Ms. Knee-Hi, who was still quietly rocking and mumbling. Nick and Livie stood quietly for a moment, her elbow in his hand waiting for the elevator, simply watching Tattoo Man and Ms. Knee-Hi engaging in their mutual soliloquies. They rode silently in the elevator, their isolation and their silence only adding to the sexual tension created by Livie's embrace of Nick moments before. He returned the court file to the clerk's office then walked out to Livie's car with her. When they reached her car she turned to him and asked,

"What if he wants to see her?"

"You do not discuss anything with him. You tell him to have his lawyer call me. Got it?"

"Yes, but..."

"No *buts*," he interrupted, "his lawyer calls me. That's how it works from here on out. We'll have to arrange visitation. Probably every other weekend, maybe a weeknight..."

"Does he have to get overnights? She's only three."

"Yes, he'll get overnights. If we don't agree to it, it will just look bad for us, like you're trying to keep her from him."

"But...he...he doesn't deserve her...he's never home...never with her. He and that mother of his will just use his time to tell Jessica how awful I am and how mean I'm being to daddy. I know these people. I know what they're like."

"We simply don't have a choice. He'll be ordered, as you will be, not to discuss the divorce with Jessica, not to talk bad about each other, but keep in mind, a court order is just a piece of paper. No one will be monitoring what goes on behind closed doors. If that's the kind of people they are, you have to be prepared to deal with it. And it won't be easy."

"Oh God, she's just a baby. I can just hear Martha...and Daniel..." The tears came faster now as the realization of the likely consequences of the course she had chosen to engage in sunk in. She looked up at him, "I'll be okay...it's just so difficult."

"I know," he responded.

"Thank you so much," she added as the tears came again. She hugged Nick again and involuntarily he tensed. Before he knew what was happening she reached up and kissed him on the left cheek and then again.

She reached into her purse, grabbed a tissue and wiped the lipstick off his cheek. She smiled through her tears. "Don't want your partner, Ms. Thomas, getting the wrong idea," she added, heavily emphasizing the *Ms.*, as she got into her car. Nick stood there for a few silent seconds as she drove off. He breathed in the last of her scent still lingering in the air. *Maybe Rosa's right,* Nick thought as he aimlessly brushed the cheek Livie had just kissed, *things are starting to get weird.*

CHAPTER 10

Nick walked to his car and began the short drive back from Butler to Selma. As Nick shifted through the Acura's gears and accelerated into traffic on the interstate, his mind raced faster than the Acura's pistons. *Just two weeks ago I was coasting. Bored even. No real relationships other than with my daughter. Putting in time at the office; doing what I had to do to get by; churning some files, making a few bucks to keep Stu off my ass. Wistfully fantasizing about Rosa, but unable, or at least unwilling to risk taking a chance at turning those fantasies into reality.*

And now, I've pocketed the biggest single fee of my career. I've got the most beautiful woman I've ever personally known as a client. She is, if I'm not totally misinterpreting, making certain feelings she has for me quite evident. She'll soon be divorced, available and... rich. I should be on cloud nine, he thought. *How come,* he asked himself, *I feel like a total schmuck? Like I'm taking this once in a lifetime opportunity with Rosa, handed to me on a silver platter, and smashing it into a thousand pieces.*

Why? For years, I've silently lusted after and fantasized about Rosa. And now my fantasies become reality. And what do I do? Go goo-goo eyes over a client. And right in front of Rosa. Was it that age-old temptation? As ancient as the Garden of Eden. The forbidden fruit? I can't have Livie, so that makes me want her even more.

Whatever it is, he told himself as he pulled into his office lot, and switched off the ignition, *it needs to stop right here and now. I'm going to march into Rosa's office and set things straight. Then, the next time I see Livinia Taylor, I'll set her straight too.* He marched into his office only long enough to deposit his briefcase on his desktop, hang up his suit coat and call George, his process server, to tell him to come by the office immediately to pick up the paperwork to serve Dr. Taylor. He instructed George to go to Dr. Taylor's office building and wait by the doctor's Mercedes until the good doctor came out and to serve him with the papers right then and there.

"How long do I wait?" George asked him.

"As long as it takes," came the reply.

"Okay," George answered, "but you know I charge by the hour."

"George," Nick smiled as he had replied, "on this case, I don't care if you charge by the damn minute. Just get him served today before he leaves the office. Period. No excuses."

At the mention of charging by the minute, Nick could almost picture George grinning as he mentally started his meter. "You're the boss," George said.

Nick marched straight to Rosa's door before his newfound fortitude deserted him. He knocked softly.

"Come in," came the reply.

He entered and smiled. Rosa glanced up from her paperwork, looked at him for a few moments, then gazed back down without speaking. She continued working.

"Hi," he said.

"Hi, just come from court?"

"Yeah, I did."

"Get the O.P. for Livinia Taylor?"

"Yeah," Nick replied, slightly befuddled. He didn't recall telling her he was going to court with Livie Taylor this morning. "Pat tell you?"

"No, you did."

"I don't recall that."

"You told me just now."

Nick's befuddlement was increasing exponentially. "No," he stammered, "no, I didn't."

She put her pen down, looked back up and tilted back in her chair, feet on her desk and gave him a sarcastic smirk. "Yeah, I'm afraid you did. But not verbally." She pointed to her left cheek. Nick, following her cue, touched his left cheek and shrugged his shoulders, still in the dark.

"Turn around," she instructed.

He obeyed and found himself facing a small mirror, one of a pair that flanked a still life. He moved closer and suddenly and sickeningly, the realization of what Rosa was referring to became obvious. There on his left cheek was the clear red lipstick imprint of half a pair of lips. He quickly pulled his handkerchief out of his front trousers' pocket and completed the job Livie Taylor had so inexpertly commenced. He turned to face her.

"Rosa," he began, "it's not what you think..."

Rosa interrupted him, "You know what I think? I think you forgot to read 'The Cheating Husband's Handbook, Chapter One: Always check yourself in a mirror after an encounter.' Very elementary mistake, Nick. But then again, you're not a husband, are you? So I guess we can excuse it this time."

"Please give me a chance to explain," he begged.

Rosa sat back upright and grabbed a pen off the desk in front of her. She held it for a second then suddenly cocked her arm and threw it at him. Her aim was skewed by her anger and she missed, striking the wall behind him.

Nick was too shocked to speak but Rosa quickly filled the void. "You've obviously already crossed the line with...with that woman...but so help me God, you cross it again and I'll be on the phone to Springfield faster than you can say disbarred. Maybe our friendship, our...relationship...means nothing to you...but I would have thought that this firm...your professional reputation...and mine and Stu's and Larry's might mean something to you. What the hell's wrong with you? Is she that fucking beautiful? Is she worth risking everything for?" Her eyes were misted over as she finished. Nick sat down across the desk from her and started to speak. "Don't bother sitting," Rosa interrupted, "this conversation's over." She grabbed a tissue and dabbed her eyes.

Nick, disregarding her admonition, stayed seated. He sat silent for a moment before speaking. "Rosa, on the drive back from Butler, I swore to myself I was going to march straight into your office and tell you that you were right. Things are getting weird. But I swear to God I've done nothing to encourage it..."

"Oh, spare me..." she interjected.

"I mean it. I swear. We got the O.P. entered and then we walked out to her car and...and she hugged me and kissed me on the cheek before I even knew what she was doing. I planned on telling you...like I said, it's getting weird. I was going to suggest that you and I meet with Stu and Larry and we tell them what's going on and that you take over the file. I swear I was."

Rosa did not appear impressed. "First, I can tell you right here and now that it will be a cold day in hell before I represent... that woman...."

"Why?"

"Why? Jesus, Nick, how dense are you? Can't you see what's going on? What she's up to? She hires a divorced man as her attorney. She starts coming on to you..."

"But," Nick interrupted, "she didn't even know I was divorced. She told me so."

"What?"

"When I told her I understood what she was going through because I was divorced too, she told me she didn't know that."

"Well, that's funny."

'Why?"

"Because when Pat put her on my book she said maybe it

was better if I handled it anyway and I said 'Why?' and Pat said she specifically asked if you were married and it concerned her a little."

"She did?"

"Yeah, she did. So she's not only a manipulative bitch, but she's also a lying, manipulative bitch. And didn't you hear her little smart ass comment to me when she called me 'Mrs. Thomas' and I said 'it's Ms. Thomas'" Rosa puckered up her face as if she had bitten into a lemon, raised and cocked her left hand and fluttered her eyes as she did her best Livie Taylor imitation, " '...I'm sure it is.' Then do you think it was accidental that she only wiped half her lipstick off your cheek? What happened here in this office just now is exactly what she hoped would happen. I'm sure she could tell when I ran into you two at the office that there was something between us. She's a woman. Women can sense those things. I'm the competition and I doubt that Livie Taylor is used to losing when it comes to men."

"I think you're mistaken," Nick replied while he unconsciously continued to wipe his left cheek, "I don't think she..."

"Don't you dare defend her in front of me," Rosa retorted.

"I wasn't..."

"You know Stu and Larry don't know shit about divorce and if I won't represent her, do you think Stu is going to let you refund a hundred thousand dollars? Over his dead body and yours. So, I'd say you're stuck representing the lovely Mrs. Taylor."

Nick considered what she had said. Was she right? Had Livie intentionally left lipstick all over his cheek hoping what had just happened would happen? As dense and naive as he was, even he could tell she was coming on to him. Was she just lonely, vulnerable and genuinely affectionate towards him or was she the scheming, manipulative bitch Rosa was convinced she was?

"I'm going to talk to Stu and Larry," Nick began, "tell them what's happened so far...not just regarding Livie Taylor...but between us. They need to know why you won't take over her file.

Then if they won't let me withdraw and refund her retainer..." he paused for a moment took a deep breath then continued "...I'll resign from the firm." He looked Rosa straight in the eye. "Rosa, I was thinking about you the whole drive back from Butler. Give me another chance. I don't want to lose what we could have had together. I don't."

She avoided his gaze, grabbed another tissue and dabbed her eyes again. "You'd better leave," she said, "I have work to do."

He rose, walked to the door, then paused and turned to face her. She was again feverishly writing on a yellow legal pad.

"I'm sorry," he said.

"I am too," she replied without looking up as he opened the door and left.

CHAPTER 11

"So what's the problem?" Larry asked. Nick had told both Stu and Larry that he needed to talk to them, together, and they had agreed to meet in Nick's office at five-thirty. Nick had spent fifteen minutes outlining the status of the Livie Taylor case and what had transpired between them. He had not yet informed them of his relationship with Rosa. Before Nick could respond to Larry, Stu interjected, "Goddammit, I warned you. I warned you to keep it in your pants with this broad."

"I've kept it in my pants for God's sake. I've done nothing...nothing. But Rosa is convinced this woman is intentionally coming on to me and now, I don't know, I think she may be right...I don't know why...she could have any guy she set her sights on. Maybe she thinks I'll fight harder for her if I think she's hot for me and I've got a chance. Who knows? But I don't think I should continue to represent her under these circumstances."

"So," Stu said, "give the file to Rosa. Unless this Taylor woman's a switch hitter, she won't be jumping Rosa's bones too."

"I already suggested that," Nick replied. "Rosa won't take the file."

"Why not?" Stu asked. "And where is she anyway? This concerns her too."

"She went home," Nick explained. "She wasn't feeling well."

"Why won't she take it?" Stu repeated.

"It's personal. Look, I was going to tell you guys, but the fact is…Rosa and I have been…seeing each other outside the office and…"

"God damn, Nick," Stu interrupted, "God damn. How long has this been going on? She can't sue, can she? She's a partner."

"Oh, hell," Larry chimed in, "I'd kick her ass all over the courtroom. I'd…"

"JESUS CHRIST," Nick yelled, losing his temper and not caring one bit, "that's our partner…our friend you guys are talking about. And no, she can't sue and she wouldn't if she could. I'm not her boss. It was an affair between consenting adults. No law against that. Yet."

"So, like I said, what's the problem? Rosa takes the file. Problem solved." Stu said.

"The problem, Stu," Nick replied enunciating each syllable, "is that Rosa will take Livie Taylor as a client when hell freezes over and I don't want her as a client anymore."

"Well, this is great. This is great. Fucking great." Stu answered. "You banging Rosa may be legal but do you see now the problem you've gotten us into? I approved buying that new computer system last week figuring we had Taylor's hundred grand in the bank. Now you're telling me we need to refund it because you've been boning Rosa and she's jealous of a fucking client!"

Sixteen years of Stu's pushing Nick's buttons boiled over. Before even Nick knew what he was doing he was up out of his chair and charging around his desk towards Stu. Stu stayed seated, failing to rise to the challenge, though there was no doubt of Nick's intentions. Larry stepped into Nick's path.

"Whoa, whoa, whoa!" Larry cautioned as he placed his palms on Nick's chest bringing his charge to an abrupt stop. "What the hell's the matter with you?"

Nick took several deep breaths before speaking. "Stu," he said as he gently pushed Larry out of his path, "I'm sorry. I haven't been in a fight since seventh grade. I lost my cool. But please, understand something. I have very strong feelings for Rosa and I do not appreciate you talking about our relationship in those terms. I was not 'banging' her. I was not 'boning' her. We made love. Okay? Do we have things straight?"

"I apologize to you too," Stu stammered, obviously shaken and just as obviously uncomfortable in performing an alien act: an apology. "It's just...you've created a huge, very expensive problem for this firm and I want to know how you propose solving it."

Nick walked back around his desk and retook his seat in his office chair. He was silent for a few moments before speaking. "I'll resign."

"Well, that doesn't really solve the problem, does it?" Stu responded. "If you resign from her case and Rosa won't take it what do we do about the money she paid us?"

"I meant resign from the firm, the partnership," Nick clarified.

"Well, Jesus Christ," Larry interjected, "that's hardly necessary. You get that Taylor woman in here. You sit her down and you read her the fucking riot act. Tell her no more kissing. No more hugging. No more bullshit. You want me to sit in on it? It's that simple."

"I wish it was," Nick replied.

"It is," Stu added. "There is absolutely no reason why this firm should be broken up over this and there is no reason why you can't represent her. You schedule your appointments so Larry or I can sit in on them 'til we're certain she's got the message." Stu smiled, "Come on, Nick, you're blowing this whole thing out of proportion. Your judgment's all fucked up." He paused, then nonchalantly added, "Pussy'll do that to you."

Nick glared at him and Stu put up his hands. "Easy does it, partner. No offense intended. But the bottom line is that you've created this problem, you're gonna solve it. I think I can speak for Larry and Rosa when I say if you withdraw from her case or if you break up the partnership over this, then that hundred thousand dollars...every last nickel...is coming out of your pocket, not mine, not Larry's, not Rosa's. We didn't create this problem. Are we clear on that point?"

For an instant, Nick felt like getting up again and finishing what he had almost started with Stu. But he knew, down deep, Stu was right. *I created this problem. It's entirely my fault. I can't ask my partners to bear the loss,* he thought. He also knew that he couldn't afford to write a check to the firm for a hundred thousand dollars. That would wipe out Natalie's college fund and all his savings to boot.

He leaned back in his chair and looked at Stu and Larry. "Okay. All right. You guys are right. It is my fault. I'll get Mrs. Taylor in here and let her know that her behavior towards me has to stop and that our relationship has to be entirely professional. I'll tell her that if there is one more instance of it, I'll withdraw."

"Great, great," Stu responded, "now you're talking sense." He got up from his chair and walked around to Nick and extended his hand and added, "Let me know when she's coming in so I can be there."

Nick rose and accepted Stu's offered hand. Larry followed. "Take a few days off," Larry added. "You don't look so good."

"Thanks, Larry. I wish I could," he answered, "and Stu, I appreciate the offer but I can handle this. I guess I just lost my bearings for a bit. I'll be okay."

"Yeah," Stu added, "what's the line from that Eagles' song about what a woman can do to your soul?"

Nick smiled in response and Stu and Larry left the office. *Yeah,* Nick thought as he sat back down in his office chair and propped his feet on his desk, *and what's that other line from an Eagles' song "You can check out any time you like, but you can never leave."*

***

He spent the evening drinking wine, picking at his leftover

mostaccioli and sausage and watching mindless TV, all the while with the cordless phone seated in his lap. He wanted to call Rosa and ask her if he could come over and explain everything to her. He'd finish Livie's case but he'd promise he wouldn't tolerate any more inappropriate conduct from her. He'd promise Rosa that he'd be the consummate professional. Then they would make passionate love and everything would be fine. Nick laughed at himself for thinking, even in his fantasies, that the situation with Rosa could be resolved that easily. *Just like a man,* Nick scolded himself, *to think sex will solve everything.* He woke up in the recliner at two A.M., the plate of mostaccioli still balanced precariously in his lap next to the phone, although obviously in his sleep, Felix, his cat, had helped himself to a large portion of the pasta and sausage. *Great,* he thought, as he rose from the recliner and stumbled to the kitchen, *I'll be cleaning up cat puke all over this place tomorrow.*

***

He arrived at the office at eight-fifteen and immediately saw that Rosa's Cherokee was already there. He grabbed a cup of coffee and greeted his secretary Pat.

"Morning, Pat," Nick said.

"Morning," she replied as she interrupted her typing long enough to hand him the phone messages that had already accumulated in the fifteen minutes the office has been open. "George called. He got Dr. Taylor served. Said he was mad as a wet hen. Mrs. Taylor's already called twice. Says it's urgent she talk to you as soon as you get in."

"Great," Nick replied.

"That is going to be one demanding client," Pat observed.

"Tell me about it. I need to talk to Rosa before I call Mrs. Taylor back though. If she calls again tell her I'll call her as soon as I'm free."

"Okay," Pat replied then added, "Nick?"

"Yes."

"Can I ask you something?"

"Sure."

"Is everything okay?"

"Yeah sure," he replied. "What do you mean?"

"Nothing," she answered, "it's just...you haven't seemed like you've been here lately. Like something's bothering you. And I know Rosa hasn't been herself lately either. Just concerned, that's all."

"Thanks for your concern. Everything's okay. Really," he replied, wishing desperately that he was speaking the truth.

She smiled in reply and resumed her typing. As he turned to walk to Rosa's office, he heard Pat answer the phone again and say, "Yes, Mrs. Taylor, he is, but he's tied up in a meeting. He said to tell you he'd call you back as soon as he's free."

***

He knocked softly on Rosa's door and entered. She was seated at her desk and was packing her briefcase with several files. She glanced up as he entered. "Oh, hi Nick. I'm getting ready to leave for court in a few minutes. I don't really have any time."

"That's okay," Nick replied, "this will only take a few minutes."

She continued packing her briefcase and nonchalantly replied, "Suit yourself."

He sat down and began, "I met with Stu and Larry last night."

"Oh."

"Yeah. I told them about us...and about the situation with Livie Taylor. I'm going to finish the Taylor divorce..."

Rosa stopped packing her briefcase, sat back down, and looked directly at him as he continued "...I'm going to talk to Livie Taylor. Let her know her behavior is inappropriate and I will not tolerate it further. That our relationship is and will be entirely professional." He paused for a moment, looked directly into her eyes and added, "Okay?"

"Well, it seems to me my three male partners have already decided the issue, haven't they? Did you guys set a dress code for me too? A curfew?"

"Be reasonable. You won't represent her and I can't afford to write a check to the firm for a hundred thousand dollars. I've thought about it more and I don't want to break up the firm. We're doing well. What else can we do?"

"I've had some time to think about things, too," she began in an emotionless monotone as if she was discussing strategy in a case, "and I apologize to you. I had no right to get jealous. We agreed upon all that up front. It's just...I guess the woman in me prevailed over the lawyer. I guess after the last couple of weeks I created certain expectations about you...us...that, apparently, weren't appropriate. I think we should just try to forget what happened between us and..."

"I don't want to forget," he interjected.

"Well, I do. Very much so. But I am very, very concerned with respect to this firm and that woman and her intentions."

"I understand. I'll set her straight."

"It's not her being straight I'm concerned about."

"Jesus, Rosa, don't..."

"Don't *Jesus Rosa* me," she snapped, her calm demeanor instantly gone. "You cross the line with that woman again and your former best friend...me...will be your worst enemy."

"Don't be so unforgiving," he begged. "I haven't done anything! Give me another chance."

"Look," she replied, "my dad's not well. My mom needs me. I'm going under for the third time here with this caseload Stu's dumped on me. I have other things going on in my life besides worrying about you and your feelings. Talk to me when you're done representing Livie Taylor."

"That's your decision?" he asked.

"Yeah," she said as she rose, grabbed her briefcase and strode past him and out the door, "that's my decision."

CHAPTER 12

Nick retreated to his office, told Pat to hold his calls, and closed his office doors. He sat down in his desk chair, unbuttoned the top button of his dress shirt, loosened his tie, leaned back in his chair and...thought. The more and the longer he thought the angrier he became.

His anger was unfocused and included Stu, Larry, Livie Taylor and especially Rosa. *God damn,* he told himself, *I've not done a thing wrong and I've got my partners all over my ass and pissed at me and threatening me and refusing to talk to me. Well, fuck`em. Fuck`em all! I'm sick and tired of trying to please them and everyone else.*

I'm going to represent Livie Taylor, do the absolute best job I can for her and then when it's all over and done, if she's interested in me, well just maybe I'll be interested in her. And then Stu and Larry and even Rosa can screw themselves for all I care. But, in the meantime, Livie Taylor is going to get the riot act read to her like I've never done to a client before. No more hugs, no more kisses, not so much as a God damn smile until this case is done.

Just as he finished formulating his plan, there was a soft knock on the door and Pat poked her head in, "Nick. Sorry, I know you said not to interrupt you, but Livie Taylor's called twice more...I can't even get my work done out there."

"Okay, I'll call her," he said as he picked up the phone, "Sorry." Pat smiled back and closed his door. He dialed Livie's number.

"Thank God it's you," came the answer.

"What's wrong?" he asked.

"Oh God, where do I begin?...I have to see you this evening."

"How's four?" he asked while gazing at his calendar.

"No. It has to be later," she replied, "six-thirty or after."

Nick involuntarily grimaced, not relishing the idea of being alone in the office with her. On the other hand, his partners should be gone by then and he wouldn't have to put up with their bullshit. "Okay six-thirty," he said.

"Oh, great," she continued. "Nick...he called here. Right after he got served. I've never been spoken to like that in my life. I was so scared..."

"You didn't discuss things with him, did you?"

"No, no. I did just as you said. I said...'have your lawyer call my lawyer'"

"Good. Perfect."

"But...my God, the things he said...threatened."

"Like what?"

"Like I'd made the biggest mistake of my life and he'd guarantee me that I would live to regret my actions and if I thought the courts were going to give custody to some alcoholic, schizoid, nymphomaniac..."

"Alcoholic, schizoid, nymphomaniac?" Nick interrupted. "What the hell was that about?"

"He's crazy...he's nuts. Don't expect the things he says to make sense."

"But surely he was referring to something, wasn't he?" Nick inquired.

"No...listen...I'll tell you when I come in...it's nothing...he's crazy," she responded.

Nick glanced at his watch. The day had not started well and the huge stack of files on his desk was beckoning. "Okay, all right. See you at six-thirty," he replied.

"Six-thirty," she confirmed and hung up.

While the stack of files continued their siren song to him, he could not help but devote a few moments of thought to their just-concluded conversation. Alcoholic, schizoid, nymphomaniac? It was not likely, Nick thought, that such a bizarre epithet would be hurled without at least some minute semblance of truth to it. *Well this is just great...she's going to come in this evening and let me know that she just happened to forget to tell me about her stint in the psych ward, and the fact that she puts away a fifth of Jack a day...oh and yes, that she's doing the gardener, mailman, and pool boy while Jessica takes her naps. What makes clients think,* he wondered, *that keeping information from their own attorneys would help their cases?*

***

He was able to devote an hour to the paperwork mountain on his desk before Pat buzzed him again. "Are you taking calls?" she inquired.

"Who is it?" he asked.

"Catherine Jagger. Says she's been retained by Dr. Daniel Taylor," Pat replied.

"Thanks," he said as he prepared to punch line one.

Catherine Jagger had a well-deserved reputation as a merciless and tenacious advocate. At this point in her career, it took a big case with big stakes to bring Catherine Jagger out from Metro East to the hinterlands. The Taylor case certainly qualified.

He remembered Catherine Jagger well. Her firm, Farnsworth, Livingston, Sedgeworth & Jagger was located in Alton directly across the river from St. Louis. Her firm did mostly insurance defense and corporate work but Catherine specialized in domestic matters. Nick closed his eyes and tried to picture her. Their case in Mt. Vernon was a good eight or nine years ago. She was about Nick's age, maybe a couple of years younger. Slim, long blonde hair, petite and very attractive. Short in physical stature but long in brains, talent and balls. The two of them, Nick remembered, had gone to the mat on that case in Mt. Vernon. Unfortunately, he also remembered that he had come out second best. If the Taylors were wanting to declare war, and of that, Nick had little doubt, Catherine Jagger would be the perfect general to lead them into battle. George Patton in a skirt.

He pushed line one, "Hello."

"Nick Barnett?"

"Yes."

"Catherine Jagger at Farnsworth, Livingston, Sedgeworth & Jagger. I believe we had a case in Butler...or was it Mt. Vernon... eight or nine years ago."

"It was Mt. Vernon, Catherine. I recall it well."

"I go by Cat."

"Oh right...Cat...yeah, I recall now."

"We've been retained by Dr. Taylor."

"Great. Should be some interesting issues."

"I suppose you're right. Nick, we're in the process of filing a Motion to Vacate the O.P you had entered. The clerk has set aside some time for us Friday at ten..."

"This Friday?" Nick interrupted.

"Yes."

"Well," he said, glancing at his calendar, "I'm tied up Friday. Doctor's deposition in Effingham at ten."

"Nothing I can do about that," she replied. "You'll have to rearrange your deposition. We're entitled to our hearing within ten days and Friday at ten is what the clerk gave us. We can't agree to any continuance on this one. My client believes the O.P. was obtained under false representations..."

"Just a minute," Nick interrupted, "I can't change that deposition..."

"Then file a Motion for Continuance," she said as she returned the favor and cut him off. "But we'll oppose it. We have a right to this hearing immediately. Bottom line is that we're going to be in court Friday morning. Your client shouldn't have sought an emergency O.P. without notice if she wasn't able to defend it in a timely manner."

Nick knew that if he tried to push the issue, the judge would deny his motion to continue. He could back down now and save some face, or get his hackles up, tell Cat Jagger to go to hell and end up looking like an idiot. "Okay, all right, I'll see what I can do about the deposition. Friday at ten."

"Right. Plus we'll be delivering another motion to be heard Friday. Thought I'd give you a head's up. We'll be asking the court to issue a subpoena duces tecum for her mental health records from her stay at Gateway Regional. As you know, it takes a prima facie showing of relevance to get a subpoena for mental health and psychiatric records. But we believe they'll be extremely relevant in this case...essential really."

Nick was stunned, but certainly, he did not want Cat Jagger to know that his client had failed to disclose to him that she had a psychiatric treatment history nor did he want her to know that he didn't have the faintest idea what the records would show. He hesitated only the briefest of moments before replying in as calm a demeanor as he could muster under the circumstances. "Well, of course, we've covered that thoroughly and believe you are not entitled to them. Obviously, we will vigorously object to the subpoena."

"Of course," she replied, "your client could avoid the subpoena if she'll agree to custody for Dr. Taylor. I've already discussed it with him and he's willing to be quite generous with visitation."

Nick laughed in reply, "And I suppose he doesn't even want child support. What a guy! I can tell you right now that my client will agree to her husband having custody when pigs fly."

"No harm in offering," she replied. "Speaking of visitation. My client wants Jessica tomorrow night from five to nine and every other weeknight until the order of protection is vacated.

Given that the O.P. bars him from coming to his own home, I suggest we use the police station as a transfer point. Agreed?"

"I'll have to talk to my client...she's coming in this afternoon...but every other night? Come on...that's ridiculous."

"Then e-mail me your proposal."

"Okay, I'll get you something."

"Fine."

"Oh, please tell your client not to call his wife anymore...cut out the threats," Nick added.

"What are you talking about?" she asked.

"He called her yesterday right after he was served. Threatened her. Used some pretty vile language. It doesn't help the situation any," Nick explained.

"Well, I can tell you for a fact that he called me on his cell from the parking lot of his office as he was being served and I cautioned him not to attempt to have any contact with her 'til I could talk to you. His response was, and I quote, 'I'll talk to that crazy bitch again when hell freezes.'"

"Apparently he disregarded your advice," Nick added while wondering to himself just exactly how forthright his client had been with him.

"I really doubt that," she replied, "but I guess it's *he said, she said*. By the way, has your client bothered to tell you there's a prenup here and under it, she has no right to the house...or any pre-marital property...and no claim for maintenance?"

"Yeah, she's told me," Nick answered, thankful that at least he could spring something on Cat in this conversation, "and I've already got a petition to set it aside prepared and ready to file."

"Really?" she asked. "Basis?"

"All in good time," Nick replied, "I can't show all my hand up front can I?"

"I guess not," she chuckled in reply. "One other thing. My client says his personal laptop was at the house when he was served with the Order of Protection. He needs it. He says it has some very important and very confidential records regarding his medical practice. We'd like to make arrangements for him to come out and get it. And of course, since it contains his patient's confidential records, we expect its privacy to be respected if your client comes across it. You know under HIPPA it can be a criminal offense to breach the confidentiality of medical records. Please warn your client that, if she comes across it, it's in a locked case. If that lock is broken when he gets it back there will be severe legal consequences."

"Well, that's odd," Nick commented, "my client tells me her laptop and cell phone turned up missing just a couple days ago. Looks like another *he said, she said*. Looks like this case may be more interesting than either of us suspected. See you Friday."

"Right," she replied, hesitated a moment then added, "Nick?"

"Yes?"

"I recall that case we had in Mt. Vernon years ago."

"Yeah, so do I," Nick answered while wondering what her point was.

"Well, I wanted to say I thought you did a very good job with a very tough case and that you were a real professional."

What the hell is this? he thought. *Is she buttering me up hoping to use it to advantage?* He decided to play along to see where it would lead. "Flattery will get you everywhere."

"Just be careful with this woman. If things I've been told are accurate, she has some serious problems."

For the second time in their brief conversation, Nick was stunned. Was she being truthful? Was she telling him this out of genuine concern for a colleague she respected? Or was it some sly tactic on her part to drive a wedge between him and his client? From what he remembered about Cat Jagger and from what he knew of her reputation, he guessed, unfortunately, that it was the former.

"Well thanks for the warning," he answered while forcing a nervous chuckle, "but from what I've been told about your client...and his mother...I could tell you the same thing."

"Okay. Enough said. I just thought I owed you that upfront. See you Friday."

"Friday," he repeated then hung up.

CHAPTER 13

Nick paced around his office while compulsively glancing at his watch. His caffeine and adrenaline overload made it nearly impossible for him to be still. He glanced at his watch again. Six twenty-seven. He heard a door open and then a few seconds later another door open closely followed by the sound of a car starting. He spread open and glanced through the mini-blinds covering his office window and was immensely relieved to see Rosa's Cherokee leaving. *Thank God,* he thought, *at least I can deal with Livie without worrying about a scene between her and Rosa.*

A minute later he glanced at his watch again and was disappointed, though not particularly surprised, to see it was now six twenty-eight. Sixteen glances later at six thirty-seven anger began overtaking nervousness as his primary emotion. *Goddammit,* he muttered to himself, *if Livie stands me up again, we're through...I'm done.* As he finished his muttering, he heard the door chime announce that someone had entered. He walked out to the lobby to greet her and although mentally prepared he was nevertheless taken aback for a brief moment. She was wearing a white skirt which came to well below her knees. Her pale pink silk blouse was unbuttoned enough to display a full view of her simple string of pearls and an enticingly slight bit of cleavage. The lacy scallops of her bra were clearly discernable under her blouse.

Her hair was styled differently but the difference was so subtle that Nick would have been hard-pressed to identify it. A pink rose in her hair complimented her blouse.

She wore white hose and white heeled sandals. As she took a step towards him and extended her right hand to him he could see that the skirt had a long slit on the right side that traversed halfway up her thigh. Nick doubted seriously that, an hour ago, home alone with a toddler she was dressed in this fashion and had little doubt it was for his benefit. This, he quickly concluded, is not going to be easy. He took her hand but kept a good distance from her and said, "Come on back. We have a lot of ground to cover."

They went back to his office. As she took her seat across the desk from him she crossed her right leg over her left. The slit in her skirt obligingly opened to display her thigh and just a touch of the lace top of her white stocking. *No,* Nick thought before swallowing hard and beginning, *this is not going to be easy.*

"Nick," she began before he could get the first word out, "thank you so much for seeing me so late...I just couldn't get away and I had..."

He interrupted her, "We've got several important matters to discuss first and I want to get to them before we run out of time..."

"I've got all night," she said as she smiled. "Jessica's at a friend's."

Nick smiled back, "Well, I don't. I have to be out of here by..." he glanced at his watch and quickly calculated that it would take an hour to go through everything he needed to cover with her, "seven forty-five."

She continued to smile but clearly looked perturbed that Nick had declined her not so subtle invitation. "Fine," she replied.

"I got a call from your husband's lawyer today...Catherine Jagger...from Alton...a very fine attorney...a good firm...."

"Yes."

"And they've scheduled a hearing for this Friday regarding the order of protection..."

"Well, delay it," she interjected.

"I doubt I can. They're statutorily entitled to a hearing within ten days and that's the day the court has given them...."

"But you said you could drag it out for months," she reminded him.

"I said it could drag out for months but if they insist on a timely hearing, I can't prevent it."

"Then we'll go to court Friday," she said nonchalantly.

"Yes, we will," he added, "unless we can agree to a temporary order before then."

"Which says what?"

"Well, we'll have to deal with temporary possession of the home, temporary custody, support, payment of the bills, try to get some attorney fees out of him," Nick explained.

"What about alimony?"

"We'll probably need a separate hearing on that...later. The prenup you signed bars alimony."

"But you said you could throw it out..."

"I think I can. But it will take a full evidentiary hearing, discovery, depositions. No way that will happen this Friday."

"What do you recommend?" she asked.

"You keep temporary possession of the house, primary custody of Jessica, every other weekend and Wednesday night visitation for Daniel, he pays all the household bills...utilities...insurance on the house, your car, medical insurance through his office and we'll ask for fifteen thousand dollars but if we can get close to ten thousand a month child support, we'll be doing well."

"That's ridiculous...I'm used to spending that much on clothes every month."

"It'll just be until we can schedule a hearing on the temporary alimony question. When I hit them with the evidence we have to set the prenup aside, my guess is they'll back off and agree. Jagger's firm prepared the prenup. They won't want to be embarrassed in court."

"How long will I have to get by on ten thousand dollars a month?" she asked.

Get by? Nick thought. *Ninety-nine percent of the families in this town would think they died and went to heaven if they had ten thousand dollars a month to "get by" on.* But he didn't think she would benefit from a lecture on how fortunate she was. "I'm hoping no more than sixty to ninety days," he replied, then added, "Also I'll ask for fifty thousand dollars in temporary fees from him, then I can rebate some to you."

"Okay, but you keep it. I'm afraid you're going to earn it," she said as she again smiled and shifted her legs to expose even more thigh and stocking. "I told you I had quite a bit of money put away I can tap into." She smiled again, "I trust you."

"Thanks," Nick replied. "Okay. Next. They're going to push for custody for Daniel..."

"I could have told you that," she interrupted.

"I know, but apparently there will be allegations of some serious psychological or psychiatric problems on your part..."

"What bullshit!" she exclaimed.

"They're already talking about subpoenaing records from your hospitalization at Gateway Regional. What's that about? Why didn't you tell me?"

She turned her head away and he thought for a moment she was going to cry. She looked back at Nick. Her face was devoid of tears and instead anger seemed to have overtaken her. "After Jessica was born, I had a short bout of postpartum depression. I was trying to cope with a new baby, he was never home, I was totally isolated, his bitch of a mother was all over my case. I was overwhelmed at first. I got some help and got through it."

"Was there alcohol abuse involved?"

"Yes...for a short while...it's not unusual in those situations.

You want to escape so bad...." She stopped and the tears came now, "...that bastard, that bitch." She looked up directly at Nick, leaned across the desk and grabbed his hand. "I got some help and they're going to use it against me? The court won't let that happen, will it?"

"Livie..." Nick replied as he retrieved his hand from her grasp and proceeded slowly, "when custody's at issue, everything...every little thing about a parent...their age, health, emotional history, likes, dislikes, whether you're left-handed, right-handed, whether you like coffee or tea, everything's at issue. Nothing's off-limits."

"Then let them get the fucking records," she snapped. "They'll show I loved my daughter enough to get help."

Nick slid a medical release form across the desk to her. "We better get them first. Sign here and I'll overnight this to Gateway. Okay?"

"Okay, but understand, it's a disease. It's like cancer or the flu or any other disease. It wasn't my fault I got it. And you're capable of thinking things, saying things, you would never really do," she replied as she signed.

"I do understand," he answered. "Now, is there anything else I don't know that I should? Much better that it comes out now so we can figure out how to best deal with it than to find out in court."

"No, nothing," she answered.

"What about...other men?"

She grabbed a couple of tissues, glanced back up at Nick and dabbed her eyes. "Look, I didn't want to get into this but...how shall I put it? Daniel has very severe performance problems." She glanced back down and looked embarrassed. "I've always had...a healthy appetite...and I was thirty-five when we got married. I just wasn't ready to give that part of my life up. I tried to get him to get help...Viagra, whatever, but of course, according to him, it wasn't his problem, I was causing it."

"How many?"

"I didn't count," she shrugged as she glanced downwards.

"How many does he know about?"

"I don't know, two, I think. He was always accusing me, even when I was innocent." She looked back up directly into his eyes and continued, "Please don't think I'm like that though. It was totally out of character for me. It's against everything I believe in." She paused, smiled and searched his eyes to see if he was believing her mea culpa, "I would never ever cheat on a real man."

"I have to ask you a very, very important question and do not take offense at it. But I have to know. Is there any possibility, any possibility at all, that Daniel is not Jessica's father?"

"Of course not," she replied, looking more amused than indignant. "I've already told you the circumstances surrounding her conception. He had...problems...that night too but we both had way too much to drink. It was more work than fun...it always was with Daniel...but I swear to you he's her father. There's no doubt."

"Has he ever suggested that he questions his paternity?" he asked.

"No, never. He was too damn proud that he could knock someone up," she answered. "Martha's made her little smart remarks now and then but never Daniel."

Nick leaned back in his chair and locked his hands behind his head. *So the moniker, "alcoholic, schizoid, nymphomaniac" wasn't all that far from the truth after all. Well, that was just great. And what a great time to be finding this stuff out,* he thought.

"I don't know how to put this strongly enough," he began, "I have to know this stuff. You simply cannot be withholding information from me."

"But what does any of this have to do with Jessica?" she pleaded.

"Maybe nothing. Maybe a lot. But how can I make a judgment if I don't know about it?"

"I'm sorry. Honestly, it never even occurred to me that any of this would be a concern..."

"You didn't think a history of alcohol abuse, hospitalization for depression, multiple affairs would be a concern in a divorce?" Nick asked, incredulous.

Her tears came again. "Don't put it like that...you make it sound so awful...if you had any idea what those two were putting me through..." her voice trailed off, drowned in her tears.

Nick let her cry in silence for a moment before continuing. "I've tried to tell you, we're in a war. A general better know as much about the strengths and weaknesses of his own army as he does about the enemy's. I absolutely have to know this stuff and I'd much prefer learning it from you than from Cat Jagger. Do you understand?"

"Yes," she replied, "I'm sorry...I promise I wasn't trying to keep things from you. God, what a nightmare this is."

"It's just beginning. This could go on for a year. Remember what I told you about being in it for the long haul."

"I do. I will. I'm okay. Thank you," she replied with another smile.

"All right. Two other things before we talk about court Friday."

"Okay."

"One. Jagger says you have Daniel's laptop, not vice versa. She says it's in a locked case. There are confidential medical records in it and if you find it and open it they'll see to it you're charged with a crime for violating confidentiality."

"Well, where is it supposed to be?" she asked.

"She wouldn't say."

"Then how am I supposed to find it?"

"He wants to come to the house and get it."

"No way, Nick. No way he sets foot in that house until this is over. He'd probably plant a bug in the house. You don't know these people. They're capable of anything."

"Well, if you come across it, don't open it. Just bring it to me."

"If it's at the house, I'm certainly not aware of it. I'll bring it to you if I find it, but it's probably just another one of his crazy games."

"Okay. Please do. Now, point number two: Livie, attorneys have certain rules of conduct; of ethics. Rules that, if they are broken, can cause a lawyer to be sued, suspended from practice, even disbarred."

"Yes."

"One of those rules is that a lawyer and a client cannot become..." he paused searching his mind for the right words "...romantically involved...in any way." At the mention of "romantic involvement," a small smile came across Livie's face.

Nick continued, "You're already aware that I'm divorced. You're an extremely attractive woman. And I just want to make it crystal clear that these rules will be abided by. To be honest, some of your behavior to date has crossed the line...the hugs, the kisses. In fact, my partner, Rosa, was convinced that you left lipstick on my cheek on purpose just to...cause a problem..."

"She said that? I didn't realize I left lipstick on your cheek. That's crazy! What's her problem?"

"I told her she was wrong. But if there is any misunderstanding on this issue I want it to be corrected right here and now before anything else happens. There are to be no more hugs, no more kisses, no flirtation. We have serious work to do here and those are the rules. Okay? Any questions before we start preparing for court Friday?"

Livie smiled coquettishly, looked directly into his eyes and replied, "Only one."

"What's that?" he asked.

"Do the rules still apply when the divorce is over?"

Nick blushed. She had recrossed her legs and was exposing even more of her stockinged thigh. She continued to smile. Nick studied her intently. Her beauty and femininity were overpowering. He knew he should read her the riot act and again let her know he was deadly serious about what he was telling her. But as those very thoughts were swirling in his head, he nevertheless heard himself say, "No. No, they don't."

CHAPTER 14

Nick nervously paced back and forth in front of the west entrance to the courthouse. The weather was continuing its springtime moodiness. Menacing dark clouds had returned after a brief respite and were swirling in from the southwestern sky threatening another round of intense thunderstorms.

Nick continued pacing while keeping a lookout for Livie Taylor's white Lexus. *Times like this,* he thought to himself, *make me wish I'd never quit smoking.* If it wasn't for the solemn promise he had made to Natalie, he might even consider taking the filthy habit up again. After ten years of abstinence, he missed them almost as much as the day he had quit.

The week about to conclude had been one of the longest and most difficult he could remember. He had felt, in his own office, as alien and uncomfortable as a politician at confession. Stu and Larry were, uncharacteristically, poking their heads into his office four or five times daily just to say hi. What bullshit! He could count the number of "hi's" he had gotten from Stu and Larry in the previous sixteen years on one hand. He knew they were checking up on him, making sure he wasn't diddling Livie Taylor on his desk and more importantly letting him know that his office was no longer private. That they could and would open his door and check things out any damn time they pleased. And Rosa and her God damn excruciating politeness. Absolutely refusing to truly talk to him. He could not even remember the last time he had heard her laugh.

Even the secretaries. Obviously, word had gotten out that there was a major problem in the firm and just as certainly they knew the problem somehow involved Nick, Rosa and Livinia Taylor He didn't even want to imagine the rumors that were probably circulating around the office water cooler. He had little doubt that Sarah, Larry's secretary, who loved gossip more than life, had informed the others that she knew for a fact that Nick, Rosa, and Livie Taylor had gotten caught in flagrante delicto in a threesome on Nick's desk. No wonder every time he went back there the conversation suddenly turned to the weather or the Cardinals or something equally safe. And they all gave him their polite, almost apologetic smiles. *Jesus, how did things get so haywire so quick?* he asked himself.

Livie Taylor had been in yesterday to prepare for today's hearing. She had again insisted on an evening appointment and Nick had been happy to comply. He had no doubt that if he had Livie Taylor in his office during the day, Stu, Larry, Rosa, half the secretaries, the mailman, the UPS guy and the lady who cleaned the office on the weekends would all find an excuse to poke their heads in.

Their appointment had been at seven-thirty. The thunderstorms had finally bored of pummeling Martin County and had moved on to other targets of opportunity. In their wake, the weather had turned gloriously and unseasonably warm, hot even. It was a perfect spring evening, a gentle breeze carrying spring's signature scent of rebirth with it. Nick had gotten back to the office at seven intending to get some work done before Livie Taylor came in, but the beauty of the day's transformation into dusk overwhelmed him and instead he simply sat on the front steps of his office and reveled in the serenity of it. Life, he mused, with a slight chuckle, was a lot like Midwestern weather.

Chaotic, unpredictable and heartbreaking one moment. Then, an instant later, serene, perfect, intoxicatingly beautiful. *I suppose,* he thought, *it teaches us to take the bad with the good. If life was like San Diego weather, I'd complain it was boring.* He felt sorry, momentarily, for San Diegans before recognizing that, likely, they neither desired nor warranted his sympathy.

As he had concluded his philosophizing about whether it could be possible to truly appreciate a life devoid of shitty weather, Livie Taylor's Lexus pulled to a stop in front of his office. Excepting only the time she had appeared in a skirt, sweatshirt and tears, she had always been dressed immaculately. Classic, refined and elegant...regal even...were all adjectives that came easily to mind. After their initial discussion about inappropriate conduct, he had talked to her twice more on the phone about the fact that he would not tolerate any more such behavior on her part. He wanted to make sure she got the message loud and clear. Each time she had given the appropriate responses. But each time Nick had gotten the distinct impression that she was reciting the answers by rote. Giving the perfect answer she knew the teacher wanted to hear so she could get a passing grade, but also letting the teacher know that when school was over, maybe it would be time for recess and a little fun.

Livie Taylor was thirty-nine. She was beautiful in a way women under thirty-five are incapable of, regardless of their physical attributes. In describing Livie Taylor, "beautiful" was such a pathetically inadequate adjective. This evening was beautiful, a Ferrari was beautiful, Hawaii was beautiful: Livie Taylor was...well...divine...in the truly religious sense of the word. Unassailable proof of the existence of God.

Nick could not help but wonder about her ancestry. Clearly, she was a menagerie. Her maiden name, "Lawrence" was not much help other than to indicate there was some amount of Anglo Saxon somewhere in the mix. Likely he guessed there was also some Mediterranean in her...Italian perhaps, or Greek maybe, or Spanish...the olive shading of her skin, the brunette hair (he was certain it was her natural color), the beautiful brown eyes told him that. And if pressed, he would almost guess that...maybe generations back...there was some Asian mixed in, or maybe some American Indian. The ever so slight oriental look to her eyes complemented perfectly her otherwise occidental face. It was as if God had picked and chosen from His best work over the past hundred thousand years and had produced, finally, His masterpiece. Nick could almost picture Him in heaven, seated on His throne, with a self-congratulatory smile thinking, "Damn, I'm good."

He recalled last night that Livie had exited and walked around her car. Although he had tried to be emotionally prepared, she nevertheless, once again, had taken his breath away. And last night she had not looked refined or elegant and certainly not regal. Her hair, always previously perfectly coifed had been liberated and was bouncing unrestrained about her shoulders as she walked. Sunglasses were propped up on her head. A delicate gold chain disappeared into her decolletage. She was wearing a lacy white sleeveless spaghetti strap blouse of which the top three or four buttons were unbuttoned; a very short, very black, very leather skirt, and black high heeled boots that came to just below her knees.

Previously his mental image of her was Aubrey Hepburn in *Breakfast at Tiffany's*. Refined, elegant, cultured. But last night as she had strode up the walk towards him, an intoxicating mixture of leather and lace, the imagery was of Barbarella. Dangerous, sexual and oh so incredibly fuckable. He had never seen her like this before nor could he have even imagined it. It would have been like trying to picture the Pope on a Harley wearing chaps and a muscle tee and sporting tattoos. The raw sexuality of her appearance immobilized him briefly.

He had overcome his momentary paralysis and rose to meet her. He willed himself to be a lawyer instead of a man. But will power was a feeble match against the countervailing force of a million years of evolutionary biology and he was engorged even before he was completely upright. He was mortified and his mortification was obvious. He placed his left hand in his pants pocket hoping to mask the source of his mortification but he saw Livie look down at the obvious bulge in his khakis. They smiled at each other and engaged in a silent conspiracy to pretend that neither was aware of what they were both acutely aware of.

"Beautiful evening," Nick commented nervously.

"Yes it is," she confirmed through her triumphant smile.

"Yes, well, come on in. We've got a lot to cover," he stammered.

Biology gradually loosened its grip on Nick as his genes eventually concluded it was a false alarm and they would not have the opportunity tonight, at least, to propagate themselves. They had had their conference and had prepared for the hearing today. Nick had forced himself to again remind her that their relationship was to be entirely professional although, given the manner in which he had greeted her, his lecture lacked a certain moral clarity. Both of them seemed to sense that he didn't mean a word he was saying. Although he doubted he needed to remind her, he made sure to tell her to come to court as Aubrey Hepburn and not Barbarella.

To say that Nick Barnett's feelings about Livie Taylor were ambivalent was an understatement of enormous magnitude. Other than financially, her appearance in his life had been a complete disaster. Rosa barely spoke to him. Stu and Larry hovered over him protectively as if he was Poland and she was Hitler. Professionally, he had already done things in her case which skirted and perhaps even crossed the line. He had already been given substantial reason to doubt his client's ability to be truthful.

Yet, standing on the courthouse steps, waiting for her to arrive, picturing her in his mind, he knew that if he was given the choice today to have her disappear forever from his life without consequence, he would decline. It wasn't, he convinced himself, just that she was, far and away, the most beautiful woman he had ever known. His attraction for her went beyond her mere physical beauty. Her speech, her laughter, her tears, her mannerisms, the way she moved; everything about her was everything Nick's mind told him a woman "should" be. And somehow she was able to explain rationally and to Nick's satisfaction the myriad accusations being hurled at her. It did not then occur to Nick that, perhaps, he wanted, too much, to believe her. Whenever she completed an explanation, she had the uncanny ability to cause Nick to feel guilty and apologetic that he had even questioned her in the first place. She had come to him for help in the most difficult time of her life to save her from a detestable, sexless, loveless marriage to a man apparently incapable of love. She was a beautiful princess tied to a stake and the fire-breathing dragon was circling ever closer and preparing to dive towards her. Sir Nick, lance in hand, clad in a suit of shining armor, on his pure white steed had arrived to rescue the damsel in distress. There was something so compelling, so primeval about the whole scenario. Nick knew, deep in his subconscious, how the fairy tale always ended after the knight in shining armor slew the dragon. The fair damsel would be his reward. And he had little doubt that Livie Taylor was a damsel capable of providing a reward that would make dragon-slaying worth the occupational risks.

His ruminations about the prior evening had been so focused that he had overlooked her Lexus circle by and pull into a parking space. But she immediately caught his eye as she exited the car. She was again Audrey Hepburn, this time dressed in a pale purple suit and a white blouse, with, of course, pearls, and a matching bag and pumps. He had been so overwhelmed when he had seen her last night that, before he even knew what he was saying, he had mentioned that he liked her hair down. She was again wearing it down and unstructured. He noted several men and one woman simply stop dead in their tracks on the sidewalk to watch her walk by. As he watched them stare at her, he felt a masculine pride usually reserved for husbands or boyfriends.

He greeted her with a handshake. "Ready?" he asked.

She smiled uncertainly and squeezed his hand, "As long as you're with me."

"Let's go."

They silently took the elevator to the third floor of the courthouse. He quickly ascertained that there was no jury today and he seated Livie in the jury room. "I'm going to find your husband's lawyer and we'll probably both meet with the judge first. I'll come get you when I need you. Will you be okay?"

"Yeah, I'm fine," she replied as she reached for and squeezed his hand. "Fight for me."

Nick smiled back and closed the jury room door. As he walked towards the judge's chambers a very short, very stocky woman with masculinely short dark hair in a navy blue business suit holding a briefcase in one hand approached him and extended her hand "Nick, hi," she said. "Should we try and grab Judge Swanson?"

Nick extended his hand in reply but was befuddled. Obviously, this woman was either a lawyer or a damn good impersonation of one but he was certain he had never set eyes upon her in his life. He tried but was unsuccessful in his efforts to conceal his confusion. She smiled as she took his extended hand in hers and said, "It's me. Cat Jagger."

Shock proved no easier for Nick to conceal than befuddlement. His mind was screaming the question, *What the hell happened to you?* The last time he had seen her she had been very attractive, very petite, very blonde. His voice instead said, "Oh sure...Cat. I'm sorry. I guess it's been a while."

"No need to apologize. I hardly recognize myself anymore. The long blonde hair and size twos are long gone," she laughed, then explained, "I've had some medical problems and this damn prednisone they put me on made me blow up like a balloon. But, hey, my husband says it just makes for more of me to love."

"Oh, jeez, I'm sorry," Nick stammered.

"Don't be. I'm still here. I've learned to enjoy every day like I never could before. And I've got a great husband and an excuse to never go on a fucking diet in my life, ever again. Every woman's dream," she chuckled.

"Well," Nick replied, "that's a great attitude. If I was a betting man, I'd bet on you."

"Thanks," she said. "What do you say we find Judge Leslie Jones-Swanson and see what she thinks about our not so happy couple?"

"Fine," he said while opening the door to the judge's chambers. "Ladies first," he added.

Cat looked up at him and laughed. "Thanks, but once I cross through that doorway I'm no lady. I'm your worst nightmare."

Nick chuckled in reply but only hoped that Cat Jagger was right and that his worst nightmare would not prove to be his own client, patiently seated in the jury room in a pale purple designer suit.

CHAPTER 15

Nick and Cat were informed that Judge Swanson was on a conference call in her chambers that was expected to last another ten minutes or more. Nick took a seat in the judge's chambers to wait while Cat saw another lawyer she had not seen in years and reintroduced the new her to him.

Nick glanced about the judge's chambers. Court reporters, bailiffs, clerks, lawyers and the occasional judge were milling about, sipping coffee and trading war stories, just as they had sixteen years earlier when Nick had gone to court for the very first time right here in this very same courthouse, a very new, very in-experienced, very nervous young lawyer. Many of the names had changed, many of the faces, the hairstyles, the fashions, the haze of smoke that was ever-present sixteen years ago but long since banned. Otherwise, it was almost like a time warp. *If I knew then what I know now*, he waxed nostalgic before recognizing that, back then, he knew nothing. He glanced at the portrait of Judge Walter Samuels hanging on the wall.

He remembered it like it was yesterday. His first case in court. The haze of smoke might be gone now, but through the haze of his reminiscing, he could almost hear old Judge Samuels call his first case. A default divorce. No opponent. All issues settled. All he had to do was get through a checklist of questions with his client, Mrs. Brown, and hand Judge Samuels the paperwork. He smiled slightly as he recalled his performance. Nervous, sweating, stumbling over his words, dropping the paperwork all over the courtroom floor, calling Mrs. Brown, Mrs. Black. What would today take him four or five minutes to accomplish had dragged on for fifteen long torturous minutes. The longest fifteen minutes of his...and, he was quite sure, anyone's life. When, mercifully, it was over and Judge Samuels had sorted through the disorganized jumble of paperwork Nick had gathered from the floor and handed to him, the judge had excused Mrs. Brown and declared a recess. He then quietly added to Nick that he would like to see him in his chambers.

Nick followed the gray-haired, black-robed judge back to his chambers fully expecting to get excoriated for his performance. Judge Samuels slowly removed his robe, hung it on the coat tree, sat down, lit a cigarette and poured himself a cup of coffee.

"Sit down, Nick," he said as he gestured to a chair. "Smoke if you like." Nick obliged him.

"First time in court?" he asked.

"Um...yes...I'm sorry sir, I guess I was pretty nervous," Nick replied.

Judge Samuels laughed, "Well, I'm glad."

"Glad, sir?"

"Yes, glad. And 'judge' will do fine. No need for 'sir'. I'm not a general. Just an old man in a black robe. I'm glad because being nervous means you have some reverence for what you're going to be doing for the next fifty years. A reason to be nervous. And you're not trying to cover up with some false bravado. The nervousness will go away, trust me. Replaced, a lot of the time, by boredom, frustration, cynicism even. But don't lose the reverence. Reverence for your clients, for what you do, for the law itself." He paused a minute and took a long drag on his cigarette and a sip of his coffee. "Mrs. Brown out there you just got divorced, barely..." he paused again and chuckled, then added "you won't remember her name or her case in twenty years. But she'll remember today. It might well be her only personal contact with our legal system in her entire life. And she'll base her opinion of this system...on lawyers and judges...more on this, her personal experience, than on all the TV shows or movies she'll ever see. Remember that, Nick. Remember who it is this whole system is designed to serve. Not you. Not me. But Mrs. Brown. Remember that and you'll be a good lawyer."

Nick smiled fondly as he remembered. Judge Samuels had been so right about so much, but he had been wrong too. Nick remembered Mrs. Brown, and always would, because of their conversation.

The door to Judge Swanson's office opened, she stepped out and made eye contact with Nick.

"Nick," she barked, "Ms. Jagger here yet?"

"Yes."

"Find her and get her in here," she commanded, "we've got a lot to cover."

Nick smiled in reply, rose, interrupted Cat's conversation and led her to Judge Swanson's office. They entered. Nick closed the door behind him and they seated themselves. Judge Swanson was turned away checking stock quotes on her computer. She finished, then spun on her chair to face them. She looked at them both for an instant then asked with her customary lack of tact, "Where the hell is Ms. Jagger?"

"Right here," Cat replied as she extended her hand across the desk. Nick was amused to see that the judge's shock appeared to exceed the level of his own only minutes before. He could picture the same question formulating in Judge Swanson's brain, *What in the hell happened to you?*

Poor woman, Nick thought, she's probably ready to print up cards to have available to pass out to the morbidly curious stating, "What the hell happened to me? I got sick and I've been on steroids and I blew up like a fucking balloon and I quit dying my hair and cut it short but you know what? I'm just God damn happy to be alive. That's what happened. Any more stupid questions that are none of your business?"

In the years Nick had known Judge Swanson he had never seen her at a loss for words, not that, at times, he hadn't wished she was. But for the moment she was flustered, stammering. Cat, being a lawyer in the unusual and thoroughly enjoyable position of having a judge at a disadvantage, failed to offer an explanation as she had to Nick. Judge Swanson stammered and fidgeted for another few seconds before realizing she was not going to get an answer to her unasked question.

"Okay, counsel," she began, "we've got quite a bit to cover and one hour of court time to cover it in. First off, the order of protection is vacated..."

"But Judge" Nick protested, "you..."

She cut him off with an upraised hand and continued, "Counsel, I seem to remember you approaching me in chambers awhile back seeking an emergency O.P. with a remarkably similar set of facts. Am I wrong?"

"No, your Honor," he conceded.

"And I also seem to recall that I advised you in no uncertain terms that I did not see a basis for an ex parte order. Correct again?"

"Yes."

"Then I see where Judge Hanson who was assigned the criminal docket that day was apparently talked into entering an order in that same case. True?"

"Yes."

"For future reference, Mr. Barnett, when I am the judge assigned to civil and make a decision you do not like I do not expect counsel who practice in front of me to do an end-run to another judge. This isn't *The Dating Game*. You don't get to pick and choose. Either boot me off the whole case or live with my decisions. Clear?"

"Yes, ma'am."

"Okay. That's settled. Now, as I've said, we've got one hour of court time. From review of the pleadings, we've got enough issues pending to consume two or three days of trial already. Each side has filed petitions for temporary custody, temporary exclusive possession of the home, there are petitions from Mrs. Taylor for temporary maintenance and attorney fees, Dr. Taylor has a motion for a subpoena duces tecum for psychiatric records, a motion seeking enforcement of a prenup, a motion to bar certain temporary relief. Have I missed anything, counsel?"

Nick reached into his briefcase and handed the judge and Cat each a large stack of papers. "I'm filing right now a motion to set aside the prenup with supporting documents attached which I believe conclusively demonstrate that Dr. Taylor substantially understated his net worth. We've also included a brief on the issue."

"Well...." Cat started to reply but was instantly cut off.

"No need to reply now. But I take back what I said. We may have a week's worth of trial time just on what's already pending. As I see it, you two have two choices. One, you can sit down and talk turkey. Cut the crap, cut the bullshit, and come to a temporary arrangement which I'll be pleased to approve. Or we can call Carla up here with the court's calendar and get a date for a three or four-day temporary hearing that will probably be in six to eight weeks. So, in the meantime, there will be no orders entered. No custody order, no visitation order, no support order, no exclusive possession order, no shit. If your clients don't kill each other before we get to the hearing, then we'll get some orders entered then. Now," she said as she picked up her phone, "should I call Carla or do you two want to get down to business?"

Nick and Cat glanced at each other and said simultaneously, "We'll talk."

Cat continued, "But, we would certainly like some guidance today on the issue of these psychiatric records of Mrs. Taylor. We can't possibly seriously address any permanent custody arrangement without them. As we've noted in our motion some very serious issues are raised. Issues that go to whether this young child is substantially at risk if the mother gets custody."

"What's wrong with her?" the judge asked.

"That's the problem. We really don't know. She's always refused to discuss it with her own husband or let her doctors do so. But, as Dr. Taylor has set forth in his affidavit accompanying the motion she was an inpatient in the PCU at Gateway Regional for approximately two weeks..."

"When?"

"Shortly after the child was born, maybe three years ago. When she was discharged she was on an antipsychotic medicine which Dr. Taylor, as a physician, knows is often prescribed for schizophrenia. She self-terminated her medication and treatment. There's been substantial alcohol abuse, rampant sexual promiscuity..."

"Judge, please," Nick barged in, "I object to having my client crucified in chambers. She had a brief bout of postpartum depression. She got help. She shouldn't be punished for that."

"Ms. Jagger," the judge asked, "any known history of mental health treatment since the discharge three years ago?"

"Not that we're aware of."

"And apparently for the last three years, your client has not been so concerned that it prevented him from going to work every day and leaving the child in the care of his wife?"

"Well no, Judge, he was very concerned. But he had to work."

"Really?" she replied as she glanced at some of the financial papers Nick had handed her. "If I had his net worth I'm not at all sure I'd work."

"But Judge..." Cat began.

"I'm sorry Counsel," Judge Swanson interrupted, "but I get rather tired of having parents come in here complaining that their spouse is a child abuser when there's a history that they voluntarily left the kids with that very same parent day in and day out for years. Your motion will not be granted today. Notice it up for formal hearing, but you better have more than what you've told me today if you expect it to be granted."

"Judge..." Cat pleaded.

Judge Swanson glanced at her watch. "You've got fifty minutes. I'd start talking if I were you."

Nick and Cat left the judge's chambers to tell their clients that the judge had let them know, in no uncertain terms, that they would agree upon a temporary order whether they wanted to or not. By now they were both used to how the system worked and neither was particularly surprised at what had transpired in chambers. It's just that...it was so different from what they had been taught in law school or what you saw on TV and movies where cases were decided in open court amidst brilliant oratory, withering cross-examinations, or "O.J." moments. Most cases, they knew, were hammered out in the courthouse library, or an unused jury room, or an out of the way corner. Tempers frayed, nerves on edge, until finally, both sides relented, walked away with half of what they had insisted upon getting, and some ugly, rough parity of justice was somehow achieved.

Before entering the jury room to tell Livie what had happened he watched Cat as she walked up to the middle-aged man and an older matronly looking woman who rose to greet Cat in unison from the hardback wooden chairs lining the third floor of the courthouse. It would not have taken a seer to guess that it was Dr. Taylor and his mother.

He had not inquired of Livie about a physical description of either Daniel Taylor or Martha. But, when he saw them, he instantly realized he had subconsciously created a mental picture of both...just as one puts a face to a familiar, but unseen, voice on the radio. He was amused that his mental picture of Martha was right on...nearly a perfect match. His mental picture of Dr. Daniel Taylor, however, could not have been further from the reality now standing twenty feet from him. His mental picture of

Daniel had been short, stocky, a bit of a belly, bald on the top, dark black glasses; a nerd, a momma's boy. The kind of guy that looks, to other guys, like a pathetic excuse for a guy. A prissy little mouse who never had grease under his fingernails. A guy who looked like he never swigged a beer in one gulp, or wiped his nose on his sleeve.

But Daniel Taylor was none of those things. If possible, he was a male version of Livie. *Jesus,* Nick thought, *we're dealing with Ken and Barbie.* Taylor was clearly an inch or two taller than Nick's six foot three. His immaculately tailored navy blue suit, starched white shirt and patterned gold and navy tie could not even begin to hide the chiseled body underneath. The slightest movement on Taylor's part caused unseen muscles to tense, relax, ripple and flex like a lion stalking its prey.

He was as handsome as Livie was beautiful. He had wavy jet black hair combed straight back. Perhaps a little too much gel to suit Nick's taste, but that was nitpicking, like criticizing the Grand Canyon for an excess of rock. His face, clean-shaven, was as chiseled and rugged-looking as his body. Deep penetrating blue eyes completed the picture of a perfect man's man.

At first glance of Daniel Taylor, Nick felt an undeniable pang of jealousy. *Why should one guy have it all? Handsome, muscular and rich.* He then remembered Livie's descriptions of Daniel's "performance problems" and a triumphant smirk came across his face. *I guess you can't judge a book by its cover,* he thought. Apparently, Daniel Taylor was all show and no go.

If Dr. Taylor was the opposite of the mental image Nick had constructed of him, Martha Taylor was the spitting image. Mrs. Thurston Howell, III. in the flesh. He had to work to keep from laughing out loud as he pictured her on a desert island in a formal gown whining about the fact that they had no caviar. Everything about her, her physical appearance, her clothes, her hair, even the small snippets of her speech he could catch as she talked to Cat Jagger screamed "patrician."

Nick concluded his observations of his opponents and entered the jury room. Livie was standing by the far window, which she had propped open. She was facing away from him. She turned to face him. Nick's eyes were immediately drawn to the cigarette in her right hand.

"Livie," he said, "I didn't know you smoked."

She waved her cigarette around, smiled and replied, "Very rarely. Only when my nerves get the best of me." She smiled nervously and laughed a moment. "God, it would drive Daniel nuts when I did. Excuse me." She opened the door to the bathroom, walked in and a second later he heard the toilet flush. She exited. "Sorry."

"No problem. It's just...it's a no smoking building."

"What, they're going to...arrest...me? For smoking? Will you defend me?" she asked with another nervous laugh.

Nick explained to her what had transpired in the judge's chambers and that he would meet with Cat in the courthouse library and try to hammer out a deal.

"Okay," she replied as she grabbed his right hand with both of hers, "but please, don't let that bastard have my baby any more than you have to."

He retrieved his hand and answered, "I'll do my best."

Nick walked up to Cat, Dr. Taylor and Martha still huddled together and having an animated conversation. As he approached they abruptly stopped their conversation. "Nick," Cat said as she introduced her client, "Dr. Daniel Taylor."

"Morning," Nick replied. Dr. Taylor took Nick's extended hand but did not reply verbally.

Martha Taylor stepped forward and introduced herself, "Mrs. Henry Taylor," she said. She extended her hand as if she was the Queen of England and Nick was to take it, bow, and kiss it. He took her hand and shook it lightly.

"Well, Mr. Barnett," she began, "I certainly do not envy you, being required to represent the type of people you do, and..."

"Martha, please," Cat interrupted.

"Quite right, dear," Martha replied to Cat, "the gentleman is just doing his job." She glanced back at Nick. "No offense intended."

"None taken," Nick replied.

Nick and Cat retreated to the library.

Nick began. "First thing...your prenup is toast. Just glance at those figures. He lied. He's worth three times what he said. And it's one thing to lie to his fiancé but if he lies on his financial affidavit he files in court, well, that's perjury. I know your partner, Harry Sedgeworth, prepared the prenup. But Taylor lied to Harry too. You don't want Harry in court trying to defend it. He'd end up with shit all over him just like Taylor will."

Cat was furiously thumbing through the Motion to Set Aside the prenup Nick had filed with an ever-increasing scowl on her face. "Okay," she replied, "obviously we can't stipulate at this point to tossing the prenup. I've got to go through all this and talk to Harry but I understand your point. For purposes of our discussion today we'll assume no prenup. Now, what about the kid?"

"Temporary custody to mom," Nick began, "Every other weekend with dad. I'll have to twist her arm but I think I can sell it...oh, and fifteen grand a month temporary support."

Cat laughed. "Joint custody. Every other weekend. Tuesday and Thursday nights. Ten grand a month."

Nick paused a minute then said, "How about every other weekend and Wednesday nights and I'll see what I can do. Will you agree to temporary exclusive possession of the house by her and Dr. Taylor paying all bills? Plus I need fifty grand for me for fees."

"I'll see if he'll agree. But he's not paying her plastic or her personal expenses."

Nick smiled, "I think we'll be able to do business."

It took a good ten minutes for Nick to convince Livie that

joint custody was just a fancy legal phrase and that what really mattered was that they'd prevailed, at least for the time being, on the psychiatric records, on throwing out the prenup and on getting her the home and primary custody of Jessica.

A few minutes later the four of them, along with Judge Swanson and Helen the court reporter, were all in the courtroom. Martha Taylor sat in the spectator benches. The temporary agreement was recited into the record and both Livie and Dr. Taylor stood and openly acknowledged that they agreed to those terms and would abide by them. Nick noted Livie and Dr. Taylor exchanging icy glares at each other as they unconvincingly smiled at the judge.

"All right," Judge Swanson concluded, "order entered this day." She consulted with the attorneys and assigned a date for hearing on the motions regarding the psychiatric records and the prenup. She then closed the file and stepped down from the bench. Nick watched as Cat and Dr. Taylor and Martha held a brief, hushed discussion before Dr. Taylor and his mother left the courtroom.

Cat walked over and extended her hand to Nick. "Nick, nice seeing you again. I'll be in touch."

Nick shook her hand and replied, "Yeah. Always a pleasure working with you. I'll call you next week."

Cat then extended her hand to Livie, "Mrs. Taylor, sorry to be making your acquaintance under these circumstances."

Livie did not take her hand and only answered, "Yes, well, I'm sorry too."

Cat shrugged her shoulders at Nick and left.

Livie looked back to Nick and her facial expression instantly went from retributive to adoring. She grabbed his hand with both of hers. "I don't know how to thank you. You were...wonderful." She let go of his hand and hugged him tightly.

"Please..." he objected.

She abruptly let loose. "I'm sorry," she said, "I forgot." She then smiled and added, "naughty me. Can I see you tonight? I want to make sure I understand all this and try to figure out where we go from here." As she spoke, she lightly placed her hand on his thigh.

Nick rose and began packing his briefcase. "I'm sorry, I'm really booked today."

"Monday?" she pleaded.

"No, I have a trial Monday and Tuesday. It will have to be Wednesday. Call Pat for a time."

"I don't have a sitter for Wednesday but I guess he'll be picking up Jessica at six. How's seven?"

Nick zipped his briefcase up and smiled. "Wednesday, seven," he replied.

CHAPTER 16

Wednesday. Nick glanced quickly at his watch. Five-thirty. He was bone tired and wanted to get out of the office in time to go home, have a drink, grab some leftovers and take a shower before returning for his seven o'clock appointment with Livie Taylor.

Monday and Tuesday had been spent trying a boundary line dispute between his client, a farmer, and the neighboring farmer. They were contesting a strip of land twelve feet wide that wasn't even farmable. But you would have thought it was the Gaza strip the way they had gone at it. Nick was sure that each side had spent at least a hundred times what the damn piece of dirt was worth but he had learned long ago, that with a farmer you could question his parentage or his wife's virtue, shoot his dog even, but never ever try to steal his dirt.

He closed a file he was working on and placed it, teetering precipitously on top of his "Done" stack of files on his desk. He then transferred the whole stack of done files to Pat's "To Do" stack on her desk. He made a mental note to be late tomorrow so he wouldn't have to deal with Pat when she first saw the altitude of her "To Do" stack.

He walked out to the parking lot and noted Rosa's Cherokee was still there. They had been passing each other in the hall and encountering one another at the office coffee pot and water cooler, all the while exchanging insincere smiles and inane pleasantries with a brevity that was in direct proportion to their discomfort level. He decided to talk to her, not that he thought there was any chance they could resume their out of office relationship so long as he was still representing Livie Taylor. But, good Lord, the tension at the office was enough to give him an ulcer. They had to talk like adults and resolve this thing enough to at least have a civil working relationship. He went back into the office and knocked softly on Rosa's door.

"Come in," came the reply.

Nick entered and started talking before he even noticed that someone was seated across from her. "Rosa, can we..." He stopped midsentence when he saw the someone. A man in a suit.

"Oh, I'm sorry", he muttered, "I didn't know you had a client." The man turned around in his chair to face Nick. "Not a client, Nick," the man said as he extended his hand to shake. "Alex Hixenbaugh, new P.D. Been on the job three months. Don't think we've been formally introduced."

Nick looked at Rosa quizzically. *What business would she have with a public defender?* he wondered. She didn't do any criminal work.

"Oh sure," he replied taking Alex's hand in his and squeezing much harder than appropriate. "Seen you at the courthouse. Welcome to Martin County."

"Thanks," Alex answered while rubbing his hand, "some grip you've got there, Nick."

"Sorry," Nick replied as he smirked at Rosa.

Alex got up and, uninvited, walked behind Rosa's desk. She rose to meet him. He put his hands on her hips, gave her a peck on the cheek, and said "Great, Rosa. See you Friday night."

"Yeah. Seven, right?" Rosa replied.

"Seven," Alex confirmed as he turned to leave. As he passed Nick he added, "Nice meeting you," and extended his hand again then pulled it back quickly, laughed and added, "Once bitten, twice wary."

Nick could feel the anger and jealousy boiling up inside him like a pressure cooker about to explode. Rosa sat back down while Nick continued to stand there, his face reddening by the moment.

"What?" she finally said.

"Well, that's cute, Rosa, real cute. What is he, twenty-five?"

"You know what?" she responded, "it's none of your God damn business how old he is. Maybe you should just leave."

"So you just had to get revenge, huh?"

"Revenge!" she snapped. "Boy, I just had no idea how egotistical you could be. Did it ever occur to you that he just might be a nice guy and he just might be interested in me and that it has absolutely nothing to do with you?"

"Yeah, right," Nick answered. "I was coming in here to try and declare a truce; to try and set things straight between us. But obviously, you're in no mood for a truce, are you? Not...not while you're playing kissy-face in your office with your new boy toy."

Rosa stood up and pointed to her door. "LEAVE! NOW! And tomorrow if you can get over your self-centered, egotistical bullshit I might consider accepting an apology from you."

Nick spun on his heels, and while storming out of her office, yelled over his shoulder, "Fat chance of that!"

***

Nick stayed in the shower at least ten minutes longer than necessary to remove the day's sweat and grime. The water heater finally declared unconditional surrender and, as the water cooled, he turned the shower off. The bathroom was a sauna; filled to the ceiling with steam, mist and raging emotion. He had hoped that the hot water would soothe those emotions along with the tenseness of his muscles but the intensity of his rage, jealousy and anger had grossly overmatched the water's consoling powers. He was surprised at the intensity of his primal rage at seeing Alex kiss Rosa right in front of him, even if it was just a peck on the cheek. *God damn*, he thought, *I wish I coulda squeezed his balls like I squeezed his hand, the little wimp.*

As he toweled off he began to wonder if it was even possible to continue to work at the firm. Things had gone from bad to worse to now absolutely intolerable with Rosa. How could he work, focus, get anything done tomorrow with Rosa there? He knew if he left the firm Livie would go with him. Rosa had already made it crystal clear that she wouldn't represent her. Neither Stu nor Larry were capable of doing it. But what about the fee? Who got it? And would it mean a lawsuit between him and his partners? The mere thought of it almost made him physically sick. If anyone knew what a nightmare litigation could be Nick, a lawyer, certainly did. No, the only reasonable course of action was to suck it up, soldier through it, try to have as little contact with Rosa as possible for the foreseeable future and, hopefully, to let time eventually heal some of the wounds he had self-inflicted.

He got back to the office at six forty-five p.m. and was quietly relieved to see that Rosa's Cherokee was gone. His anger had subsided little and prevented him from recognizing his own culpability. Precisely at seven, the front door chimed and Nick went out to the waiting room. She had been Audrey Hepburn in her demure purple suit in court the last time he had seen her. Previous to that she was Barbarella in her leather skirt and boots. Tonight she was somewhere on the gamut between Hepburn and Fonda. Black slacks, spiky black stilettos, and a spaghetti-strapped purple blouse with a neckline that plunged to reveal more of Mrs. Livinia Taylor than had previously made Nick's acquaintance. She was crying.

"Livie, what's wrong?" he asked.

"He picked her up an hour ago. Her first visitation. I can just imagine what they're putting her through right now...oh God...

my poor baby..." Her sobs increased and Nick, disregarding his own repeated admonitions to her, and in a not so subtle effort to get back at Rosa, put an arm around Livie's shoulder.

"It's okay. She'll be okay. She has you," he comforted her.

Her tears increased and she turned into him and wrapped her arms around him. "Oh my poor baby," she repeated over and over. She was pressed tightly against him. His chin, buried in her hair, breathing in her scent, it was only a matter of time before he was fully aroused. He placed both his arms around her. The feel of the warm skin of her bare shoulders added to his arousal. There was no doubt, pressed as close as they were, that she was as cognizant of his arousal as he was of her tears. He let go of her but she failed to reciprocate.

"Oh God," she said, still pressed to him, "I'm so sorry. I know this breaks your rules. But it feels so good to be held by a man capable of caring and compassion." She tilted her head back and looked into his eyes. "Please don't stop, just yet."

Nick complied and put his arms back around her until she stopped crying. Finally, he let go and this time she did too. They backed away from each other.

"I'm sorry," she repeated.

He smiled. "It's okay. It's my fault. I hugged you. Let's go back to my office."

She followed him back to the office and took a seat as did Nick. They sat silently for an instant gazing at each other. Finally, Nick broke the awkward silence. "What can I do for you tonight?"

"Oh yes, well," she stammered, "I guess I just wanted to be sure I understood the temporary order and where things go from here."

"We discussed all that on the phone Monday, didn't we?" he pointed out.

"Yes...but...I just wanted to hear it from you personally and...well...the truth is...I didn't think I could be alone tonight...

her first visitation with him." She paused a moment then proceeded. "The truth is, I wanted, very much, to see you tonight."

Nick leaned back in his chair, grabbed a pencil off his desk and rolled it between his palms.

"Am I allowed to say that, Nick?" she asked through a plaintive smile.

He set the pencil down and stared into her eyes. She was smiling demurely and breathing slowly and heavily. With each slow breath, her breasts heaved within the minimal confinement of her low cut blouse. He was overcome with an aching desire for her that he no longer had the motivation or the ability to resist. *Rosa's taunting me with her little boy toy. Everyone's already tried and convicted us anyway,* he told himself. He continued to stare into her eyes but was incapable of replying.

"Am I?" she asked again as she rose and began to walk ever so slowly around his desk to him. She approached him and swiveled his chair towards her. "Am I?" she repeated. She looked into his eyes and saw the answer he was incapable of verbalizing. She spread his legs and knelt between them.

"Am I?" she asked once more as she continued to look into his eyes.

"Yes," he finally replied as she slowly unbelted and unzipped him. "Yes," he said again as he leaned back in his chair and closed his eyes.

***

Nick tilted back in his office chair, his feet propped on his desk. Muted jazz floated by his ears unheard. He glanced at his watch. Nine-twenty p.m. She had left the office at eight-fifteen. Dr. Taylor was scheduled to return Jessica at nine. For the last hour and five minutes, Nick had thought. He engaged in no other activity. He did not eat, he did not drink, he did not work, he did not hear the music emanating from his stereo. He thought.

I'm forty-one years old. He mentally went through the list of lovers he had had in his life. Ten, before tonight. Not a lot, he was certain, for a forty-one-year-old guy. Not a lot at all. But certainly, he was not a virgin either. But nothing in his past experiences had prepared him for Livie Taylor. It was as if he was Dorothy opening the door after the tornado. He was leaving his black and white world behind and entering the kaleidoscopic colors of Oz. He had been introduced to a whole new world, a world he scarcely knew existed only two hours ago. He was fully aware that he had just broken every rule in the book. But instead of feeling guilty, remorseful, he felt defiant. Like a little kid sticking his tongue out at the teacher after having been caught throwing spit wads.

He finally willed himself to get up and walk out to his car and drive home. *"My God,"* he asked himself over and over, *"what have I done? What am I getting myself into?"*

And each time he asked, the answer was the same, *"I don't care."*

CHAPTER 17

Although it was only nine a.m., Nick was already tired and stressed. He had spent a restless night tossing and turning and replaying the evening's events over and over in his mind. First the altercation with Rosa and that little wimp Alex. Then the encounter with Livie, over and over and over until every word, every movement, every sight, sound, and smell of their encounter was engraved into his brain as if etched into glass.

What happens from here? What are the repercussions? How do I act towards Livie the next time we talk? There were a thousand questions but, as of yet, no answers. He was fully cognizant that he had now crossed whatever line had been left between them. He had knowingly, intentionally, with malice aforethought, breached the Canons of Ethics. No different, in theory, than if he had stolen money from a client or knowingly used perjured testimony. He was now no better, no worse, than the scumbag lawyers he knew that had gotten themselves suspended or disbarred. Lawyers he vowed he was different from. Breaking all the rules, then, once they got caught, pleading with the disciplinary committee that drugs or alcohol or a bad marriage or a bad secretary had gotten them into trouble. *Well, I may have broken the rules, just like them,* he thought, *but if the shit hits the fan at least I'll be a man about it and take full responsibility. No "my dick made me do it" defense from me.*

He could foresee only two possible courses of action. One, withdraw from Livie Taylor's case, refund her fees, reimburse the firm and resign and then see where things went with Livie and hope and pray that if their relationship went south she would not seek retribution and report him.

Two, continue representing Livie, swear her to secrecy, hope against hope that her divorce would get resolved within a reasonable time and hope and pray that, in the interim, she didn't turn on him.

He tried to think rationally about the situation, about Livie, although he recognized that in the heady euphoria of his sexual high, rational thought was all but impossible. Livie Taylor was beautiful. That much was a given. She was also intelligent, well-educated and well-read. She had gotten her bachelor's degree in art history before embarking on her career in pharmaceutical sales. The real world, she had learned, apparently valued drugs substantially more than art. At least it was willing to pay her substantially more to sell drugs than to sell her knowledge of French impressionists. Besides her formal education, his discussions with her had revealed that she was well-read and well informed.

She had opinions on nearly any topic and was not shy about sharing them. And Nick had to admit that, for the most part, he agreed with those that she had shared. They had spent a good ten minutes one day trumping each other on who was more rabidly anti-Trump.

She was obviously also a concerned, loving mother and had talked adoringly of Jessica. She had confided that she had actually grown to like being a stay at home mom and had gotten into decorating and baking cookies and being "Mommy". Things she would never have imagined for herself five years ago. "I'm turning into a damn Martha Stewart," she had laughed. She could hardly wait, she said, for PTA's, and room mothering and field trips, and Brownies and the whole "Mommy" trip.

And despite the serious, even somber nature of most of their discussions, she obviously also had a well-developed sense of humor. Granted, most of her punch lines had been at her husband's or mother-in-law's expense, but clearly, she was capable of uninhibited laughter.

So, he summarized, Livie Taylor was drop-dead gorgeous, a lover that was in a category far beyond any in his prior experience, educated, smart, well-read, cultured and funny. The perfect woman. And, after supporting Sheila all those years, he had to admit to himself, however mercenary it seemed, the fact that she was and would be financially secure, simply added to his attraction for her. And finally, there was the whole ego thing. Nick was forty-one and doing pretty good by most people's standards. But, certainly, he knew he wasn't going to be going around breaking hearts or causing women to swoon. Yet, here was a stunningly beautiful woman, a woman who would not only fit in but stand out, dressed in a designer gown on the red carpet on Oscar night...and she was after him! It was causing neurons to fire and chemicals to ebb and flow in his brain (and elsewhere) that he had no more ability to control than his need to take his next breath.

So what's the problem? he asked himself. *Well, first off,* he answered, *it's against every rule in the book, second I don't trust her, third these feelings for Rosa that just won't go away, made impossible to deny by my reaction to seeing her with Alex.*

But his feelings for Rosa were, he concluded, unilateral. He had blown it with her and he might as well face facts and get over it. He had broken a cardinal rule early on in their relationship... never ever look at another woman with "that look." He had committed the crime right in front of her and capital punishment had been imposed. A lethal injection to their relationship.

His phone buzzed. "Who is it Pat?" he asked more gruffly than he intended.

"She won't say. Sounds like an older woman. Says it's personal," Pat replied.

"Okay," he answered as he pushed line one. "Nick Barnett here. What can I do for you?"

"Mr. Barnett, this is Mrs. Henry Taylor."

"Who?" Nick asked, not recognizing the name.

"Dr. Taylor's mother," came the reply. Nick was stunned. It was a breach of the ethical rules for an attorney to talk directly to someone represented by another attorney. For an instant, he thought of simply hanging up and calling Cat Jagger and reporting the call to her. But on reflection, he recognized that Martha Taylor was not Cat's client. She was not even a party to the case. He quickly concluded that he had the legal and ethical right to talk to her. As his mind worked at warp speed debating the pros and cons of continuing the conversation he decided that, if he played his cards right, he might learn something of value.

"Oh, yes," he finally replied, "I should advise you, Mrs. Taylor, before you begin, that you calling me is highly unusual and of course nothing you tell me is privileged. Does Dr. Taylor's attorney know you're calling me?"

"Mrs. Jagger is not my attorney, Mr. Barnett. And I talk to whomever I choose to talk to."

"Fine," Nick replied feeling better now that he had *Mirandized* her. "What can I do for you?"

"I think it would behoove you to be made aware of certain things about your client."

Behoove? he asked silently to himself. *Who the hell says 'behoove'?*

"Such as?" he asked.

"Such as, were you aware that Danny caught your client... how shall I put this...in the act...with a colored gentleman?"

"Mrs. Taylor," he interjected. He had no idea who or what she was referring to but did not want to let her know, "there's little point in you telling me this. My client certainly has a different version of what supposedly occurred. And I believe the current phraseology is a 'black man', not 'colored gentleman'."

She ignored his rebuke and continued. "Are you aware of her psychiatric diagnosis?"

"Yes, I certainly am."

"Well, then you should be well aware that people with her... condition...are incapable of telling the truth."

There was a pause as if she was expecting him to reply. When none was forthcoming, she continued. "Mr. Barnett, I have virtually unlimited resources at my disposal. I am used to getting what I want and I do not give up easily. My dear departed Henry used to say 'Martha, you're one part Irish, one part German and two parts bulldog.' As you're aware I, and Danny and his sister, control a very substantial trust fund and have numerous investments and business ventures in the area. In fact...this is rather ironic... TFI Holdings, LLC...the owner of your firm's office building, is controlled by one of our trusts..."

"I wasn't aware of that," he answered while jotting down notes.

"Indeed it is," she continued, "T.F.I. stands for Taylor Family Investments. Small world, isn't it?"

"Certainly is," he replied concluding there was, no doubt, an implied threat that their rent would double if he didn't drop Livie Taylor like a hot potato.

"In fact, our holdings have become so extensive in this area that, just before all this between Danny Boy and that woman blew up, we were discussing putting a local firm on retainer. A very generous retainer. Your firm's name was prominently mentioned."

"Really?" Nick replied. "Well, as you say, it's a small world. Too bad we're no longer in a position to be able to represent you if you got a God damn parking ticket."

The other end of the line was silent for a moment. Finally, she spoke, "Well, I can see from your attitude that apparently it was a mistake to think you might be a reasonable man...."

"You're right, Martha," he snapped, "you were mistaken. I'm totally fucking unreasonable when people try to intimidate or bribe me."

"Fine," she replied, "my mistake. I won't bother you any-more."

"Fine."

"Just one other thing before I hang up."

"Yes."

"Do you really think it appropriate for you to be meeting with attractive female clients who dress as she does at all hours of the night?"

Click!

"You GOD DAMN BITCH!" he barked at the dial tone. "Don't you ever call me again or I'll call the fucking cops!" He slammed the receiver down. Fear streaked through his body like an electric shock. *My God,* he wondered, *were Livie and I videoed in my office that night?* He spun in his chair and looked at the mini-blinds covering his lone office window. They were closed and all the way down. He was certain they were also closed that night. The fear subsided only slightly.

A second later there was a knock on his door. Pat opened it and walked in, concern evident on her face. "Nick, what...what's going on?"

Nick's face was beet red. He picked up the receiver and slammed it down again. "God damn bitch. God damn bitch," he repeated. "You wouldn't believe that bitch, she calls me...."

"Who?"

"Martha Taylor." Nick could see from the expression on her face that the name meant nothing to Pat.

"Livie Taylor's mother-in-law."

"She called you?"

"Yes, can you believe it?"

"What did she say?"

"She owns this God damn building. Can you believe it?"

"What?"

"Yes. And when intimidation didn't work, she tried to bribe me! The bitch tried to bribe me! Can you believe it?"

"How?"

"She offered to put the firm on retainer."

"No," Pat replied, clearly astounded.

"I swear," he answered. "God, I've never had a conversation like that in my life. Threatened and bribed all in the space of thirty seconds. Oh, and get this; apparently they've had someone tailing Livie. She knows when Livie comes to the office and what she's been wearing."

"What do you mean about what she's been wearing? What does she mean?" Pat asked, confused.

"Oh..." Nick stammered not wanting Pat to know he had been entertaining Barbarella in his office after hours, "you know how she dresses...like Aubrey Hepburn."

"Oh. What are you going to do?" Pat asked.

"I don't know," he conceded. "If I thought David Rathman might prosecute the bitch, I'd call him. But I'm not sure she really broke the criminal laws. Plus, it would be my word versus hers. God, I really don't know what to do. But Pat, please, a favor?"

"Sure, what?"

"This is between us, okay? I don't want to involve Stu or Larry or Rosa in on it and I don't want the rest of the girls to know."

"Sure," she replied, "if that's how you feel."

At that moment the other door to Nick's office opened and Stu walked in. "What's going on? Thought I heard a commotion."

"Nothing," Nick answered. "I stubbed my toe on the damn desk leg. Hurt like a son of a bitch. I cussed. Sorry."

Stu looked skeptical and looked to Pat for confirmation. She smiled, turned and left Nick's office.

"So, partner," Stu continued, "everything going okay?"

"Yeah, everything's fine."

"What's the latest on the Taylor divorce?"

"This," Nick said as he searched through a stack of paperwork on his desk and produced a letter from Cat Jagger with a check paper-clipped to it. He handed it to Stu.

Stu flipped over the letter and looked at the check. "Damn. Another fifty grand. This time from her husband? Do we have to endorse it to her?"

"No. She says I'll earn it. Says to keep it."

"You're kidding?"

"No."

"A hundred and fifty grand for a divorce?"

"Yep."

"Well, Jesus H. Christ," he said as he whistled, "two months in a row as Partner of the Month. I just might make that permanent. See, we were right on how we handled this thing. She's been behaving?"

"A perfect lady," Nick lied in response.

"Perfect is right," Stu added as he continued to ogle the check. "Absolutely perfect."

CHAPTER 18

Nick paced back and forth in his office. He was a bubbling cauldron of nervous energy, unable to sit. Had the phone call with Martha Taylor happened a month ago, he would have marched straight into Rosa's office and would have told her all about it. She would have calmed him down, coolly analyzed the situation and pointed him in the right direction. He was sure of that. But discussing anything with Rosa, most particularly anything to do with the Taylor divorce, was out of the question. He had obstinately refused to apologize to Rosa following his encounter with her and Alex Hixenbaugh and she had just as obstinately refused to speak so much as a word to him at their partners' meeting this morning.

Just as certainly, it would not do any good to try to talk to either Stu or Larry. Stu would be concerned only that he do nothing to jeopardize the hundred and fifty grand the firm had already received on the Taylor divorce. Larry would be telling him how if it was him, he'd be kicking Martha Taylor's ass right this moment. No, he was on his own on this one. But what should he do? Call Cat Jagger and tell her? File some kind of motion with the court? Of course, it would be his word versus hers and what could anyone really do? The bottom line was that Martha Taylor was not a party to the divorce, the judge did not have jurisdiction over her, and Cat Jagger was not her lawyer. He wondered if her veiled threats could be construed as intimidation or as a bribe. Could a criminal law have been violated? Should he call David Rathman, the state's attorney? But, as far as he knew, bribery laws only applied to public officials and he doubted that mentioning she was his firm's landlord would be considered criminal intimidation. He was about to conclude that there was nothing to do but try to forget it and put it behind him when his phone again buzzed.

"Yeah," Nick barked.

"Your favorite client," Pat answered. Nick knew immediately that she was referring to Livie. What he didn't know was whether she was being sarcastic or whether she knew more about his relationship with Livie Taylor than he gave her credit for.

"Okay," he said as he sat down and pushed line two.

"Livie, hi."

"Hi to you," she said in a sultry tone. "Have you been thinking of me since…you know?"

Nick, extremely uncomfortable about even acknowledging what had transpired that night in the very chair he was seated on stammered in reply, "Well…yeah…sure…Livie…look….we need to talk…."

"We need to do more than talk," she replied.

"Please," he begged, "someone could pick up on this line by mistake."

"I'm sorry, Nicky," she replied, "I promise I'll be a good girl…it's just…you were really something. I needed to tell you that."

"Well…thanks…so were you," he answered, embarrassed but truthful. "But please, this has to be kept quiet. We have to be careful. It's dangerous."

"Maybe I like danger."

"Livie, PLEASE," he begged.

"Okay, all right, I'm sorry. Don't be mad. It's just been so long. When can I see you?"

"Umm…how about Friday. But, please, I can't risk getting

caught at the office. I just can't. You'll have to start coming during regular office hours and it will have to be strictly business."

"Well, okay, but then when can we...be together?"

"We'll figure it out. Please. We still have your divorce to get through. We have a lot of work we have to do. See, that's why lawyers have these rules in the first place."

The other end was silent for a few seconds before she finally replied. "You're not trying to tell me you don't want to be with me, are you, Nicky? You're not one of those guys are you?"

"What guys?" Nick asked.

"The kind that takes advantage of a girl then moves on to greener pastures."

Takes advantage? Nick thought. *That's sure not how I remember our encounter.* "No, of course not. It's just what I've said. It's dangerous...for both of us...we have to be very, very careful."

"When Friday?"

"How's ten?"

"Okay, Nicky, ten. I'll behave myself. I promise."

"Oh and please don't call me Nicky in the office."

She giggled, "Okay...Mr. Barnett...see you Friday."

Nick tried to focus on getting some routine work done but found it impossible. His mind and his penis and all parts in between were consumed with all things Taylor; Livie Taylor, Martha Taylor, Daniel Taylor, the Taylor divorce. He glanced at his daily calendar and was glad, for once, to see it booked solid with clients coming in all day starting at ten. *Thank God,* he thought, *if ever I needed a distraction, today's the day.*

***

At twelve-fifteen, he finished up with the last of his morning appointments and went out and grabbed the day's stack of mail off its appointed spot on Pat's desk. He quickly thumbed through with disinterest until he came across a cover letter from Gateway

Regional Hospital with a large stack of medical records clipped to it. He deposited them on his office desk and went back to the coffee room to grab a yogurt out of the office refrigerator. No time for lunch today. The parade of clients started up again at one and he desperately wanted to quickly review Livie Taylor's psychiatric records. *Maybe*, he thought, *I'll find out exactly who it is I've had sex with.*

As he turned the corner to the coffee room door he immediately saw a shapely pair of high heeled legs in a short skirt protruding from behind the refrigerator door. Rosa stood upright and closed the door just as Nick had started a pirouette to exit in an attempt to avoid being seen by her.

"Nick," she called out. It was the first word she had spoken to him in days.

He turned back around, "Oh, Rosa...didn't see you," he lied. She was holding a Tupperware bowl of salad and a diet Coke.

"You got a minute?" she asked.

"Well...umm..." Nick stuttered as he glanced at his watch for added emphasis, "umm...not really. Been like a barbershop in my office all morning. Haven't even looked at the mail. I was just going to grab a yogurt."

"Well, grab it and come to my office. I'll just be a minute." she smiled her smile. That sweet "Rosa" smile Nick had come to miss so much recently. "Okay?"

Nick smiled in return. "Okay," he replied as he maneuvered behind her, opened the refrigerator and grabbed a yogurt and a plastic spoon. He followed her to her office. She sat down behind her desk, opened her diet Coke and took a drink. Nick took a seat in one of the client chairs facing her and set his yogurt and plastic spoon down. He smiled awkwardly at her.

Rosa began, "I'm sorry. There, I said it..."

"Please," Nick interrupted, "you don't have to..."

She continued, ignoring his interruption, "It's not one of my strong suits, admitting I'm wrong. Apologizing. So it's not easy for me. My mom tells me that's why I'm still single. She says I can always be right and I'll always be single. What do you think?"

"Rosa, look, I need to apologize too."

"No...I didn't ask you back here for you to apologize to me. I just wanted to explain something to you."

"You don't need..."

"Yeah, I do. Not for you. For me. Please, just listen."

Nick shrugged "okay" in response.

"I'm an only child. My dad is an English literature professor at Carbondale. My mom was working on her Ph.D. when she got pregnant with me. Have I told you this stuff?"

"Yeah."

"I thought so. Anyway, I was raised with certain expectations. College was a given. A post-graduate degree was expected." She laughed slightly as she reminisced. "My parents were almost disappointed when I decided to go to law school. My dad expected another 'Dr. Thomas' in the family and I think me getting a Ph.D. would have filled in a blank in my mom's life. But anyway...the point is I've always known since I was a little girl that my education and my career would be the most important thing. My little girlfriends would fantasize about their wedding day. I'd fantasize about being named a professor at Harvard. Lord, I thought my parents would have a stroke when I got engaged to Stan. They actually had a party for me when I broke it off," she added chuckling again. "Can you believe that?"

"Well, you know ever since I broke my engagement with Stan, I...umm...haven't had a lot of luck with the guys around here. And I tried to act like I didn't care. Rosa Thomas need a man? No way! Then I turned thirty. Pretty soon I'll be thirty-one. I guess I finally just admitted the truth to myself. Yeah, I still want my career, but I do want a white dress, a wedding, a husband, kids, a dog, a white picket fence..." She started to cry and grabbed a tissue off her desk and dabbed her eyes. "I'm sorry. I promised myself I wouldn't cry."

Nick was close to tears himself, "Jesus, don't apologize."

"Anyway," she continued as she dabbed the last of her tears, "when you came over that night and we talked and laughed...and made love...I guess I just realized you were my best friend and I thought we could just talk and laugh and make love like that every night...forever. And I guess it never even occurred to me that you weren't in the same space as me. You've been married. You have a child. You've had the picket fence. Maybe that's not what you want or need in your life right now. And it was selfish of me to presume you wanted those things just because I did. Honestly, I've never been the jealous type. But when I saw...that woman... hug you...and the way you were looking at her...right after we... you know...how could I compete with her?" The tears started again and she grabbed more tissue. She continued through her tears. "Anyway, that's all I wanted to say. I'm sorry. I had no right to treat you the way I did. I had no right to insinuate you would actually do anything with her. I hope we can work together as we always did. I'm sorry. Oh...one other thing...you were right about Alex. I had him come here hoping you'd see him and get jealous. Pretty childish, huh?" The tears stopped again and she laughed once more. "By the way, he's a little dweeb. I canceled our date for Friday and broke it off with him."

Nick smiled in reply but was too overwhelmed with emotion to answer. His mind swirled with a paralyzing mix of guilt, shame, regret and desire. After several silent moments, Rosa took another sip of her diet Coke, glanced at her watch and spoke again, "Well, I know you're busy today. Can we at least be friends again?"

Nick was still temporarily incapable of replying. *If life was a movie,* Nick thought, *James Taylor would start singing "You've Got a Friend," I'd get up, charge behind her desk, pick her up, carry her out to my car, and we'd drive off laughing and crying and listening to J.T. Then they'd cut and, as the credits rolled, they'd show us laughing and playing with our two little kids and a dog behind our white picket fence. If only life had a script and a director,* Nick mused.

Finally, he spoke. "I know what you've just told me was probably very hard for you. And I appreciate your honesty. And I do...very much...want to be friends and be able to work with you...and I feel like I should apologize to you more than you to me. I just really, really screwed things up and I am so sorry I hurt you. I never meant to."

"I know that," she replied.

"Anyway," Nick continued, "I think maybe...it might be best if I tried to get this situation...you know, the Taylor divorce...resolved before...we try moving beyond friendship. What do you think?"

"Sure," she replied, smiling sadly. "That's probably wise."

Nick rose and grabbed his yogurt and spoon. "Okay, then," he said as he turned to leave.

"Okay, then," Rosa repeated and then added, "Nick?"

"Yes?"

"I just want you to know that I do trust you...you know... around Livie Taylor."

Although he felt as if he had just been stabbed in the heart and the knife was now being twisted, he smiled back at her, "Thanks. That means a lot to me."

CHAPTER 19

Nick groaned as he surveyed the ever-increasing mound of files on his desk. Livie had been right on at least one thing. He was earning his retainer. Apart from the hours he was actually devoting to her case, he was finding it increasingly difficult to focus on his dozens of other files. Files that needed attention. Clients that needed hand-holding. Phone calls that needed returning. Briefs that needed writing. But Livie Taylor had invaded and occupied his brain as if she were the tentacles of a malignant tumor. He glanced at his watch. Two forty-five. She would be in the office in fifteen minutes and there were a thousand things he wanted and needed to cover with her...but where did he start?

Clearly, he had to warn her about the fact that she was being followed and probably photographed or videoed. Maybe, he thought, it would serve as an opening to suggest that their "extra-curricular" activities be suspended. He already knew that he had made a serious mistake in crossing the line with Livie. Rosa's conversation with him yesterday only reinforced that. It was becoming increasingly obvious that at least some of the things being said about Livie were the truth. The woman had some serious problems. He knew that, even if a relationship with her wasn't a breach of the rules of his profession, he'd already be having second thoughts. Yes, she was beautiful beyond description. Yes, she had a body to die for and yes she was incredibly skilled in using that body. But, it had become painfully clear that the woman was more than a few bricks shy of a load.

He decided he wouldn't tell her about Martha Taylor's phone call to him. He had no idea how she would react. She had made no secret of the vitriol she harbored for Martha and he didn't want to do anything that might push her over the edge. He would simply tell her that he had found out through an anonymous source that she was being followed and that prudence dictated that they meet only during office hours and avoid any improprieties. Dr. Taylor had responded to the Petition for Dissolution of Marriage Nick had filed on Livie's behalf with a counter-petition alleging adultery as a grounds for divorce. It didn't take a legal scholar to conclude that it was not wise for Nick to be having sex with a client whose husband was charging her with adultery. When Cat Jagger asked Livie in depositions if she had committed adultery and she denied it, what would Nick do? Ethically, he could not knowingly allow perjured testimony, but what then? Interrupt and say "Livie, did you overlook the time you fucked my brains out right here in the chair I'm seated in?" *If, somehow,* he mused, *I get through this mess with my law license intact, I'll write an anonymous treatise for the Bar Journal, "How to Fuck up in a Divorce Case Six Ways to Sunday without Really Trying."*

The next issue was the medical records he had received from Gateway Regional. He had only had time to hurriedly read through them once. He needed to spend a good part of the weekend going through them in detail googling the medical terminology and translating them into English until he fully understood them. But even a cursory reading was enough to know the records would be devastating to their custody case if Cat Jagger got ahold of them. Livie's description of her diagnosis as a "bout of postpartum depression" was akin to describing a massive heart attack as some chest discomfort.

Livie's diagnosis was not postpartum depression but postpartum psychosis. He had not yet researched it but knew enough to know there was a world of difference between depression and psychosis. The record was complete with references to her suicidal, and even more damaging, her homicidal ideations. Ideations directed towards her newborn infant, the subject of the ongoing custody dispute: Jessica Erin Taylor. He could picture Cat Jagger on cross-examination, "By the way Mrs. Taylor, did you tell Dr. Ahmad that you had an overpowering urge to drown little Jessica in the bathtub and then deliver her dead body to your husband at his office?"

Almost as disturbing was the secondary, psychological diagnosis: narcissistic personality disorder. Again he had not had time to research it but the psychologist's notes clearly indicated that such persons were grandiose, haughty, lacking in empathy and interpersonally exploitive. *Hard to argue with much of that when it comes to Livie,* he thought.

As he started going through the records a second time, he paused. *Exactly what am I doing?* he asked himself. *I'm going through these records hoping I can find a way to keep them out of Cat Jagger's hands. If I succeed, am I putting a little three-year-old girl in danger? Should Livie even have custody? And if her interests conflict with this little girl's, where do my loyalties lie? Who's my client? And do I even have any business asking myself these questions?* Lawyers are hired guns, he had always been taught. *Our duty is to represent our client's interests, whether our clients are neo-Nazis marching through Skokie, serial killers or a psychotic mom seeking custody of her little girl, right? God,* he thought to himself, *I wish I'd never heard the name Livie Taylor.*

There was a soft knock on the door, it half-opened and Rosa poked her head in. "Got a second?"

He smiled, "Sure."

"Any chance you could handle some motions for me in Mt. Vernon Thursday at one?" she asked.

He glanced at his calendar "Yeah, have to move a couple appointments but it's no big deal. What's up?"

"Oh, nothing...doctor's appointment. Thanks."

"Everything all right?" Nick inquired, clearly concerned.

"Yeah, I think," she replied then added with a grimace, "some routine female problems."

"Oh, well," Nick said, at a loss for words, "if I can do anything else."

"No. Thanks. I'll get the files to Pat."

"Okay."

As Rosa turned to leave, Pat appeared at Nick's door escorting Livie Taylor.

"Oh," Pat said, "I'm sorry. I thought you were free."

"No problem," Rosa replied as she extended her hand, "I was just leaving. Mrs. Taylor, we were introduced before."

Livie took her hand, "Yes, I recall. Ms. Thomas, right?" she said with a decided emphasis on the "Ms."

"Yes, it is. Nick and I were just discussing your case," Rosa continued, "weren't we Nick? Seems as if I'll be helping him some after all." She looked at Nick for confirmation.

"Oh, right, sure," he stammered, "your file's getting pretty complicated."

"Well, fine," Livie replied. "Does that mean you'll be sitting in on our conferences?"

Pat could stand the tension no more, smiled, turned and retreated to her office.

"If necessary," Rosa replied. "Nice seeing you again, Mrs. Taylor." She then turned towards Nick. "Later, Nick."

Livie closed the door behind Rosa. She was more casually dressed than was her norm, but still elegant. White linen slacks, white heeled sandals, and a white blouse with pale turquoise piping and a matching turquoise short sleeve jacket.

She took a seat. "She's rather pretty in a kind of odd sort of way, isn't she Nicky?"

"Who?"

"Why, Ms. Thomas of course."

"Well...I suppose so."

"Likes to wear her skirts pretty short, doesn't she?"

"Please, we've got a lot to go over and we really don't have time to discuss Rosa's hemlines."

"I'll bet you find time to look at them though, don't you Nicky?"

"Livie...Jesus...please...I asked you...don't call me Nicky... and Rosa's my partner and she's a helluva lawyer and I just need some help on your file."

"Is there anything else I should know about her?"

"Like what?" he asked exasperated.

"Like, is there anything going on between you two?"

"God, no...there's nothing going on between us and we just really have to focus on your case and stop all this...this bullshit."

He looked up at her and could see her eyes were misting over.

"I'm sorry, Nicky...I mean Nick...I trust you...it's just...I guess I'm afraid of losing you. I'm not losing you, am I?"

How do I respond? he wondered. *Losing me? I didn't even know you had me.* "No...but please...you see this is why we have the rules we talked about..."

There was a knock on the door and a second later Stu poked his head in.

"Oh, sorry. Thought you were free." He smiled at Livie who had turned slightly in her chair. "Everything okay?" he asked.

"Fine. Great." Nick answered before adding a silent "*Fuck you, Stu*" in his mind.

"Great," Stu said as he smiled at Livie again and closed the door.

"What was I saying?" Nick asked.

Livie smiled and spoke quietly, "I think you were saying you couldn't wait to get that big hard cock of yours inside me again."

Nick grimaced. "Let's get to work, please, shall we?"

"Oh...okay, if we have to" she answered.

"We have to," Nick replied.

CHAPTER 20

He had decided not to even bring up the medical records with Livie until he could read them more thoroughly and research postpartum psychosis and narcissistic personality disorder. She had been fit to be tied when he had told her that she was being followed and they knew when she was coming to the office and what she had been wearing. He concluded he had been right not to share with her the source of that information.

Nick stood in his gym shorts and gray tee shirt and sipped his coffee as he mixed the waffle batter. He loved those Saturday mornings when Natalie was with him. When they had still been a "family" it had become a Barnett tradition for Nick to fix a big Saturday morning breakfast. Sheila usually slept in, so generally, it was just Nick and Natalie. And how he treasured the memory of those times. As hectic as his life had been when Natalie had been a toddler, he looked back at those days through a haze of nostalgia and with the fond remembrance of a simpler time.

The doorbell rang and Nick dolloped some batter onto the waffle maker before setting his coffee down and walking to the front door, wondering who would be ringing his doorbell at eight-thirty on a Saturday morning. He opened the door and wonder turned to shock. There was a sunglassed Livie Taylor in a haltered white tennis dress with a tennis racket over one shoulder. A tennis bag was slung over the other shoulder. A broad smile traversed her face. She set her bag down, propped her sunglasses on her head and spoke, "Wanna play, Nicky?"

Nick was too stunned to reply. He quickly poked his head outside, looked for spies, saw none, grabbed Livie by the elbow with one hand, picked up her tennis bag with the other, ushered her into the house and closed the door.

"Livie...what the...how did you find my house?"

"You're in the book, silly," she replied. "It didn't take the CIA." She took a mock swing with her racket. "Wanna play?" she asked again.

"I don't play tennis," he answered.

She put an arm around his waist, stretched on her tiptoes, kissed him on the lips, then pulled his ear down towards her mouth. "I wasn't referring to tennis," she whispered.

He broke their hug. "My daughter's here. You shouldn't be here. You were probably followed..."

"Fuck them," she said petulantly, "so I stopped at my lawyer's house on a Saturday morning on my way to tennis lessons to sign some papers. So what?"

"No...please, you have to go. I've tried to tell you how dangerous this is."

"And I've told you; maybe I like danger."

He looked even more exasperated and she laughed. "Oh...okay...I'm sorry Mr. Party Pooper," she then shifted to a whisper again, "...I just wanted you so bad..." before speaking normally again. "At least a cup of coffee before I go."

"Okay," Nick relented, "just one cup, then please, you'll have to go."

"Oh, all right," she said as she playfully slapped him on the shoulder and followed him into the kitchen.

He grabbed a cup from the cabinet, replenished his cup, then filled hers. "What do you take?" he asked while still facing the coffee pot.

"Black," came the reply.

He turned to hand her the cup. She was standing a few feet away, a mischievous grin on her face. She was twirling her tennis panties on her index finger, then let them fly off her finger. They landed on the kitchen table.

"Sure you don't want to play?" she asked as she reached down with both hands and raised her tennis dress.

As she did, they both heard the unmistakable noise of a teenager rapidly clumping down a flight of stairs. Livie let her dress back down. She started to reach for her panties but before she could Natalie was in the kitchen facing them. "Hey, Daddy..." She immediately stopped talking as she entered the kitchen and saw Livie. Nick's heart was thumping as if it was about to explode. He stood there, a cup of coffee in each hand, his face red, unable to speak.

Livie broke the silence. "Well...you must be Natalie. Your father has told me so much about you. Hi," she added as she extended her hand, "Livie Taylor."

Natalie grabbed Livie's hand and they shook briefly. Livie turned and playfully slapped Nick on the shoulder. "Nicky, she's even prettier than you told me."

Nick was trying to maintain eye contact with Natalie, but involuntarily his eyes kept darting to the panties sitting next to the salt and pepper shakers on the kitchen table. He saw Natalie's eyes follow his glances to the table. She smirked and he could see she was trying to suppress a laugh.

Livie continued, "Well, it is so nice to finally meet you, Natalie."

"Thanks," Natalie finally replied.

"Who does your hair sweetie?" Livie asked.

"I do."

"No, really?"

"Yeah."

"Well, it looks great...but, I wonder...just a minute..." she said as she walked out of the kitchen. While she was gone, Natalie gave Nick a huge grin. Livie walked back out to the living room and grabbed her tennis bag. She returned to the kitchen, set the bag on the table, and in one sweeping move she scooped up her panties and put them in it.

"Let me try something...just a second..." she said, reaching into her bag and pulling out a couple barrettes. She played with Natalie's hair for a minute and pinned one side slightly up. "There," she said triumphantly as she reached into her bag again and pulled out a compact. "What do you think?"

Natalie intently gazed at herself in the small mirror. "Yeah," she said, "I like it. Makes me look older."

Livie gave her a brief hug. "Have you got a second honey?" she asked Natalie.

"Sure."

"One other thing," Livie said as she dug into her bag again. She emerged with a small case of eye shadow which she expertly applied above each of Natalie's eyes.

Natalie perused the result in the mirror. "Oh my God...I do look older. That looks great."

"It's the perfect shade for you. Here," Livie said as she handed the eye shadow to Natalie. "Keep it. The trick is to be subtle. Don't overdo it."

"Thanks, Livie. Daddy, what do you think?" Natalie asked as she batted her eyes.

"I don't think you need to look older," he replied somberly.

"I have to finish getting ready," Natalie said. "Kendra's mom's picking me up. Nice meeting you."

Livie eschewed Natalie's offered hand and instead hugged her. "My pleasure." She broke her hug then added, "Hey, let's do a girls' day out sometime. Hair and makeup and nails. All day. What do you say?"

"Sure," Natalie replied as she started to leave.

"Oh, Natalie?" Livie asked.

"Yeah?"

"Do you ever babysit?"

"Sure."

"Well, I have a precious little three-year-old named Jessica. Would you be available sometimes when your father and I have plans?"

"Yeah, sure."

"Great."

"Just call," Natalie said as she smiled, turned and left.

Nick silently handed Livie her coffee. She took a sip. "Oh God, I can see why you're so proud of her. She's beautiful. I'll bet her and Jessica will be best friends." She started giggling, then added, "You don't think she saw my panties do you?"

"I'm pretty sure she did," Nick replied.

"Oh my God," she shrieked, "how embarrassing. Oh, Nicky, I'm so sorry."

"Please," Nick began, "...you're really putting me at risk... we can't be..."

She set her coffee down. "Oh...okay...I can see when I'm not wanted. I'll go take my tennis lesson. But you can at least walk me to the door."

Nick followed her obediently. When they reached the door, she stopped, reached into her bag and grabbed her panties. She stepped into them and pulled them up. "Almost forgot," she smiled. "That would have been quite a sight on the tennis court, wouldn't it?"

"Okay," Nick said while ushering her out the door, "we'll talk next week."

She turned towards him and immediately became somber. She grabbed his right hand in both of hers and spoke softly, "Nick, I want you to know something very important."

"What?" he asked, not at all certain he wanted to know whatever it was she had to tell him.

"Well...I can see how you are with Natalie. How much she obviously loves you and what a good dad you are..."

"I try," he interjected.

"I just want to make sure that you know...I'm not too old."

"Too old?" Nick asked, "too old for what?"

"Too old to have more children, silly," she replied as she reached up, kissed him full on the lips, grabbed her bag and racket and left.

***

Nick sat at the kitchen table, too overwhelmed for rational thought. *Good Christ in Heaven,* he asked himself, *how am I going to get out of this fucking mess?* He heard Natalie coming back down the stairs. She entered the kitchen.

"Uhh...Daddy...the waffles are like burning up," she said as she pointed to the counter.

He snapped out of his trance and jumped up. "Shit!" he yelled as he touched the hot waffle iron. He unplugged it, grabbed some hot pads and deposited the whole smoking mess in the sink and ran cold water over it.

"How about cereal?" he said.

"Sure," she answered.

"Honey, look," he began, "I'm really sorry about all that. I had no idea..."

"Daddy...don't apologize. Mom's been remarried for four years. I was wondering when you'd get a girlfriend. And, oh my God, she's so beautiful. I can't believe it! Where did you meet her?"

"A friend," he shrugged.

"Do you like her?"

"Well, yeah...but it's a little hard to explain..."

"Daddy. I'm fifteen. I know about these things. I have a boyfriend."

"You do?"

"Yes."

"Who? How old is he? Who are his folks?"

"His name's Ryan. He's seventeen…"

"Seventeen!" Nick exclaimed.

"Yeah…and, oh my God, he's so cute and he's a senior and he has a Mustang."

"Why can't you find a boy your age? Seventeen's too old. And you haven't been riding in his car have you?"

"Duh! Of course. Mom said it was okay. And it is so sweet for a sophomore to be dating a senior. He's taking me to prom next Friday."

"Well, I have to meet him. I have to talk to him. I have…"

"Daddy! Okay. How about prom night? We'll stop by for pictures. But you have to promise not to scare him."

"Okay," he said, "I promise." He stepped forward and hugged his daughter.

"Thanks," she replied. "You know, I like Livie. She seems really nice."

"Yeah," Nick replied. They heard a horn honk.

"Oh, that's Kendra's mom, gotta run. I'll eat later. Love you," she added as she kissed him on the cheek.

"Bye, honey," he answered. "Be careful. Love you, too."

CHAPTER 21

Nick sat in his office and thought about the weekend just past. He had spent the balance of the weekend analyzing and researching Livie Taylor's medical records in greater detail. Further analysis simply led to further concern. The more he learned about postpartum psychosis and narcissistic personality disorder, the more he learned about his client, the more concerned he became.

When he wasn't worrying about the Taylor file, he was worrying about the fact that his baby girl was apparently riding around in cars with boys. *When did she grow up and become a young woman?* he asked himself. *Just yesterday I was playing ball with her and now she's riding in cars with boys? What happened?*

In a perfect world, he knew he should and could devote one hundred percent of his worry quotient to his teenage daughter. But Livie Taylor had become so omnipresent in his life, both professionally and now personally that she left little time, energy, or ability to worry about anything else.

He had managed to avoid four or five phone calls at home from Livie but he knew he was postponing the inevitable. Eventually, he relented and answered her call Sunday afternoon. Talking to her gave him the distinct impression that he was in an episode of the Twilight Zone. One minute she'd be talking dirty to him describing in explicit detail what she intended to do to him the next time they were alone together, the next she'd be talking as if they had been married for years and as if Jessica and Natalie were step-sisters. She talked of taking "the girls" shopping; of having Natalie babysit so "we" could have "our time together." The next minute she'd be discussing the case with Nick. And she made it all sound so normal, so natural. At times he had to ask himself if she was crazy or if he was. He had somehow managed to avoid committing to her as to their next "alone time" but he knew it was only a matter of time. While he doubted her veracity on many things, there was no doubt she had been truthful when she had told him she had a healthy appetite. That first night, in Nick's office she had worn him out. He was physically sore the next day.

The phone buzzed and he picked up, "Yeah."

"Cat Jagger, line one," Pat said.

"Thanks," he said as he connected.

"Morning, Cat."

"Hi, Nick. Those storms hit you guys yesterday?"

"No, passed to the north for a change."

"You're lucky. We got walloped here."

"We've had our share this spring. What's up?"

"Friday we have the motion set on your client's psychiatric records."

"I know."

"Well, I'm e-mailing to you some additional documentation we're filing in support of our motion. "We've got an affidavit from a psychiatrist, Dr. Nathan Bowman from St. Louis U. Based on what Dr. Taylor advised him and based on review of the coding on the insurance E.O.B.'s and the medicine prescribed, he concludes that your client's diagnosis was an unspecified psychosis together with an underlying personality disorder. Likely histrionic or narcissistic disorder..."

"Jesus," Nick interrupted, "quite a magician this guy is. He's diagnosing people he's never talked to?"

"Hey, shrinks are diagnosing Napoleon and he's been dead two hundred years," she retorted. "The point is, he concludes that a patient with such a diagnosis could present a danger to a young child."

Nick was deeply worried. The records scared him. If Cat got ahold of them he wouldn't give a plug nickel for their chances. But he couldn't give Cat any hint that he was concerned.

"I don't know. Didn't seem to me Judge Swanson liked your motion very much. Wouldn't bet on your chances."

"I'm sending you some citations to some recent cases on the issue. I really don't see how she can say no. If she does, we'll take an interlocutory appeal. We think it's that important and we're that convinced."

"Well. I guess you do what you have to do," he replied.

"But that's not really the purpose of my call. I had a long conference with Dr. Taylor and his mother..."

Nick interrupted her, "Speaking of Martha Taylor, I wasn't going to tell you this but on second thought I think you should know."

"What?"

"She called me up."

"You?"

"Yes."

Nick heard a muffled "that bitch" that obviously snuck through Cat's hand over the receiver. "You're shitting me," Cat finally said.

"No."

"What the hell did she say?"

"In the space of thirty seconds, she managed to inform me that one of her trusts controls the LLC that owns our office building..."

"No...."

"Yes...and second she let me know she's looking for a local firm...maybe Ford, Ford, Osgood, Barnett & Thomas...to put on a very generous retainer."

"Oh, for Christ's sake. I am so sorry. I'll talk to her. What did you tell her?"

"Well, in so many words, I told her to go fuck herself."

"Good for you."

"That's not all."

"Do I want to hear this?"

"Probably not, but you're going to. She's had someone tailing my client even when she comes here, to my office."

"Shit. I swear I had nothing to do with it."

"I know that. That's why I didn't call you immediately."

"I'll talk to her, I promise. Let her know if anything else like that occurs, Danny Boy's looking for new counsel. I don't give a damn what she's paying me."

"Thanks. I appreciate that."

"Jesus, I am so sorry. Listen, the real reason for my call is I think there's a chance...an outside chance...we could wrap this whole thing up and settle it before the shit hits the fan on this medical stuff."

"Really?" Nick replied with unconcealed interest. If they could settle the whole thing, Livie would no longer be his client. He'd have to refund a chunk of her retainer but at this point, so what? He'd have Livie Taylor out of his life. And, if thereafter she turned on him, he'd hate doing it, but he'd deny everything. He'd say it was the sick ravings of a psychotic, narcissistic scorned woman. His word versus hers. Who would believe her?

"On what terms?" he continued. Nick took detailed notes as Cat recited the terms of a proposed settlement offer. Nick was surprised at how generous it was.

They'd agree to toss the prenup. Dr. Taylor would pay her three million dollars cash for a permanent waive of alimony and for surrendering all claims to the house and his medical practice and his investments. He would continue to pay ten thousand dollars a month child support and agree to pay all college costs when Jessica turned eighteen. They would equitably divide the household contents fifty-fifty, which was estimated to be worth three hundred thousand dollars. She would get her Lexus free and clear and all her jewelry he had given her, worth at least another two hundred thousand dollars.

But the key, the tough sell, he knew was that Dr. Taylor had insisted upon true joint custody of Jessica. Not just in name, but in deed. Jessica would spend half her time with Dr. Taylor and half with Livie. The parties would have to agree upon any major decisions affecting Jessica and neither would move outside the Selma school district.

When Cat finished reciting the terms, she gave Nick a second to catch up with his note-taking. "I'm emailing you a summary of this offer. It's not a gimmick. Dr. Taylor wants to avoid a war and to do what's best for Jessica. This was all his idea. Martha didn't like it one bit even though she's funding it. But he absolutely wants this thing settled right now. We've cut straight to the chase. No b.s., no negotiating. It's all I've got to offer. You know as well as I that even without the prenup almost all the assets are pre-marital anyway. No way, no way she'll come out this good financially if she litigates. You're smart enough to know that. And we really think if we get our hands on these psych records, we've got a shot at full custody, besides…."

Nick interrupted her, "Cat, you're preaching to the choir. You don't have to sell me on this one."

"Well, sell it to your client. Neither one of us needs this headache."

"I'll do my best," he replied, "I'll get her in this afternoon. Get me that email."

"It's on its way," she answered before hanging up.

In a minute, Nick checked his email, clicked "print" and walked straight back to the printer and hovered over it waiting for Cat's correspondence to arrive. As each sheet came in he pulled it out of the printer, unable to tolerate the machine's lackadaisical worth ethic.

He took the papers back to his office and compared them to his notes. They conformed to each other. He quickly glanced at the affidavit of Dr. Nathan Bowman and his curriculum vitae. He had little doubt that when Judge Swanson reconsidered the motion, particularly in light of Dr. Bowman's affidavit, she would issue the subpoena for Livie's records.

Once Cat got those records, the game was over as far as Nick was concerned. What judge in her right mind would grant custody to a mother who had voiced an intent to drown her baby and plop the dead body on her husband's desk? Not one that wanted to get re-elected. If the shit ever hit the fan and Livie did harm Jessica, Judge Swanson would be crucified.

He dialed Livie's number. She picked up on the third ring and began speaking immediately "Hey, Nicky...have you been missing me as much as I've missed you?"

"Livie, please," Nick cautioned, "someone else from my office could be calling you."

"Oh, honey, I'm sorry...I didn't think of that. You're not mad are you?"

Oh Christ, he thought, *now I'm "honey"*. "No, I am not mad...just, please, be careful."

"I'm sorry. I will."

"Listen, can you get into the office this afternoon?"

"Why, what's happened?" she asked.

"Quite a bit, but I don't want to discuss it on the phone."

"Yeah, I guess, but I'll have to bring Jessica."

"Fine...I'd like to meet her anyway. Is she okay with strangers? Can Pat watch her while we talk?" he asked.

"Yeah, with women she's okay. Now, men, that's another story. She's usually scared of men."

"Okay, three?"

"Sure, three. Nick?"

"Yes?"

"It's been a while. When can we make time for us?"

"I don't know. Things are really at a crucial point in your divorce right now. We just can't afford to be doing things that could jeopardize the case. Do you understand that?"

"Yes," she replied, "I understand, but I don't have to like it. I'll see you at three. Oh, I'll bring a little treat so I'll always be on your mind."

"Don't worry about that," Nick assured her, "you are always on my mind."

"You're so sweet," she said as she hung up.

Nick leaned back in his chair. *So now I'm "honey" she's bringing me "little treats", she's acting like Jessica and Natalie are stepsisters and she's letting me know that "we" can have more kids. No wonder she's always on my mind. My God,* he asked himself, *could the situation be any crazier?* He declined to answer his own question. He walked down the hall, checked with Betty to make sure Rosa didn't have a client in the office and knocked softly on her door and opened it.

Rosa was on the phone but gestured towards one of the chairs facing her desk. Nick sat down. He half-heartedly listened to Rosa's end of the conversation which had something to do with a woman who had run off to Alaska with her kids and her ex-con boyfriend. Apparently, Rosa represented the woman. She was patiently trying to explain to her client why both her husband and the judge might frown upon her preferences in both companions and locale. She hung up and chuckled slightly. "Clients," she said.

"Tell me about it," Nick replied. "Listen, I really need a second opinion on something."

"Shoot," she replied. "What file?"

He gulped hard, "The Taylor divorce."

"Jeez, Nick, I hate to get involved in that one...why don't you ask Larry when he gets back."

"Oh, God, you know how Larry is. By the way, where is he?"

"Chicago," she replied. "He'll be back Monday."

"Why is he always going there? What the hell does he do there anyway?" Nick asked.

"What do you think? His boyfriend lives there."

"Boyfriend!" Nick exclaimed. "Larry's gay?"

Rosa laughed, "My God, you didn't know?"

"Well...gee...no...not really...I mean...I kinda wondered why he never talked about women or a girlfriend or anything but I thought he was just such a prick, women couldn't stand him either. Gay? Jesus, no...I didn't know. How come he doesn't act gay?"

"And just what, exactly," Rosa asked, "is '*acting gay*'? You're not some kind of closet homophobe are you?"

"Of course not. I'm a card-carrying liberal...and you know...I didn't mean anything about acting gay...God...I'm just so surprised. You think you know someone..."

Rosa laughed again, "Guys are so observant. I wonder how you guys avoid walking into walls your whole life."

Nick chuckled in reply. "I'm feeling like I have been. Hey, about my second opinion?"

"Okay, but one time only. Please don't involve me in that situation anymore."

Nick briefly explained what he had learned from the medical records and outlined Cat Jagger's settlement offer. He did not tell her his personal reasons for wanting to settle the Taylor divorce as soon as possible.

"What do you think?" he concluded.

"What do I think?" she repeated. "I think you'd better take it and run. In a New York minute."

"Boy," Nick replied, "my thoughts exactly. I'm so glad you confirmed it. Thanks. She's coming in at three. I'm going to twist her arm like I've never arm twisted a client in my life."

"Great," Rosa said as Nick got up to leave, "and while you're at it..."

"What?" Nick asked.

"Break it...for me," she said with a wry smile.

CHAPTER 22

Nick walked out to the waiting room to escort Livie back to his office. His overwhelmed mind apparently lacked the storage capacity to recall that Livie was bringing Jessica with her. He entered the waiting room and was stopped dead in his tracks.

Livie was kneeling down facing away from him. She was wearing a pale yellow sundress with a halter top and bare back. She was adjusting a barrette in Jessica's hair. Jessica, who was facing Nick, glanced at him for an instant then hurriedly returned her gaze to her mother. Jessica was also wearing a sundress, pink in color. Her hair was long and curled and just one shade lighter than Livie's. She had her mother's olive shading to her skin, darkened even more by her obvious tan. But she did not have her mother's eyes. Her eyes were blue like her father's. Nick's previous doubts concerning Jessica's paternity were assuaged. The overall effect was stunning. Nick would not have believed it possible, but it appeared likely that, in twenty years, Jessica would be even more beautiful than her mother.

"Hi, ladies," Nick said. Livie rose and turned to face him. She looked absolutely radiant and for the briefest of instants the insanity of the last weeks was purged from his mind and he felt that familiar, overpowering desire for her.

"You must be Jessica," Nick said as he bent down to her level and extended his hand. "I'm Nick."

Jessica grabbed her mother's dress and pulled it in front of her, hiding behind it.

"She's a little bashful," Livie explained. She then looked down at Jessica. "Honey, this is Nick. I told you about him. He's the nice man who's helping us so Daddy and Grandma will stop being so mean to us and quit trying to take you away from Mommy."

Nick looked at Livie in disbelief. His renewed desire for her evaporated in an instant. This was the Livie he had, unfortunately, recently become acquainted with.

"Well, yes," he said, "let's go back to my office."

Livie grabbed her purse off the chair and a large three-ring notebook. She slung the purse over her shoulder, grabbed Jessica's hand in hers and followed Nick back to his office.

Nick tried to engage Jessica in conversation but she refused to respond or make eye contact with him. He called Pat to take her and entertain her while he and Livie talked. Pat had four kids, and, if he had it right, the grandkid count was up to seven. Jessica jumped into her arms without hesitation.

"Sorry," Livie apologized. "Told you she was shy around men."

"Guess I'm scarier than I thought," he joked.

"Sometimes..."

"What?"

"Oh, never mind. Nothing. Here," she said reaching across the desk and handed him the notebook. "This is your treat I promised you."

"What is it?" he asked.

"Well, look, silly. I think you'll like it."

He set the notebook down on his desk and flipped it open. His eyes grew wide in amazement as he flipped through the pages. "Livie, what the...I can't...what is this?"

"They're called 'boudoir photos'. I had them done a couple of years ago by a professional. They were for Daniel. I'd hoped they might help with...you know...with his problem. But he couldn't have cared less. He looked at them once and said, 'You let someone take pictures of you like this?' and put it up in his closet. What do you think?"

He flipped through some more pages. "Well, Jesus...I mean...I can't keep this. They're beautiful, unbelievable. But, what if someone found them? I mean...you're naked in most of these!" He heard footsteps in the hall outside his office and quickly slammed the notebook shut and placed it on top of a stack of files on his desk. The footsteps passed by.

"Well of course I'm naked, Nicky," she laughed. "That's the whole point, isn't it? I told you I wanted to make sure I'm always on your mind. God, it was so much fun doing those. When this is all over, I want to do some more, just for you."

"Please, it's just..." he began, but then realized he didn't want to waste valuable time debating with Livie Taylor the pros and cons of him keeping a portfolio of nude photos of her. "Um... okay, all right. We'll deal with it later. We have two very important things to talk about."

"Okay," she replied, "I'm glad you like them."

"First, I got the medical records."

He looked at her and could see concern come over her face. "Remember what I said about postpartum depression."

"I do. I know. I've done a lot of research. But first, your diagnosis wasn't postpartum depression."

"It wasn't?"

"No. It was postpartum psychosis and..."

"Same difference," she interjected.

"No, no it's not. Psychosis, by definition, is a very, very serious psychiatric disorder..."

"But I'm over it..."

"Yes, maybe. But the problem, you see, is that you never really completed treatment...you self-terminated. Dr. Ahmad..."

"Oh, for God's sake, he's a quack. I insisted upon the head of the department seeing me and they sent me...that...that little quack who could barely speak English. What a joke!"

"Regardless, he was your treating physician. He made the diagnosis."

"Well, okay, what's your point?"

"There's also a secondary diagnosis."

"What?...That quack never said anything about another diagnosis."

"You were also diagnosed with a psychological personality disorder."

"Oh, bullshit. What?"

"It's called narcissistic personality disorder."

"Oh my God...what bullshit! Can we sue him?"

"No, we can't sue...but to answer your first question the point of all this is it's potentially devastating to our custody claim."

"But, you said the judge wouldn't let them get the records."

"At that point in time she didn't. But they've filed some additional paperwork including an affidavit from a psychiatrist..."

"Who?"

"You've never seen him."

"Then how the hell is his word worth anything?"

"Please. You're paying me a lot of money for my skill, my judgment. My judgment is that Judge Swanson will issue the subpoena. They'll get those records."

"So what if they do? I told you. Ahmad's a quack. No one in their right mind will listen to him."

"He's a psychiatrist, an associate professor. The judge will listen."

He leaned back in his chair and looked at her. He could see her mind working a thousand miles an hour. Finally, she smiled "Nick...honey...I hired you because of your reputation. I did a lot of research first. Of course, I didn't know I was going to fall for you. But you've already told me our chances are excellent. He'd just have to dump her on babysitters. I'm a full-time mom. What judge would do that to a little girl? Come on, honey, you're getting yourself all worked up over nothing. Do I look crazy to you?"

It took all Nick's willpower not to respond, "Look, sound, feel, smell and act crazy." He paused a moment to collect his thoughts before replying "No one's saying you're crazy. But the test here is the best interest of Jessica. Not yours. Not Daniel's. Not Martha's. The judge has one question to answer, 'What is in Jessica's best interest?' You don't have to be crazy to lose."

"We're not going to lose. I just know it."

"Look, my real point in telling you this is that Cat Jagger made a settlement offer this morning on the whole thing. And I believe it to be a very reasonable, even generous settlement. We could have this all done and have you divorced in two weeks."

A broad smile came across her face. "My God! You're kidding! I wondered if Daniel would have the balls to fight."

Nick smiled in return. "Yes. I was really surprised."

"Well," she added with a mischievous grin, "guess maybe I'll have to get on the phone and schedule another photography session."

"Um...well...let me tell you the terms," Nick interjected. Nick spent at least fifteen minutes going through Cat Jagger's letter point by point in extreme detail. With each new financial detail, particularly, the three million dollar lump-sum payment, her grin broadened.

"My God," she said as he concluded, "that's wonderful. I just can't believe it. And his visitation will stay every other weekend and Wednesday evenings?"

"Well, no," Nick began. "That's the thing. He wants joint custody."

"Well, as you said, it's just a word. I don't like it but I think I can live with one evening and alternate weekends."

"Livie, he's talking about true joint custody. Half the time with you. Half with him. Joint decision making on all major decisions. The whole nine yards."

Her smile evaporated instantly. Before she responded, tears began to slowly trickle down her cheeks. "I'm sorry. I can't. He could offer me ten million and I wouldn't do it. Never. That's my baby. They're already putting her through hell. Tell them no deal."

Nick begged, pleaded and cajoled for another fifteen minutes. But it was pointless. No deal.

CHAPTER 23

Nick escorted Livie and Jessica to the front door. "I'll see if I can get them to come down on the fifty-fifty custody but I really doubt it. Please think it over some more."

"Look at her," she responded, "and tell me from your heart that I should let him have her half the time. I can't. But call me, regardless" she replied, then smiled and added, "And in the meantime, you'll have your little souvenir to remember me."

"Shit," Nick mumbled.

"Nick, please," Livie scolded while nodding her head towards Jessica. "Your language. What's wrong?"

"Umm...your souvenir...I think I left it on my desk. I gotta go."

Livie smiled, "Call me."

Nicked headed back to his office as if he was an Olympic walker in the home stretch. He was almost to his office when Stu opened his door and entered the hall.

"Nick, how's it going?" Stu asked. "Got a minute?"

"No, not really," he replied glancing at his watch. "I've got to return an important call."

"Just take a second," Stu continued. "I know you're really buried, but I signed up a new client, could be a really good one, and it's really more up your alley, probably take litigation to resolve it and..."

"Yeah, I'll take it," Nick interrupted, desperate to get back to his office.

"Jeez, great. I'll have Paula get the file to Pat," Stu said as Nick walked away.

Nick raced back into his office to see Pat sitting in one of the client chairs. "Pat?" he said, his heart beating like a rabbit, "looking for something?"

Pat got up and faced him "Close the door," she instructed. He complied then turned to face her. "Um...what?"

"What's going on? No bullshit."

"What do you mean?"

"What the hell is that?" she demanded, pointing to the notebook. "I was looking for a file."

"Oh, Christ," he began as his mind raced, "it's not what you think. She had them done for her husband. She didn't want them at the house. Afraid someone might find them."

"Really?"

"Yeah, Pat. Really."

She walked over to his desk and grabbed the notebook and flipped it open. "Wonder why the inside cover says 'To my Nicky, Enjoy. Love, Livie.?'" She handed the notebook to him.

Nick took it and read the inscription. His eyes had been so focused on the photos he had not even noticed it. He closed the notebook and sat down. "Look, I'm sorry I lied to you. She did have them done for her husband, but it's just...things have gotten a little out of control. The truth is, she's...she's not right. I'm trying to deal with it...trying to get her case resolved so I can get her out of my life. Please, I'm really sorry."

"You know, I've been your secretary what, six years? But I just don't think I want to be part of this. To lie for you. To cover-up. I had a boss like that. Cheating on his wife with the other secretary and I was the one who had to cover for them. It gave me an ulcer. I don't need another one. A while back Betty told me she thought you and Rosa had something going on. Well, for the last month Betty says Rosa's been a royal bitch to work for. Sometimes she finds her crying in her office. She thought it was over her dad's health problems. But I'll bet there's another reason, isn't there? Rosa's a sweet girl. She reminds me of my oldest. How could you do this to her?"

"Pat, it's not what you think."

"I think it's exactly what I think," she said, "and I don't want any part of it. Friday will be my last day."

"Please," he begged as she turned and left his office.

Rage and anger...at himself...overcame him. He had a nearly uncontrollable desire to break something but there were no immediate targets of opportunity. "Shit," he mumbled. He grabbed Livie's notebook and threw it in his trash can until recognizing that that was a less than optimal solution to his problem. He retrieved it from the trash can and placed it in his bottom desk drawer until he could think of a permanent solution.

He picked up his phone and buzzed Pat, "Pat?"

"What?"

"Cancel the rest of my appointments," he said. "I've got to make a phone call then I need to leave."

"Okay," she responded, "I think I'll leave too."

Nick dialed Cat Jagger's number. He silently fumed as he listened to the electronic message and menu. He had forgotten Cat's personal extension and had to listen to the whole thing. Stu had been talking about getting an electronic receptionist. Supposedly it made the secretaries more efficient and the firm more profitable, he had said. But as Nick listened to the interminable menu and fumed he silently swore he'd be God damned to eternal damnation before they put one in at his firm.

He finally heard Cat's extension...nine...and pushed nine so hard he hurt his finger. Cat's secretary answered and put him through.

"Well?" she said without pleasantries or introductions.

"No deal," he replied.

"Oh, shit, come on. What the hell does she want? Are you serious?"

"Like a heart attack," he replied. "Everything's okay except the fifty-fifty custody. She wants it kept as is."

"Well, for God's sake, we made the financial offer as generous as we did to get fifty-fifty custody. Dan Taylor was buying his little girl."

"You think I don't know that?" he replied, exasperated. "I already told you...you're preaching to the choir."

"Fine. But make sure she knows...we get those psych records...and if they're what we think they are, all bets are off. We're going for full custody. That means no child support."

"She knows."

"All right. Guess there's nothing else I can say. You've got your ass exposed big time. Hope you've covered it for your file nice and tight. See you Friday."

"Right, Friday," he said then added quietly after hanging up, *"Only it's more than my ass that's been exposed."*

He grabbed his briefcase, took Livie's notebook out of his desk drawer and placed it in his briefcase. He opened his office door to leave. Stu was rapidly approaching in the hall. "Nick. Need to talk," he shouted.

Nick retreated back into his office. Stu entered and closed the door.

"I'm in a big hurry, Stu. We'll talk later."

"No, now. What's going on? Pat just told me she's leaving. Last day is Friday."

"Did you ask her?"

"Of course."

"And?"

"She said it was personal."

Nick breathed an involuntary sigh of relief. "Same thing she told me."

"Well, for Christ's sake, do you have any idea how hard it's going to be to replace her? God damn, did she want more money?"

"No."

"Then what? Why no two-weeks' notice?"

"It's personal. Personal means personal. How the hell should I know?" He picked his briefcase back up and started to proceed past Stu. He was stopped by Stu's hand around his bicep.

"Goddammit, Nick," Stu barked, "I'm managing partner. This is my father's firm. Something the hell is going on and I want a fucking answer."

Nick stopped. Everything in his life was spinning wildly out of control. Both his professional life and his personal life were imploding like the final death throes of a supernova. But here, now, at this instant in time, was a problem he could and would fix. He turned to face Stu. One glance at the look in Nick's eyes and Stu knew instantly that he had overplayed his hand.

"Stuart, take your hand off my arm and don't you ever touch me again or I'll knock your fucking teeth down your fucking throat," he commanded coolly and calmly, enunciating each word as if it would be the last word Stuart Ford would ever hear.

Stu not only let go of Nick's arm, he backed away from Nick with such alacrity he bumped into one of Nick's client chairs causing him to stumble and knocking the chair over.

"Thank you," Nick replied as he turned and left an utterly dumbfounded financial management partner in his office.

***

Nick sat on his couch. With his right hand, he aimlessly stroked Felix. Each time Nick stopped, even momentarily, Felix clawed his arm, reminding him as to who was in control of terminating the grooming session.

With his left hand, Nick alternatively took sips from the gin and tonic perched on the end table next to him and flipped through the pages of the notebook Livie had given him. It was his fourth gin and tonic and his fifth time through the notebook. He rarely drank hard liquor anymore and the three and half drinks he had already consumed were more than sufficient to render him legally and morally drunk. He also rarely looked at pictures of naked women anymore, but Livie's notebook was controlling his left arm as surely as Felix was controlling his right.

The pictures were as perfect and professional as if they were Playboy centerfolds. And Livie had a body that would have shamed most of the centerfolds he had ever seen. She had themed the pictures as a calendar shoot and Livinia Taylor was Miss January through Miss December, costumed, just barely, in each picture to represent something to do with that month.

One more look through, he told himself. How, he wondered, could someone so beautiful be so totally fucked up? He concluded, however, before his drunkenness robbed him of all analytical ability, that beauty and fuckedupness bore no correlation whatsoever.

He flipped from Miss June...Livie wearing a Cardinals baseball hat and an unbuttoned Cardinals jersey and holding a bat, to Miss July...Livie wearing a red, white and blue top hat and holding a small American flag in each hand. As he did, there was a brief knock on the door and, before he could even close the notebook or stand up, the door flew open. Nick slammed the notebook shut as Natalie walked in trailed by a tall, gangly teenage boy holding her hand. The boy had a bad case of acne and an even worse excuse for a mustache and he immediately reminded Nick of himself at that age.

"Hey, Daddy," she said.

"Sweetie," he said as he got to his feet. "What are you doing here?"

"I wanted you to meet Ryan," she explained. "We were decorating the gym. Friday's prom...remember?"

"Yeah...sure," he said. His rapid and unanticipated ascent

from the couch had left Nicky dizzy. In the matter of seconds it took for Nick to overcome his vertigo he stumbled and bumped into the coffee table. He nearly fell and as he bumped the table, Livie's notebook slid off and fell onto the floor. Panic seized Nick but subsided slightly when he realized the notebook had not come open.

"Daddy," Natalie asked glancing from the drink on the end table to her father, "are you okay?"

Nick was certain that Natalie had never seen him drunk or even close to it. He had no doubt that he smelled like a brewery. The room had started to spin slowly and Nick was doubtful of his ability to successfully walk the three or four steps over to Natalie and Ryan. He stood still and prayed that the room would follow his example and stop spinning.

"Umm...yeah...I had one of my migraines...really bad...I took some Imitrex with a drink...probably shouldn't have. It kinda knocked me for a loop. So," he added, desperate to change the topic, "you're Ryan?"

"Yes, sir," Ryan said, "pleased to meet you. Natalie's told me so much about you." He strode up to Nick and extended his hand. Nick took it in his and firmly shook.

"Here," Ryan added, "let me get that for you." Ryan bent over and picked Livie's notebook off the floor as Nick yelled, "No, it's okay..."

"No problem," Ryan said as he set it back on the coffee table, "already got it."

"Thanks," Nick said.

"Well, we need to run," Natalie said as she glanced at her watch. "I told Mom I'd be home by nine." She walked up to Nick and hugged him. He held his breath, refusing to exhale during her hug, hoping to minimize the evidence of his drinking. Finally, Natalie broke the hug and stepped back to Ryan.

"Sure," Nick replied. "Ryan, nice meeting you. You drive careful with my little girl in your car."

"Daddy," she scolded him, "please. I'm not a little girl." They looked at each other and Nick smiled in return. "Sorry," he said.

"You sure you're okay?" she asked. Nick could see the concern on her face.

"Yeah, honey. I'm fine. I'm going to bed," he replied. "See you next Friday for pictures."

"Okay, bye."

Nick managed to follow them to the door without stumbling. He stood and watched them get into Ryan's Mustang and drive away until they were out of sight. He doubted Ryan drove over twenty mph, at least so long as he was within sight. Nick closed the door, walked over to the coffee table and picked up Livie's notebook. He took it with him out to the back porch. Felix followed.

He took out Miss January and placed it on the grill. He squirted lighter fluid all over it then struck his match. Miss February through December were followed by the notebook itself.

As he tossed each photo into the barbeque and watched the flames curl and ultimately consume them, he spoke to Livie, "You cost me Rosa. You cost me Pat. I'll be God damned if you'll cost me Natalie."

CHAPTER 24

"I will say for the record," Judge Swanson began, "that I do not like doing this..."

"But, Judge, just one more point..." Nick pleaded.

She silenced him with an upraised hand. "Mr. Barnett, I've listened patiently, I believe, to you and Ms. Jagger for an hour because I think this is an important issue. And I truly believe that mental health records should be privileged except under the most extraordinary circumstances. People have to be able to trust that when they see a psychologist or a psychiatrist, that what they say in that office stays in that office, just as clients must with their lawyers. But ultimately, my main concern here is with a little girl and her future. I'm charged with deciding what is in her best interest and I take that responsibility very seriously. Your client voluntarily asked this court to award her sole custody, asserting, in her pleadings, under oath, that it was in the child's best interest that I do so. I now have in front of me what I believe to be significant evidence that your client has some substantial psychiatric problems, problems that go beyond a 'bout of postpartum depression' as you have described it and may, and I emphasize the word 'may', have some impact on the decision I will be called upon to make. What I find particularly troubling is that your client apparently terminated all treatment against medical advice.

So, reluctantly, I am going to grant the motion and order

189

the subpoena to issue. I will also grant a protective order that no one..." she looked directly at Cat Jagger for emphasis as she continued, "...no one, besides Ms. Jagger and Dr. Taylor are to view these records or receive any information concerning them without further order from me."

"But, Judge," Cat interrupted, "we'll have to have them reviewed by our expert Dr. Nathan Bowman."

"Yes, okay," Judge Swanson continued, "but Dr. Bowman must understand he is subject to the same protective order. No secondary disclosures.

Finally, sua sponte, I am ordering that Mrs. Taylor, Dr. Taylor and Jessica are to be evaluated by a psychologist appointed by the court." She paused a moment and consulted a list before continuing. "Does Dr. Benjamin James have any connection to any of the parties or to this case in any way?"

"No," both Cat and Nick replied simultaneously

Judge Swanson continued, "Then does anyone have an objection to Dr. James serving as the court's expert?"

Cat and Nick each briefly conferred with their clients. "No," they both responded.

"Fine, then each of the parties is ordered to make themselves and the minor child available for whatever evaluation and testing Dr. James deems necessary. Dr. Taylor will pay the cost for himself and Jessica. Mrs. Taylor, you will pay for your evaluation."

"Anything else on today's agenda, counselors?" she asked.

"No, your Honor," they both replied.

"Then we are adjourned," Judge Swanson said as she called the next case.

***

Nick took Livie back into the empty jury room to discuss the implications of the judge's rulings. Livie was dressed more casually than she had previously been but still looked striking and elegant. She was wearing a longer, flowing, flower print skirt, white blouse and a pale lime green summer jacket that matched perfectly the green splashed here and there in her skirt. White heeled sandals and matching bag completed today's ensemble.

He closed the jury room door and turned to face her. "Livie..." before he could get another word out she threw her hands around his neck and kissed him full on the lips.

"God," she said as she finally broke her kiss and hug. "I've missed you so much. We have to make time for each other this weekend. Daniel will have Jessica."

"Livie..." he started to reply.

She smiled mischievously and added, "I promise I'll make it worth your while."

"Please sit down. We have to talk." He pulled out a chair for her.

"What's wrong honey?" she asked.

"Please...don't call me honey...not here..." he begged, "no kissing, no hugging, please..."

She smiled and slapped his knee, "Oh all right, Mr. Serious. But what's wrong?"

"What's wrong?" he repeated, totally dumbfounded. "You were in court. You heard her. By five today, Cat Jagger will have those records. She's hand delivering the subpoena to the hospital and doctor today. Then...then there's going to be the psychological evaluations. I'm very, very concerned. Maybe if I called Cat on her cell right now they'd still go with the settlement offer they made. It may not be too late."

Livie smiled again. "You worry too much, honey...oops...I mean Mr. Barnett..." she giggled before proceeding. "I told you I'm not worried about the records. That was well over three years ago. I'm fine now. My God, you know that. And as far as the evaluations are concerned, I say 'bring it on.' If he's any kind of a shrink at all he'll see what a prick Daniel is. And I'm sure Jessica will tell him she wants to be with me. Besides, this Dr. Benjamin

James is a man..." she paused and smiled lecherously, "and in case you haven't noticed, men find it rather difficult to say 'no' to me. But don't get jealous, Nicky, I won't actually do anything. I won't have to. Why are you so worried?"

He was going to attempt a detailed explanation of the likely legal ramifications of the judge's ruling but quickly decided that it would be pointless. "I've been practicing law for over sixteen years. The majority of my practice is divorce. I've handled hundreds of custody cases, tried dozens and dozens of them. I know, believe me, I know how this system works and I am telling you right now, not warning you, not cautioning you, but telling you...if this goes down the way I think it's going to go down, you will lose custody of Jessica. Period. End of story. It's that simple."

She took her hand back from his knee and looked stunned for an instant. Tears welled up in her eyes. She was silent for a few moments, then grabbed a tissue from her bag and dabbed her eyes and stood up. She regained her composure, bent over, kissed Nick and smiled. "It's not going to happen. It is simply not going to happen. He will not get custody of her. Ever. Mark my words." She walked to the door and grabbed the handle. She paused and turned to face him. "I'm going home to be with Jessica before that bastard picks her up at six. Call me tomorrow. Please. I need you. I need you more than ever." With that, she opened the door and left.

Nick's mind was a disorganized jumble of conflicting emotions as he pulled into his office lot. He was still thinking just clearly enough to realize that he was nearly incapable of a clear thought. He dreaded thinking about the work he had put out this week. Thank God Pat was still here...until five today at least...to prevent him from committing malpractice. He had begged and pleaded with her to stay, but she had remained resolute. She had made it clear that she wanted no more of Nick Barnett.

The temporary service had sent over Misty, a twenty-two-year-old with frizzy unkempt blonde hair and apparently an intellect to match. Pat was to show her the ropes today on this, her last day. He walked up to Pat and Misty and forced himself to smile. "So, how's it going?"

Pat looked back at him and rolled her eyes in answer.

"Oh great," Misty squealed, "I'm gonna love it here. Mr. Ford has been soo nice to me."

"Yeah," Nick replied, "Stu's a gem. Hold my calls, please."

"Sure thing, Mr. Barnett," Misty answered. "But then, should I take messages?"

Nick smiled and glanced back up at Pat before replying, "Yeah, Misty, that would probably be a good idea." He dumped his briefcase on his desk, loosened his tie, hung his suit coat up, grabbed his coffee cup and headed back to the coffee pot. Betty, Sarah and Michelle were all there. *Damn,* thought Nick silently, *we don't pay 'em to stand around here and gossip.*

"Betty," he called out, "is Rosa back yet?" Nick knew that Rosa had been gone the last two days. Her father's health had taken another turn for the worse. Betty turned around, a tear rolling down each cheek.

"Betty, what?" Nick asked.

"Rosa just called...he...he passed away late last night. She's really taking it hard."

"Her dad?"

"Yeah. Visitation's tomorrow night."

"Oh my God...oh poor Rosa. She was so close to her dad. Oh, shit. Where at, Carbondale?"

"Yeah," Betty continued. "I'll call the funeral home for details. Stu told me to send flowers in the firm name. Said to spend no more than fifty dollars."

Nick filled his coffee cup, then turned to face Betty. "Spend a hundred. Not a nickel less," he instructed. He went back to his office and tried calling Rosa on her cell. There was no answer. He thought about trying to make a dent in the huge stack of files on his desk. But it was pointless. He buzzed Pat's desk.

"Ford, Osgood and Barnett," came Misty's voice, forgetting the second "Ford" and the first "Thomas" in the firm name. "How may I help you?"

"Misty," Nick explained, "this is a local line. It's me."

"Who?"

"Nick Barnett, your boss."

"Oh, Mr. Barnett, how may I help you then?"

"Well, for one, when you answer the outside lines, the firm name is Ford, Ford, Osgood, Barnett & Thomas..."

"That's what I said," she protested.

"No...no..." Nick began before deciding it wasn't worth pursuing, "...and second...could you send Pat in."

"Sure...send her in where?"

"My office, Misty. My office."

"Oh, sure."

A second later Pat entered. Despite the somber nature of her last day she smiled and chuckled. "Good luck. You're gonna need it."

"Where in the hell did they find her?" he asked.

"Beats me."

"Pat, I just want to say one more time I'm really sorry. I just hope we can part as friends despite everything."

"Sure," Pat replied.

"I've gotta leave early. I wanted to check with you to make sure the Fullerten complaint gets filed. The statute runs Monday. Don't think I'll rely on Misty to make sure it gets done."

"All done and filed," she replied.

"Great. You heard?" he inquired.

"About what?"

"Rosa's dad passed away."

"No. When?"

"Late last night, I guess. Betty's getting the details on the visitation."

"Oh, poor girl. Thanks for telling me." She paused a few moments. As Nick got up, grabbed his suit coat and briefcase and prepared to leave, she continued. "Nick?"

"Yes?"

"Do what's right."

"Thanks, Pat," he answered as he opened the door to leave.

"I only wish I knew what that was," he added quietly to himself as he walked down the hallway and out to his car.

CHAPTER 25

Nick went straight home. He again tried to work on some of the files he had brought home with him. They desperately needed his attention but he knew after fifteen minutes that it was pointless. Even if he actually did any work on them, odds are they would be as fucked up as his life was right now. And he obviously would not be able to count on Misty to catch any mistakes. Hell, if he handed her the lyrics to "Mary had a Little Lamb" to type, odds were good she'd screw it up.

He wanted a drink, but his mind was still functioning well enough to remember that Natalie and her boyfriend...he still had such difficulty formulating the word "boyfriend" in his mind when thinking about his little girl...were stopping by around six on their way to the prom for pictures. He made sure his iPhone was charged, made some coffee, and sat on one of the wooden rockers on the front porch. It had continued to be unseasonably hot and he sweated out of every pore in his body as he drank the piping hot coffee. He welcomed both the heat and the sweat it was producing. It felt purifying, as if a torrid fever had just broken and the sweat rolling off his forehead, back, chest and arms was purging him of the poison within his body.

He wasn't sure he felt like reading but nevertheless picked up the collection of short stories lying on the end table next to his rocker. He needed a distraction. It was only two fifteen. He opened the book and despite his mood, the power of the writing soon transported Nick to places, characters and cultures from across the universe. He was envious of the author's skill but not envious in the pejorative sense. Maybe "awe" was a better adverb, he thought. *Someday,* he mused, *someday I'll finish my novel.* It had been patiently gathering dust in the bottom left drawer of his desk. Four years...he had started it shortly after the divorce and had found writing therapeutic. Four years of work and seventy-two pages to show for it. *Christ,* he wondered, *how do Grisham and Patterson do it?*

He refilled his coffee cup then microwaved it to make up for Mr. Coffee's less than sincere efforts to keep the pot hot. Probably the result of some God damn lawyer suing Mr. Coffee for keeping their coffee too hot, he figured. "Fucking lawyers," he mumbled to himself. "We'd all be better off without them," he added, before chuckling at his own masochism.

For the first year after the divorce, he had lived in an apartment in downtown Selma within walking distance of his office. It was convenient but he soon found that convenience was too high a price to pay for soullessness. An apartment...a rental apartment...simply lacked a soul. A Ted Bundy with two bedrooms and two bathrooms instead of two arms and two legs.

A house, a real house with real dirt and real grass and real creaks, groans, cantankerousness and personality...he found that he needed that. He had bought a modest three-bedroom two-story on the very outskirts of town. Directly across the road was a farm field that alternated in an endless cycle, depending upon the season and the mood of the farmer between corn, soybeans, wheat and barrenness. He sometimes rocked on his porch, stared at the field and wondered if the dirt yearned for something different. For a break from the endless cycle of corn, soybeans and wheat. If it was able, would it beg for something else to be impregnated with? Just once. A tomato plant perhaps? Some asparagus shoots? A tree? Maybe even grass?

A little over three years now and the house was definitely his home. He had slowly conformed it to his will, painting, wallpapering and decorating it with as much dedication and interest as a heterosexual adult male could muster. The house had previously been owned for over thirty years by a widow and it had been thoroughly and utterly feminized. He had tackled the job slowly and gently. In increments, gradually, over protest, the house had accepted its inevitable transformation and had come to terms with its sex change.

He took his coffee back out to the porch and picked the short story collection back up. He was still reading at six when the cordless rang. He picked it up and looked at the caller I.D. "Livie's TracFone". *Shit,* he thought, *Jessica's been gone five minutes and she's already calling me.* He did not answer. Livie was persistent but after seventeen rings, her perseverance finally exhausted itself and the ringing stopped. A moment later a white limo rolled to a stop in front of his home. A rotund black-suited man with a cap too small for his oversized head got out, walked around, opened the back door and extended his hand.

Natalie exited. His baby girl, standing in front of him in what looked like acres of purple chiffon and organza. Her hair was up and strewn with baby's breath and topped by a tiny tiara. Ryan exited too and walked around the back of the limo and took Natalie's hand from the driver. A moment later, a second girl, who Nick barely recognized as Jennifer, Natalie's best friend, exited swathed in swirling yards of blue chiffon. Her date followed. Nick grabbed his iPhone and walked down to greet them. The girls had smiles from ear to ear. The boys, looking, in their ill-fitting tuxedos, as stiff, awkward and uncomfortable as grooms at a shotgun wedding, exchanged nervous glances at each other.

He walked up to hug Natalie, but she stopped him. "Daddy, please be careful...my dress...and my hair."

"Okay," he said, "I'll be careful." He stepped up to her and hugged her as awkwardly and gently as if every bone in her body was made of fragile china. "My God," he gushed, "you look so...

so beautiful." He stepped back then added, "You too Jennifer. By the way, when did you grow up?"

The girls giggled in reply. "Here," Natalie added, "Mom said to give this to you." She handed him an envelope. He took it from her and stuck it in the back pocket of his shorts. They walked to his small flower garden and he took a dozen pictures. At the girls' insistence, he finally invited their dates to be in the last three or four pictures.

"Daddy, we have to go," Natalie firmly reminded him.

"Okay, honey," he said, giving her another fragile hug before she entered the limo. Jennifer reentered next. Nick grabbed both boys by the arms before they could escape into the limo. He assumed his most menacing *you touch my baby girl and I'll break your fucking arm* father look. "You boys be gentlemen and behave yourselves," he said. "Yes, sir," came the simultaneous reply from the two boys.

He stood silently and watched the limo drive away before walking back to the porch. He glanced at his watch: six twenty-seven. He picked up the cordless and scrolled through the recent call list on his phone. Four more calls from Livie. He pulled the envelope Natalie had given him out of his pocket and tore it open. There was a note from Sheila "Nick; Hair $150.00, Dress $596.50, Shoes $93.42, Limo (half) $200.00. Plus you still owe me $156.00 for the eye doctor last month. Orthodontist needs $2,500.00 up front to start. Please write me a check. Sheila."

"I'm thinking of you too on this night, Sheila," Nick said aloud to no one. *Jesus,* he thought, *love gone bad is not a pretty sight. Not at all.*

The phone rang again. Nick looked at the display; Livie. "Shit," he said aloud. It ended after nineteen rings and he quickly dialed Rosa's cell before Livie could call again.

She answered.

"Rosa," he said, "oh God, I'm so sorry."

"Thanks," she answered. "Can you come to the visitation?"

"Sure. Of course," he replied. "Is there anything I can do?"

"Um...no..." she answered, "nothing that I can think of. Just...next week...my mom's not doing very well. I don't know when I'll be back at the office. I know you're buried..." as the word "buried" came out of her mouth she stopped and he could hear her sobbing for a moment before she continued, "I know you're snowed under but can you check with Betty? Keep an eye on things. I know I've got two or three hearings next week that will have to be continued."

"No problem," he assured her. "Don't worry about the office. I'll take care of it. Take as much time as you need."

"Thanks."

"Hey, anything I can do just let me know."

"Okay, thanks. Maybe there is just one thing..."

"Sure, what?"

"Um...the visitation starts at six. Do you think maybe you could come a little early? And I wonder if we could maybe go together. I just don't want to be alone and have to answer all the questions from all the relatives about why I'm alone."

"My God, of course. Do you want me to come tonight?"

"No, I couldn't ask you to..."

"I'm on my way," he said as he hung up.

***

Sunday afternoon. He cringed as his cell rang again. He picked it up off the front passenger seat knowing what it would say before he even looked. "Livie." "Shit," he mumbled. He had given up counting the number of times she had called over the weekend. *How the hell did she even get my cell number?* he wondered. He got off the interstate at Mt. Vernon to gas up and to run through McDonald's. He glanced at his watch. Three-fifteen p.m. What a strange, even surreal, weekend it had been.

He had gotten to Rosa's parents' home about eight-thirty on Friday. He met Rosa's mom and tried to chit chat and exchange pleasantries until she finally tired of it and declared that she was going to bed. A few other relatives, Rosa's aunt and uncle and some cousins and their spouses, stayed until about ten and then they too left. Rosa made more coffee and they dabbled at the cakes and pies some neighbors and friends had brought over. Rosa talked about her dad. He had, she told him, been one of the wisest and smartest and kindest men she had ever known. But there had been something missing. Rosa had known that from as far back as she could remember. It was only in the last few years that she had, she thought, figured it out. Her dad, for all his outward calm and genteelness, was an angry man inside. Angry that, for all his success, he wasn't successful enough. Angry when colleagues from the Ivy League or the Big Ten universities would look down their noses disdainfully at him when he would announce that he was a Professor at Southern Illinois University. Angry that, early in his career, he had been forced to turn down associate professorship at Michigan because Lillian had been in the last months of a difficult pregnancy. Angry, maybe, even at her, at his little girl, for being the reason why he had been unable to climb the ladder of academia. And finally, angry at the world of books he loved so reverentially. Angry at it for the seven unpublished novels stacked in boxes in his library and for the accompanying boxes of rejection letters. Maybe, she told Nick, it was the anger, unable to be vented and allowed to destroy the veneer of civility and genteelness so necessary to the persona of "Professor of English Literature", that had turned on his own heart and caused it to destroy itself at sixty-one. Maybe, she added, that's why I decided to be a lawyer. We're supposed to be angry. We're supposed to express it.

When she had finished her eulogy, the tears came anew. Nick sat next to her on the couch and put his arm around her and held her. Her tears increased and she slowly maneuvered herself such that she was under him. "Make love to me," she asked through her tears. He did. And then he wanted to cry too and he was unable to tell her why.

Nick walked into his house, threw his keys on the end table, walked straight to the refrigerator, grabbed a cold beer, then sat down in the recliner. He ratcheted the handle, elevating his feet and ran the cold bottle across his forehead.

He grabbed the cordless and scrolled through the caller I.D. Livie had called incessantly all weekend, both on his cell and on his home phone. He glanced at his watch: six-ten p.m. Jessica would just be back from visitation. He suspected the calls would start up again any second. He knew she would be pissed that he had failed to answer any of her calls. He was quite certain that Livie Taylor was not used to being stood up, especially by men, and he had little doubt there would be hell to pay. He had done considerable research on narcissistic personality disorder and was convinced from his own research that the diagnosis was right on. And narcissists did not take well to rejection. Not at all. But he no longer cared. He had been given a second chance with Rosa and this time he was determined not to blow it. Rosa could not come close to matching Livie in physical beauty, nor her skills in bed. Who could? But Rosa...Rosa...was a real person with real feelings and real emotions and the ability to recognize and empathize with other people's feelings. Livie, he had come to realize, was a shell. Living behind a mask, saying, doing, whatever it took to get what she wanted and to hell with the consequences to other people. Nick paused in his ruminations for a second. *I've just described myself and my actions ever since Livie walked into my life,* he realized. The epiphany scared him. It scared the shit out of him. He would finish Livie Taylor's divorce...what choice did he have? But it would be strictly professional. He would explain that he had made a serious lapse in judgment. That he, by his actions, was jeopardizing her case and he could not allow that to continue. He thought he finally had her scared about the custody issue and hoped that if she thought their relationship could truly jeopardize her custody claim, she would back off. He knew she desperately wanted custody of Jessica. But now he realized it was not so much because she thought it was in Jessica's best interest. No, rather, it was because it was a way to kick sand in Daniel and Martha's faces. And he doubted she would turn on him and report him to the disciplinary committee. Reporting him would, by necessity, mean stating under oath that she was an adulteress. It would mean getting a new attorney, all of which would play right into Daniel's hands in the divorce. He vowed he would get the Taylor divorce over, one way or another, and then get Livie Taylor the hell out of his life once and forever.

He spent a good part of Monday dealing with Betty, trying to make sure Rosa's files would be under control until she came back to the office. The time he had not spent with Betty had been spent exercising damage control with Misty hoping that the things she was screwing up were little things that would be fixable when he got a real secretary with a functioning brain. But, by four-thirty, he could take it no more.

"Misty," he said, "I really appreciate you pitching in, but I really think we need someone with some more law office experience. Sorry."

"You're firing me after two days?" she asked, close to tears.

"Well no...not really...see the temp agency is really your employer. We were just kinda renting you and...well...the lease has expired." He smiled broadly, hoping this explanation would assuage her hurt feelings.

"Well, I liked it here," she said, obviously not consoled one bit. "I think that's kind of poopy of you, Mr. Barnett. Not to give me a chance."

"Sorry. It's for the best," he said as he retreated to his office. As soon as he closed the door he said quietly to himself 'Poopy?' Did she really say 'poopy'? he chuckled and immediately realized it had been weeks since he had last laughed.

There was a knock on the door and Larry entered. "Hey Nick," he said, "how's the new girl working out?"

"Fired."

"Jesus. Two days. Think that's a record for the firm."

"Two days longer than it should have been," Nick replied. "How was Chicago?" Nick asked hoping to get some confirmation of Larry's "status" straight from the horse's mouth.

"Chicago's Chicago," came the curt reply.

"So..." Nick pressed on, "what do you do there?"

Larry looked back at him quizzically. "I stay with my boyfriend. At least I did. But he can fuck himself for all I care."

Nick breathed a sigh of relief. There it was. The barrier broken. It was all out in the open now. "Jesus, Larry, how come you never told me? I feel like an idiot. We've known each other all these years."

"We just broke up this last weekend. How could I tell you before now?"

"I'm talking, about you being gay. That's what I'm talking about."

Larry started laughing, "Oh my God. You're telling me, that until right now, this very moment, you didn't know? I never tried to hide it."

"Well no, not exactly. Rosa told me last week."

"Oh, Jesus, Rosa, I heard about her dad. Sorry I missed the visitation and funeral."

"Does everyone else at the firm know?"

"Sure, of course. I can't believe it. Rosa was right."

"About what?"

"Oh, she told me a while back that you, let's see how did she put it...you were blind as a bat. At first, I thought she was commenting on your eyesight. But she had something else in mind. After you told me and Stu about you and her, I talked to her about it once and she told me she'd had a crush on you for a long time, that she tried to show her interest, but that she finally decided she'd have to stick her tits in your face and shake 'em to give you a hint."

"She said that?"

"Yeah. By the way, how's she doing?"

"Not well. You'll have to help me cover her files 'til she's back."

"No problem. You got any time tomorrow? I got a trial coming up I want you to second chair me on. I'd like to go over it with you."

"Yeah, I think so. How's ten-thirty?"

"Good. Okay. See you then."

"Yeah...Larry?"

"Yeah?"

"Sorry...you know, about not knowing all these years, and sorry about your boyfriend." Spontaneously he hugged Larry, something he would have thought himself incapable of before now. But suddenly, Larry too was a human being, capable of loving, or at least trying to love, capable of being hurt, capable of needing a hug.

Larry did not respond to the hug. Nick let go and stepped back. Larry shrugged, "Love's a bitch. Ain't it?"

"It sure is," Nick agreed, "it sure is."

***

Although he was relieved that Livie Taylor had quit calling, by Tuesday afternoon he found himself getting concerned. The calls had stopped right before six p.m. on Sunday, right when Jessica would have come back from visitation.

Maybe she was so pissed at him for not taking her calls all weekend that she was out hiring another lawyer. Maybe she was writing a letter to the attorney disciplinary committee right now. He didn't even want to think about it. Screwing a client in the middle of a divorce when her husband was charging her with adultery? If they believed her, that would certainly warrant a suspension at a minimum. One year, maybe two. No doubt he'd have to take some kind of sexual abuse counseling. How could he survive a year or two with no income? Who would hire him when he got his license back? How would it affect Natalie? And, of course, Rosa would never talk to him again. As he thought about it more and convinced himself that that was exactly what Livie was doing at this very moment, he decided there was only one answer. If she reported him, he'd lie. He'd deny everything. The psych records demonstrated she had severe psychiatric and psychological problems, not the least of which was a pathological ability to say or do anything to get her way. He'd convince the hearing board that she had turned on him when he had rejected her advances and had told her she was going to lose custody. A classic case of a woman scorned. There was no physical proof. A case of "he said, she said" only in this case "she" was a diagnosed pathological liar.

As he was mentally constructing his case for the hearing board, Mona, the new temp, buzzed him. She was grossly overweight and not at all attractive but that was fine with Nick, even preferred at this point. But she was pleasant and appeared to be relatively competent.

"Cat Jagger, Mr. Barnett, line two," she said.

"Thanks...oh, call me 'Nick,' okay?"

"Sure."

He pushed line two. "So tell me," he began, "you've decided

to throw in the towel, right? You're terrified of litigating this case against me and we can have whatever we ask for."

"And what exactly have you been smoking?" Cat asked.

"Shit, Cat," he replied, "can't an old man fantasize?"

She laughed. "You are getting old if that's what you fantasize about. I thought old men fantasized about young blondes with big boobs."

"Some old men," he answered, "not divorce lawyers."

"Okay," she said, chuckling again, "down to business. Those records are some interesting reading. Talk about fantasies. She wanted to drown her baby in the bathtub and plop the dead body on hubby's desk? Not exactly mother of the year."

"I've read it. What's your point?"

"We've already got a new affidavit from Dr. Bowman. He says custody in your client seriously endangers the child. We're filing an emergency motion today to modify the temporary custody. We want her evaluated before she can get the kid back from visitation. She's sick, Nick. Really sick."

"It was over three years ago," Nick replied, unconvinced himself.

"This motion will be on file today. I want to get Judge Swanson on the phone for a conference call at eight-thirty tomorrow. Are you free?"

He checked his calendar, "Yeah."

"Okay. I'm e-mailing you a copy now."

"Thanks...I think."

"You're welcome...oh and Nick?"

"Yeah?"

"Come up with some better fantasies will you?"

"I'll try," he replied as he hung up.

He walked back to the printer and retrieved the paperwork as it arrived. He went back to his office and read it with an ever-increasing sense of dread. *We're going to lose,* he thought, *no ifs, ands or buts.*

He decided to face the inevitable and picked up the phone

to call Livie. Her phone went to voicemail after the sixth ring. He left a mumbled message apologizing for not taking her calls during the weekend and telling her to call him. It was urgent.

Finally, he called Rosa but, again, got voice mail. *Shit,* he thought, *I spend half my life talking to other people's machines and the other half having my machine listen to them.* He left her a message again expressing his concern for her and telling her not to worry about the office. Everything was under control.

He grabbed his suit coat off the coat rack and walked out to Mona. She smiled and handed him some letters to sign. "Thanks, Mona," he said, "you did good for your first day. Any thoughts of maybe making it permanent?"

She smiled again. "I think I'd like that," she said. Nick smiled back, then left and drove home.

CHAPTER 27

Nick had brought a briefcase full of work home with him but it sat upright and unopened by his desk in his home office all night. He knew it would. He'd just work doubly hard at the office tomorrow, he lied unconvincingly to himself. He had spent the evening reading, listening to the classic rock station and expecting Rosa and Livie to call. Rosa did. Livie didn't.

She had told him that her mom wasn't doing very well and it would be Monday at the earliest before she would be back in the office. He assured her that they had things covered. Finally, she had broached the subject on both their minds, "Listen, about the weekend, I know I came on pretty strong and we had agreed to slow down and I just want to say, I'm sorry. I guess I just needed something."

"Rosa, my God," he answered, "don't you think I needed it too?"

"Did you? Really?"

"Yeah. Of course, I did."

"That's nice to hear, but you were right...let's take it slow. Just like you said."

"Sure."

"So, no problems at the office then?"

"No, everything's fine."

"Everything?"

"Are you asking about the Taylor divorce?"

"I suppose I am."

"She's crazy. Literally. I think she's going to lose custody."

"What about...her behavior towards you?"

Nick's mind raced. He stuttered, "Well...um...I think she's pissed at me. I told her she's going to lose. She's not returning my calls. I haven't heard from her for several days. I don't know what's going on. I'm afraid she's capable of just about anything. I just want to get it over and get her out of my life."

"My God, she sounds dangerous. Be careful, please."

"I will. Give my best to your mom."

"Thanks, I will."

***

He glanced at his watch. Three-thirty on Wednesday afternoon. Although he dreaded it, in some strange way he wanted to talk to Livie to satisfy his morbid curiosity. What in the hell was going on?

As if conjured up by his ruminations, Mona buzzed him. "A Mrs. Livinia Taylor for you on line three, Nick."

"Thanks," he answered as he pushed line three.

"Nick," she began before he had a chance even to say "hello." "Please come to the house. I have to see you this afternoon and it's very, very important."

"Please...I can't..."

"I am not letting her go with Daniel tonight..."

"You'll be in contempt," he pleaded, "there's a court order. You have to."

"I don't care," she answered, "call his bitch of a lawyer and tell her to tell him not to come. Jessica won't be there. I don't care what else you tell her. But I have to see you."

"Okay, all right. Come into the office at four."

"No. At the house in fifteen minutes or I will be at your office at four, but I'll have a letter discharging you and demanding my money back. All of it. I mean it."

"Look, we can't continue...doing what we were doing. It jeopardizes your whole case. I've told you that but..."

"It's not about that. Just come." As she finished speaking the dial tone buzzed in Nick's ear.

"Shit!" he said more loudly than he had intended. Mona opened the door a second later. "Everything okay?"

"Yeah. Listen, I've had an emergency come up. I've gotta run. Be back in tomorrow. Cover for me, will you?"

"Sure," she said.

He grabbed his briefcase and threw his suit coat over his arm. He went straight to Larry's office and knocked.

"Come in," came the reply.

"Larry," Nick began, hoping to cash in on some of their newfound closeness, "I've got a huge favor to ask."

Larry set his pen down and looked skeptical, "What?"

"Come visit a client of mine with me?"

"Where?"

"Just outside of town in the country."

"Now?"

"Yeah, now."

"You're nuts. I've got a brief due tomorrow. I'm gonna be here 'til eight as it is. Go by yourself."

"It's Livie Taylor and she says if I'm not there right now she'll fire me and ask for her retainer back and I'm...well...I'm afraid to go to her home alone. Please. I'll help you with your brief."

"You don't know shit about ERISA litigation. Some help you'd be. Ask Stu."

"Jesus, Larry, I'd rather it be you. Please."

"What is it," Larry asked, "about 'n-o' that you don't understand? No."

"God," Nick cursed in frustration, "and to think I thought you'd changed...fuck you, Larry."

Larry smiled, "A pleasant afternoon to you too."

Nick marched straight to Stu's door and was going to knock before he thought better of it. *Hell,* he thought, *Stu will tell me to go ahead and screw her if it meant saving the fee. He might even ask to join in.* He was about to leave by himself when inspiration struck. He went back to his office and buzzed Mona. She came in a second later.

"I thought you left for the day," she said.

"I was going to," he explained, "but then...listen Mona, I know this is your first week but would you mind going to a client's house with me? Some emergency has come up, and I have to see her there...and well, I thought you could take notes and..."

"I haven't used my shorthand in fifteen years."

"No problem. I won't need it word for word. Just the gist of it."

"Well, okay...I..."

"Great," Nick said as he grabbed her by the elbow and started leading her out the door.

"Wait!" she shouted.

"What?" he asked, exasperated.

"If I'm going to take notes, I might want a pad and pen."

He smiled and let go of her elbow. "Oh sure," he said as he nervously glanced at his watch.

***

The Taylor residence was about ten miles north of town out in the country. He double-checked the address on the mailbox before pulling into the long drive. The drive led to an ostentatiously large and sprawling English Tudor house. *No,* thought Nick, as he pulled up next to the familiar white Lexus and gazed around. *This ain't a house, it's a mansion.* A man was methodically traversing the acres of perfectly green grass on a John Deere mower that looked large enough to plow a farmer's field. Nick looked hard but was unable to determine which parts of the lawn were mowed and which parts were unmowed. Obsessively manicured hedges and shrubs, along with regimented rows of flowers completed a landscaping design that fit, to a tee, what Nick knew of Dr. Daniel Taylor's personality.

He grabbed his briefcase off the back seat and walked up to the front door. Mona was standing beside him with her pen and notebook in hand. He rang the bell and turned around for a moment. Nick and the mower of the lawn that did not need mowing eyed each other suspiciously as the man continued to drive the John Deere in broad circles.

"Nick?" he heard. He turned. Livie was holding the door open. She was wearing very short shorts and a tiny bikini top. Her face was streaked as if she had been crying. The two women, Livie and Mona, stared at each other in silence for a few moments. Nick glanced at Mona and saw her jaw drop an inch. He had not forewarned her.

Nick broke the silence. "Oh...oh...Livie, this is Mona. She just started this week. It sounded important. I thought Mona could take notes."

"Yes, come in," Livie finally said. They stepped in and both Nick and Mona involuntarily stopped for a second to take in the view. The entrance opened up into a huge great room. A massive stone fireplace from floor to ceiling dominated one wall. A baby grand piano complimented an eclectic assortment of furnishings and sculptures and artwork. The back wall was all glass and looked out over a huge deck with a swimming pool and hot tub. Nick doubted that he had ever been inside a private residence this opulent in his life. He half expected Robin Leach to emerge and give a guided tour. One glance at Mona, star-struck, confirmed that she was as overwhelmed as he. They took seats on a couch that was separated from a matching loveseat by a slate coffee table.

"Your house is...beautiful," Nick stammered.

"Yes, it certainly is," Mona added.

Livie sat on the loveseat opposite Nick. He could sense the outrage being directed his way for bringing along a bodyguard. "Okay," Nick began, "what's this about not letting Jessica go on visitation? You know that can only harm our case."

"Nick, I need about fifteen minutes to fill you in on what's happened since we last talked. I assume," she added while nodding towards Mona, "that it's all right to talk openly...very openly...in front of her."

Mona glanced at Nick. Confusion, maybe even fear, was in Mona's eyes. "Um, should I wait outside?" she asked.

Nick presumed that the "very open" discussion Livie intended to have included references to their extracurricular activities. He sure as hell didn't want Mona knowing anything about that. *God damn her,* he thought. *I brought Mona to act as a chaperone and she's already figured out how to get rid of her.* He smiled at Mona, "Oh well, Mona, maybe if you could just wait outside for a little while."

Mona looked relieved to be able to put as much distance as she could between herself and Livie Taylor.

"Come, dear," Livie said as she rose, "wait out by the pool. It's lovely out there." Mona obediently followed Live outside. Livie returned and sat back down.

"What's going on? Livie asked. "Why didn't you return my calls?"

"Um. I did..."

"Yeah, Monday. I called all weekend. Where were you last weekend?"

"My partner's dad died. I had to go out of town for the services. I forgot my cell phone at home. I got back late Sunday. I called you first thing Monday."

"Who?"

"Who what?"

"What partner?"

"What difference does..."

"Was it Ms. Thomas?"

"Yeah, it was. So what."

"Nick...you must sit there and look me straight in the eye and swear to God you're telling me the truth. There's nothing going on between you two is there? I cannot tolerate infidelity. I will not tolerate it."

"She's my partner. For God's sake, is that why you called me here? To threaten me? To give me the third degree? Jesus Christ, things are happening in your case. They've filed a motion to change custody. We need to talk business. Why haven't you called me back since Monday?" he asked, turning the tables.

She grabbed some tissue and dabbed at the tears forming in her eyes. "I am so scared. That bastard's not getting her again, ever. I'll do whatever I have to do to see to it."

"What? What the hell is going on?"

"Sunday night after he brought her home...she's been acting strange...I should have known. Jessica was playing in the family room. I went out there to check on her. She was playing with the dog...Sam...he's a Golden Retriever...and well..." she paused and started crying harder. After several moments she regained her composure and proceeded "Nick...I don't know how to say this... but...she...she was playing with his penis. As if she was trying to... you know...masturbate him."

Nick's eyes opened in amazement but so many questions and issues were swirling in his head that he didn't know where to begin. Livie started crying again but continued through her tears. "Oh, God, I tried to act like it was no big deal, you know, so I just said 'Honey, that's not nice. Sammy doesn't like that' And then...then she says...oh Jesus...she says...'Daddy does' and I said, 'Oh honey, Daddy doesn't play with Sam's pee-pee'. And then she says 'No Mommy. Daddy likes it when I touch his pee-pee.' And of course, I said something like, 'don't be silly, you don't touch Daddy's pee-pee.' And then, oh God, she started telling me that Daniel...that bastard..."

Nick knew exactly what was going on. He had told her she was going to lose custody so she decided to come up with something to guarantee she'd win. He had no doubt that she had brainwashed Jessica into believing that her own father had sexually abused her. He could not even imagine the psychological scars something like that could cause. But he knew better than to accuse her of making it up.

"Livie, wait, please. I have a daughter. I can just imagine how you must have felt, but you have to understand that in court you need real proof. And the timing, it's so suspicious. Kids are exposed to so much nowadays. Maybe she saw something on TV, maybe...."

"My God, she watches Sponge Bob, Sesame Street, for Christ's sake. I've never seen Cookie Monster get a hand job, have you?"

"I'm just trying to point out," he answered, "that this is a very dangerous area. You have to be sure. Maybe she got up during the night and saw something on TV...or maybe...you know... earlier...she might have seen you and your husband..."

"Please let me finish and you'll understand why I'm absolutely certain."

"Okay. It's just I can't even imagine a father doing that to his daughter."

"At first," she replied, "I was skeptical too. All the things that were just going through your mind were going through mine. I'm thinking, they're going to say I put her up to it...that she's only three, she could have seen something or heard something somewhere. I knew we'd need proof, real proof, that they wouldn't just take the word of a three-year-old and a wife involved in a bitter custody fight. So I talked to Jessica as calmly as I could. I told her that wasn't nice. That she didn't do that with Sammy or Daddy or anyone and that we shouldn't talk about it with anyone until Mommy said it was okay to. So I found an expert, a psychologist, in Belleville who specializes in this stuff..."

"Who is he?" Nick interjected. "Maybe I know of him."

"He's a she. Miranda Cox."

She noted Nick's involuntary grimace.

"What? What's wrong?"

"It's just...I've had some less than favorable experiences with Dr. Cox. I'm not sure she's really impartial when it comes to these issues. Let me think about it. We can probably find someone better."

"It's too late for that."

"What do you mean?"

"I mean that's why you haven't heard from me 'til now. I wanted to wait 'til I could get Jessica to see Dr. Cox. We were in today. She's confirmed everything...everything. She has the evidence I need. She taped her interview with Jessica. She's prepared to do whatever's necessary to make sure that sick bastard never lays a hand on my baby again.

So that's why I haven't returned your call. That's why I can't let her go. I couldn't see you until I was prepared. Until I was ready. Until I had the evidence. I didn't want you to think I was some hysterical woman or even worse that I was coaching Jessica or made it up just to get at Daniel. Do you understand now, Nick?" As she finished speaking, tears continued to run down her cheeks. She reached across the coffee table and grabbed Nick's hand in hers. "Do you?" she asked plaintively.

He retrieved his hand and glanced outside to see if Mona was watching. She had struck up a conversation with the lawn-mower man who apparently had finished the lawn and was now skimming a pool that did not appear to need skimming.

"Yes, I understand. But you need to understand something, too. The timing of this is going to look very, very suspicious. I mean...she's three and a half...and suddenly, the weekend they get ahold of your psychiatric records, he starts abusing her? Can you see how your credibility will be attacked?"

"But..."

"Let me finish. If you make this allegation and the judge doesn't believe you, if she thinks you subjected your daughter to this kind of trauma to win custody or to get at Daniel, well, then you'll be lucky if you ever see Jessica again. Do you understand the stakes involved here?"

"I do. But, I have to protect my daughter. Whatever it takes. Please. Let's go tomorrow to Dr. Cox. She can see us at three. She canceled what she had scheduled and made the appointment for us. She'll show you the tape she made. She's absolutely convinced. A three-year-old couldn't know the things she knows. Please."

Nick didn't know where to start. Livie, tears streaming down her face, sounded so convincing. Was it possible she was actually being truthful? If it was true, he'd do anything, everything he could to keep that perverted bastard away from that little girl. But how could he possibly believe Livie? And Dr. Cox wasn't a whole lot higher on his credibility scale. He glanced at the coffee table. A picture of Jessica smiled back at him. She reminded him of Natalie when she was three. He thought about how he would feel if someone had abused Natalie. He would have torn them apart with his bare hands. Literally. He looked back up at Livie. "Okay," he said, "we'll see Dr. Cox."

CHAPTER 28

He pulled up the long drive and parked. Although prepared for it this time, he was again taken aback both by the sheer size and ostentatiousness of the house and by the prissy fastidiousness of the landscaping. He glanced around and did not see the mower-pool man.

He was apprehensive about meeting Livie here alone and even more apprehensive about a round trip to Belleville with her alone in a car. But he was less apprehensive than he would have been about Livie coming to the office and then the two of them taking off in a car together. Surely, word of that would get back to Rosa. And he didn't need that right now.

He had been up half the night debating what to do. He knew he was skating where the ice was getting thinner and thinner but thought, if things worked out as he hoped, he could make it back to shore without falling through. While he personally had a big problem with Dr. Cox, he knew, nevertheless, that she was a well-qualified expert who came across proficiently in court. He had been on the losing side in trials against her enough times to have learned that lesson. Judges, men and women, apparently just trusted a woman's opinion more, even from a woman who was not a mother herself, when it came to kids. A sexism so deeply ingrained that they didn't even realize they were guilty of it.

If Dr. Cox was as persuasive as he knew she could be, Taylor might sue for peace. He might do anything to avoid a public airing of the charges, maybe even voluntarily relinquish all rights to visitation.

While Nick remained skeptical of the charges, he was hopeful that Dr. Cox could convince him. *Shit,* he thought disgustedly to himself, *am I really sitting here hoping that Taylor did abuse that little girl just so I can get this case over?*

After his visit to Livie yesterday, he had returned to the office and, although dreading it, called Cat Jagger. For once in his life, he was relieved to get voice mail and left a brief and intentionally garbled message saying that Jessica would not be available for Dr. Taylor's Wednesday night visitation. Each of the three times Cat had called him this morning, he had told Mona to tell her he was out of the office until tomorrow.

He walked up to the door and rang the bell not knowing which of the numerous Livie Taylors he had come to know would answer. The haughty aristocrat? The coquette? The man-eater? The retributive bitch? A moment later the door opened. Her overpowering beauty still had the ability to stun him. She was wearing a long multi-colored silk or chiffon skirt. Parrots, of various species and color, perched on tropical plants adorned it. A white, semi-sheer, sleeveless blouse, white heels, and despite the warm weather, a white knit shawl completed the simple, yet stunning outfit.

"Nicky," she said as she stepped forward and hugged him. She stretched upward and kissed him on the lips. "Oh God... thank you...thank you for believing and trusting in me. I knew I could count on you to keep that bastard from hurting our baby."

"Umm," Nick replied, pretending he did not hear "our baby," while glancing nervously at his watch, "we'd better go. Why don't you drive so I can review the file?"

She looked disappointed but said, "Okay."

Livie talked non-stop the entire hour drive to Dr. Cox's office. Nick added an occasional "uh-huh" or "yeah" but tried to act as if he was focused on her file. The truth was there was nothing in his file to review or to prepare for their meeting with Dr. Cox. He had been over and over Livie's file until he had it virtually memorized.

Dr. Cox's office was located in a modern low-rise office building on the west end of Belleville. Her office was flanked by lawyers on one side with a sign of the scales of justice and an orthodontist with a sign in the shape of a giant tooth on the other side. Dr. Cox's waiting room was dark and somber. Dark paneling, dim lighting and oversized dark brown leather furniture gave Nick the impression he was entering a cave. It took his eyes several seconds to adjust from the bright outdoor sunlight. In one corner was a collection of Legos, busy beads, and assorted toys and kiddie books, their bright colors clashing incongruously with the somber mood of the room.

No one else was present in the waiting room. Nick pushed the buzzer by the receptionist's sliding window and they sat down. Livie stopped talking and sat down too. She crossed her legs and was nervously tapping her foot as it dangled in the air. She put her hand on Nick's leg and squeezed and he quickly removed it.

"Please," he cautioned, "remember where you're at."

She smiled at him, "Sorry."

A moment later, the door to the waiting room opened and Dr. Miranda Cox stepped out. She was, or at least could have been, an attractive woman. She was, Nick guessed, about five feet seven. Early forties. Not thin, but certainly not overweight either. She wore an unflattering dark brown pantsuit over a tan blouse and flat brown loafers. No jewelry and, as far as Nick could tell, not a stitch of makeup. Her brown hair was pulled back into a severe bun that was pulled so tight it seemed to be stretching her face. Despite what appeared to be her best efforts to do so, she could hide neither her natural facial beauty nor her well-proportioned figure. She looked exactly the same as she had each time Nick had previously seen her. He could almost picture her closet...an unending sea of brown pantsuits, tan blouses and brown loafers. *How come,* he wondered, *every shrink I've ever met seemed to have more issues by themselves than their entire clientele put together?*

Nick rose and extended his hand, "Dr. Cox. Nice seeing you outside a courtroom for once."

She took his hand for an instant before letting go. "Yes, well, glad to see you representing someone who deserves the benefit of your skill Mr. Barnett."

Nick ignored the jab and followed Dr. Cox and Livie back to her office. Nick and Livie sat down next to each other across the desk from Dr. Cox. She slid a large envelope across the desk to Nick.

"In this envelope," she began, "are some things I think you will need. First, is my curriculum vitae. You will note that I am a graduate..."

"I'm familiar with your qualifications, Doctor," Nick interrupted.

"Fine," she said. "The c.v. is attached to an affidavit signed by me, under oath, and notarized. I believe you will find it to be extraordinarily detailed and comprehensive. I believe it came to eleven typed pages. It details the history I received from the patient and her mother, the testing I employed, my interview and examination of the child and my opinion, stated to a reasonable degree of scientific certainty, that Jessica was and has been sexually abused. I have also stated my opinion that the perpetrator of that abuse is Dr. Daniel Taylor."

Livie burst into tears and bent over, head in her lap, as Dr. Cox continued "...I have also included a DVD of my complete interview and testing of Jessica which commenced at..." she glanced at some notes..."ten thirty-seven a.m. yesterday and continued until eleven forty-five a.m., one hour and eight minutes. Mr. Barnett, there is not one shred of doubt in my mind that this little girl has been abused, horribly, by her own father. I will stake my reputation on it."

Livie sat back up and was drying her tears with a tissue. Nick glanced at Livie before returning his gaze to Dr. Cox. *I wish,* he thought silently, *you'd be willing to stake something a whole lot more valuable than that.* "Dr. Cox," Nick began, "please do not take offense but I have to play devil's advocate. It will be devastating to our case, it will cause irreparable harm if we make allegations of this nature and are unable to prove them..."

"There simply is no doubt," Dr. Cox interrupted. "I've got eighteen years' experience, I..."

"Dr. Cox," Nick said sternly, "I told you; do not take offense. But if you cannot stand up to my questioning, I can assure you, you will stand no chance whatsoever against Catherine Jagger..."

"I'm familiar with Ms. Jagger," she snipped, "and I have no doubt about my ability to 'stand up' to her, as you put it."

"Dr. Cox," Nick began with an obvious edge to his voice, "perhaps..."

"Stop it! Both of you!" Livie screamed. "We're all on the same side. Please...it's about Jessica."

"I apologize," Nick said contritely.

"Fine. Accepted." Dr. Cox replied. Nick waited a moment for mutuality which was not to be forthcoming, then continued, "Why don't you play the DVD and narrate just as you would if you were testifying in court. Then, I would like to question you as if you were under cross-examination. Is that acceptable, Doctor?"

"Perfectly," she replied as she removed the DVD from the envelope and maneuvered a TV set on a portable stand so they could all see it. She inserted the disc and pushed play as she sat back down. She glanced at Livie. "Be forewarned, Mrs. Taylor, this tape will be extremely disturbing for you to watch." And Livie started crying again.

***

Livie and Nick rode silently for the first ten minutes of the trip back to Selma. She had declined his request for her to drive again saying she was incapable of driving in the emotional state she was in. Reluctantly he took the keys from her. Nick had to admit to himself that Dr. Cox had done well. And watching the DVD, with the "anatomically correct" dolls was sickening. Dr. Cox had not appeared to be coaching Jessica in any way that Nick could ascertain.

Nick had lit into Dr. Cox with his questioning cross-examination and had failed to score many points. Of course, he was well aware that he had no opportunity to prepare nor did he have any information to impeach her with. But still, the whole thing, Cox, the DVD, it seemed persuasive. He tried to convince himself that, for once, Livie Taylor was actually telling the truth. He couldn't imagine a judge seeing and listening to what he had just seen and heard and not being concerned. But he was experienced enough to know that there were no sure things, nothing even close, when it came to court. He would have to be extremely cautious in his assessment to Livie.

He glanced her way just as she undid her seatbelt and slid closer to him. "I love you," she said. "Thank you. Thank you so much for believing us and for protecting us from that bastard."

"Livie...please...we have some good evidence...but these things are tough...very tough...they'll have experts too. Experts that will dispute everything Dr. Cox says..."

"They won't be able to dispute what Jessica says," she replied as she leaned her head against his shoulder.

"Jessica will not even be allowed to testify. She's too young," he explained.

"I mean on the DVD. The judge will see that, won't she?" she asked.

"Yeah. Sure. I believe so, but..." he abruptly stopped talking as he felt her hand migrate to his crotch. She began unzipping him.

"Livie, NO! For God's sake. We've talked about this. We can't."

She ignored him and reached inside his trousers. He let go of the steering wheel with one hand and reached down to try and stop her. "You're taking care of us. I just want to take care of you. I love you," she said as she lowered her head to his crotch.

He reached down and forcibly pulled her head up. He glanced back up at the road to see that he had swerved halfway across the centerline. He saw the approaching truck just in time. He let go of her head, grabbed the wheel with both hands and jerked the Lexus back into its lane. He watched as the truck driver extended his middle finger to Nick and laid on his horn. Livie, apparently oblivious to their near accident, had her head back down and had taken him into her mouth.

"Please. Please don't. Stop."

"I won't Nicky," she mumbled, "I won't stop."

CHAPTER 29

"Line two, Nick," Mona said.

He stared at the light blinking on line two for a good ten seconds before pushing the button. He was dreading this phone call as much, if not more than any in his life. They had seen Dr. Cox on Thursday. She already had her eleven-page affidavit typed, signed and notarized. After dropping Livie off he had gone home, showered, drunk a glass of wine, called Rosa to see how she and her mother were doing, then went back to the office. By one-thirty in the morning, he had the Motion to Suspend Visitation handwritten along with a short brief on the issue of termination of visitation. He was back at the office on Friday by seven and handed the paperwork to Mona at eight.

"Priority one," he had instructed. "Work on nothing else until this is done, then we e-file immediately."

"Sure," she had replied.

Mona was done by ten-fifteen. In the interim, Cat Jagger had called three times. Nick happened to be "in conference" each time she called. At ten an e-mail from Cat arrived. She did not attempt to conceal her anger:

"Mr. Barnett: Your client and the child were not present Wednesday night when Dr. Taylor arrived for visitation. You have refused to take my phone calls. We either have communication from someone and make up visitation or a Petition for

Order to Show Cause why your client should not be held in contempt is in tonight's mail. Catherine Jagger."

He had reviewed the paperwork Mona had typed, made some corrections, had her print out corrected copies and made two sets of copies. By eleven it had been e-filed. He left for an early lunch not wanting to be in the office when Cat Jagger first saw it. He was back at his desk at one. At 1:05 Cat Jagger called for the tenth time since Mona had e-mailed her a copy. He punched line two, "Hello," he said.

For a moment there was silence on the other end. Finally, Cat spoke. "I wouldn't have expected this from you. Lester Lange, sure. Pete Jeffries, maybe. But not you."

"Look, I know how it looks…"

"Yeah," she interrupted, "it looks like the sleaziest, most disgusting bullshit it's been my misfortune to deal with in twelve years of practice. I've never…"

"I'm Fed-Exing a copy of the DVD Cox made to you," he said, returning the favor by interrupting her. "You look at it. Look at it good, and tell me you wouldn't have done the same. He's molesting her, and it's been going on for quite a while."

"Yeah, right," she replied, "and it just so happens it surfaces right after we get the psych records and file a motion seeking full custody."

"What about Dr. Cox? Didn't you read her affidavit?"

"Don't pull that bullshit with me. I've played this game too long. I know Cox as well as you. I guess I'm not surprised you steered her to Cox…"

"I didn't…" Nick began, then abruptly stopped. He was going to explain that Livie had picked Dr. Cox out by herself but realized that attempting to defend his actions was pointless. Cat Jagger was convinced that Livie Taylor had filed false charges of sexual abuse against her client and that Nick was complicit in bringing those charges. *Maybe she doesn't believe,* he thought, *that I know they're false but she obviously believes I have serious doubts both as to my client's veracity and Dr. Cox's partiality. She thinks I'm just another sleazeball divorce attorney, a Lester Lange or a Pete Jeffries, willing to do anything or say anything to gain an advantage in a case. Well, she's going to think what she wants to think,* he thought, *and there's not a damn thing I can do about it.*

"Look, there's no point in us debating this. We have substantial, credible scientific evidence that Dr. Taylor has abused Jessica. It'll be up to Judge Swanson or the State's Attorney to sort out the truth."

Cat exploded, "The State's Attorney? Are you fucking threatening criminal charges? Because, if you are, you might be interested to know that it's a violation of the Code of Professional Responsibility to threaten criminal charges to gain an advantage in a civil case."

Nick exploded right back, "I'm not threatening shit, Cat. Look, I believe my client. I believe the fucking DVD. I've seen it. You haven't. Don't make this personal."

"Don't make it personal? Are you kidding? I'm afraid it's a little late for that," she responded.

"Fine," he countered, "make it personal. Make it as God damn personal as you want. In the meantime, if we can talk business, I've checked and Judge Swanson is available by phone at three today. Are you?"

"I'll be here," she said as he heard the receiver being slammed down.

Nick hung up slowly. His braggadocio with Cat Jagger had been intended as much to convince himself as her as to the truth of the charges. *Is it possible,* he wondered, *that Jessica was coached? That Livie put all of it into her little head and I'm engaged in an unwitting conspiracy with a pathologically sick woman bent on destroying an innocent man?* Nick could not think of any allegation that could conceivably be more destructive personally or professionally. He tried to think how he would have felt if Sheila had accused him of abusing Natalie during their divorce. He tried to think of what that would have been like but it was not possible. It was too foreign a concept to even contemplate. It was like trying to imagine what life would be like if he woke up tomorrow as a cocker spaniel. As he wondered where all this was headed, he just kept picturing Jessica in his office hiding behind her mother's dress. Beautiful. The picture of innocence. He saw her face in his mind. "I had to do this. I had to do this," he repeated over and over, trying to convince himself of the truth of that declaration.

***

Promptly at three Nick placed the conference call. First to Cat Jagger then to Judge Swanson.

"Judge," he said, "I already have Catherine Jagger on the line."

"Hello, Judge," Cat added.

"Well, counsel," the judge began, "we have a situation here, don't we?"

"Judge, I..." both Cat and Nick jumped in simultaneously trying to get the first words in.

"Just a minute," the judge said cutting them off with an icy coldness in her voice. "I intend to state a few things. When I want comment from counsel I will ask for it. We now have had filed, on both sides, motions supported by sworn affidavits making extraordinarily serious allegations. First, I will advise both counsel, that, sua sponte, I have ordered this file sealed. I have a young child to protect and I don't want to be reading about this on the front page of the Butler Times Commoner. Second, God help anyone, anyone involved in this case, party, counsel or expert if I find that any...any...of these allegations were made without good cause or not supported by substantial, credible evidence. If your clients are just using this little girl as a pawn in their own sick games there will be the most severe consequences. Each of you is directed to advise your clients of how seriously I am taking this and of the potential consequences if they persist in the actions they are pursuing if I find they are without good cause.

Third, I just got off the phone with Dr. James. You will recall that we all agreed upon Dr. James as the Court's expert witness. I have briefly explained to him the parameters of this case. As a personal favor to me, he has set aside next Thursday...canceled a conference he was to attend in St. Louis...to interview both parties and Jessica. Mr. Barnett?"

"Yes, Judge?"

"You are to overnight today to Dr. James copies of your recent pleadings and the video made by Dr. Cox."

"Yes, Judge."

"Ms. Jagger?"

"Yes?"

"You are to overnight today to Dr. James the medical records of Mrs. Taylor that you subpoenaed, your motion and your expert's affidavit. What's his name?"

"Dr. Bowman."

"Yes, Dr. Bowman."

"Okay."

"Mrs. Taylor will be at Dr. James' office Thursday at nine with Jessica. Dr. Taylor will report at one. I do not care what they have scheduled. They show up or they are defaulted. Mrs. Taylor is ordered not to discuss any of these allegations with Jessica. Dr. James will ask Jessica first thing if Mrs. Taylor has abided by this order. If I find she has not, it will not be a pretty picture. Dr. Taylor will have visitation..."

"But, Judge," Nick interrupted.

"Counsel, I'm not done," she snapped. "Dr. Taylor will have visitation Saturday and Sunday ten a.m. to two p.m. at the offices of DCFS here in Butler. Mrs. Taylor shall deliver and pick up Jessica. Someone from DCFS will be present at all times."

"Judge," Cat protested, "it's entirely inappropriate to restrict Dr. Taylor's visitation. These baseless charges…"

"COUNSEL!" Judge Swanson screamed loud enough to force Nick to move the receiver away from his ear. "I don't know," she continued in a normal tone of voice, "if these parties are playing games, but I am not. This situation will be resolved. Promptly. And in the interim, in case no one else is even thinking about her, I will protect Jessica."

"Mr. Barnett?"

"Yes?"

"Did you take notes sufficient to have your secretary type an order?"

Nick quickly glanced at his chicken scratches. "I think so. That was Saturday and Sunday ten to two at the DCFS offices in Butler?"

"Correct. Okay, get it typed, e-mail it to me and I will enter it and e-mail copies to both counsel. Dr. James has promised to have me a preliminary report within one week of his evaluations. That will be a week from next Thursday…let's see that would be the 24th. We will have another conference call on Friday the 25th at eight-thirty."

"Any questions?"

"No," they both responded.

"Fine," she replied, "talk to you both two weeks from today."

***

Nick took a long swig on his cold beer as he listened to his hamburger sizzle in his George Foreman. He looked at the bag of frozen fries sitting on the counter and realized he wasn't up to the effort it would take to cook them. He stuck the fries back in the freezer and grabbed a bag of chips instead.

He had just taken the first bite of his hamburger when the doorbell rang. He glanced at his watch. Seven thirty-five. *Shit,* he thought, *who could that be now?*

He yelled, "coming," as he strutted to the front door. He threw the door open while still having half a mouthful of un-chewed hamburger, pickle remnants and a few pieces of chips. He was clutching a half-full bottle of beer. He opened the door.

"Ro...sha," he mumbled.

She smiled, "May I come in?"

Nick chewed like a madman and took another swig of beer in order to wash it all down in one gulp. His haste and the abun-dance of food and liquid combined to make him belch loudly.

"Sorry," he said sheepishly, "yeah, come in. Sit down. Beer?"

"Sure. Just one."

He retreated to the kitchen, got her a cold beer and handed it to her. "When did you get back?"

"Just today."

"How's your mom?"

"Okay, I guess. No...no, that's not true. She's not okay. But she won't be either as long as I stay there. I had to get out of there so she could get on with things."

"Yeah, I understand."

"I'll be back at the office Monday. How's everything?"

"Oh, okay I guess," Nick lied, not wanting Rosa to have anything else to worry about.

"Listen," Rosa began, "about what happened...between us... in Carbondale...I'm sorry I put you in that position...."

"No, please..."

"No, let me finish. I know that it wasn't a good idea, that we were going to wait until you resolved some things. I just was feel-ing very alone and very scared and...well I hope you understand."

"Sure, of course. I already told you. Don't you think I want-ed to, too?"

"Really?"

"Sure. Of course."

She smiled back at him and took a drink from her beer. "So I suppose the truth is the office is a nightmare."

"A fucking nightmare," Nick conceded.

"You know," she continued, "this last week when I had time to think I really wondered whether I'd come back at all..."

"But what would you do then?" Nick asked, astounded by her confession.

"I don't know. I'm a single girl. Been making a decent living. I have some money saved. I'll be getting some from my dad's estate too. A lot more than I imagined. Maybe he never did publish any of his novels, but he sure did okay in the stock market. My mom didn't even realize how much he made. Thought maybe I'd just travel for a year or something. Who knows?"

"What convinced you to come back?" he asked.

"I'm not convinced," she answered. "I'll be in the office Monday, Tuesday for sure. Who knows after that?"

"Rosa," he asked, "are you serious? You're thinking of just... just taking off?"

"I don't know what I'm going to do. Sometimes I just think I need a break. Maybe it'll pass. Maybe by Monday, I'll be fine."

"I hope so. You can't just take off like that."

"Why not? What is there to keep me here? Look, let's talk about something else. How is your other situation...coming?"

"The Taylor divorce?"

"Yeah."

"Wait a minute," he said as he got up and headed towards the kitchen, "I think this will take another beer."

CHAPTER 30

It took Nick at least fifteen minutes to fill Rosa in on what had transpired within the last week. Livie's psychiatric records; the motion to change custody Cat Jagger had filed; the sexual abuse allegations; the conference with Miranda Cox; the videotape; the motions he had filed; Judge Swanson's order. He also casually mentioned that Pat had left "for personal reasons." He did not mention that he and Livie had driven to and from Dr. Cox's together, nor what had transpired during the car ride back. Rosa listened without comment until he finished. "So?" he asked when done.

"So, what?" she asked.

"What do you think?"

She paused a moment then drained her beer and spoke, "I think that my initial impression of Livie Taylor was correct. I think she's a lying, manipulative bitch who would stop at nothing to get what she wants including subjecting her own daughter to this. That's what I think. I just hope like hell I'm wrong. Thanks for the beers," she added as she got up and left.

***

On Thursday afternoon, Livie called.

"Oh, Nicky," she gushed, "it went so well. I had that Dr. James wrapped around my little finger. Now, don't get jealous but

I wore that little yellow sundress...you know that one you like...the one that shows a little cleavage...and well he was probably sixty but I had him practically drooling. I had him eating out of my hand..."

"What did he say?" Nick asked, more interested in Dr. James' view of the case than his appreciation of Livie's physical attributes.

"He said he thought I was very forthcoming and he said Jessica was a beautiful little girl, like her mother. Remember, I told you, don't get jealous."

"I mean what did he say about the allegation? About Dr. Cox's opinions?"

"Well, he didn't just come out and say anything specifically, but, trust me, he's on our side. I told you, men have trouble saying 'no' to me. Oh God, hopefully, it won't be long before she never has to see that bastard again. Hopefully, it won't be long before we can all be together."

"Yeah," Nick replied, "hopefully."

***

The next week crept along. Painfully slow. Nick would be at his desk and find himself staring at his wall clock. The hands moved as if the whole clock was encased in molasses. Nick wanted nothing more in the whole world than to get a positive report from Dr. James verifying Dr. Cox's opinion. He thought that if that happened, Cat Jagger would back off in a big hurry and be willing to talk about any settlement they offered. And if he could get the Taylor divorce settled, he could get Livie Taylor out of his life once and for all. He knew that if it dragged on too much longer eventually, somehow, some way Rosa would find out about what had gone on between Livie and him. It simply was not possible to lead this kind of double life forever. And if that happened he would never ever forgive himself for hurting Rosa.

But an inconclusive, or even worse, a negative report from Dr. James would mean World War III. He knew there was no way Livie would ever agree to anything that didn't involve supervised visitation for Daniel at a minimum. In fact, she was demanding termination of his parental rights altogether.

On Thursday afternoon, Mona knocked on Nick's door and entered. "Nick," she said, "we just got an e-mail from Judge Swanson with a copy of a preliminary report from Dr. James. I thought you'd want it right away. I printed it out. Here."

"Yeah, Mona, I do. Thanks," he said, not at all convinced that he really did want to read it.

He took it from Mona and she left and closed his door. He took a deep breath and started reading. The first several paragraphs were full of psychological mumble jumble and a description of his interviews with Livie, Dr. Taylor and Jessica. They gave no indication which way Dr. James was leaning. Nick's heart was thumping in his chest and his hands were sweating. Finally, he could stand the tension no more. He flipped to the last page and read the last paragraph. With each word he read, his stomach churned into an ever-tightening knot.

"In conclusion, the undersigned examiner cannot substantiate any credible evidence of sexual abuse of Jessica by Dr. Taylor, nor by anyone. To the contrary, there are clear indicia that Jessica's statements have been made in an effort by her to do what she believes, or has been told, is expected of her. Moreover, the examiner has several substantial areas of criticism, as noted in the body of this report, with respect to the conduct of the examination and interview of Jessica by Dr. Cox. It violates all accepted standards for conducting such an interview with a child of that age.

It is the recommendation of the undersigned that the supervised nature of visitation be terminated immediately. It is further recommended that Jessica begin immediate psychological counseling to deal with the likely sequela of being the subject of allegations of this nature and further that Mrs. Taylor begin further psychiatric and psychological care to understand the motivations underlying her actions.

Sincerely,

Dr. Benjamin James, Ph.D."

For an instant, Nick thought he might throw up. He took a sip of water, regained his composure and flipped back to the front page and read the entire report. It was an unsparing indictment of Livie Taylor and of Dr. Cox's methodology and examination and confirmed his worst suspicions about both women.

"Oh, Christ," he muttered to himself, "where do we go from here?" He had no doubt that Cat Jagger was reading the same report at this very moment. Judge Swanson's e-mail had notified him that a conference call was set for eight-thirty a.m. Friday.

It's over, he thought to himself. He had Mona make a copy of the report. "I've gotta leave," he told her. "I need to meet with someone."

"Sure, Nick. See you in the morning," she replied.

"Right," he replied. His mind and his stomach competed during the drive to Livie's to see which could make him more miserable. Her white Lexus was parked in front as he drove up the long drive. He grabbed the large manila envelope off the seat, walked up to the door and rang the bell. Sweat was running in rivulets down his forehead and soaking the underarms of his dark blue dress shirt. A few moments later Livie opened the door. She was casually dressed in linen shorts and a sleeveless blouse, but her hair, nails and makeup were, as usual, immaculate. Jessica stood next to her, hiding behind her legs.

"Nicky!" she exclaimed. "What a wonderful surprise, come in..." It took a moment for the deadly somber look on his face to register with her. When it did she added, "What's wrong?"

"Umm...Livie," he began, "we need to talk." He glanced down at Jessica and added "Privately."

"Well, all right, okay," she said, "but ever since...you know... all of this has surfaced, she's been so clingy. I'll have to see if her sitter's available and run her over there. Is that okay?"

"Yeah, fine," he replied.

"Okay, let me call. Then I'll change. I can't go out looking like this," she said gesturing to herself. She led him to the couch. "Can I get you anything?"

"I'm fine," he lied.

"Okay, I'll call," she said.

Five minutes later she returned wearing a light summer dress and heeled sandals. Her makeup, though not needing it, had been retouched and she now wore a full complement of jewelry. "Okay," she said, "it'll take me about twenty minutes. Make yourself at home, honey." She smiled, leaned down and kissed him on the lips. He did not return the kiss. When he heard the ignition of her car start, he got up and walked to the bay window that overlooked the front yard. He pulled back the curtains and watched her Lexus negotiate the long driveway and pull out onto the road.

He decided to use the twenty minutes he had to reconnoiter. He went first to what quite obviously was the master bedroom. He opened the closet, a double walk-in closet that had at least twice the square footage of his entire bedroom. There were racks upon racks of clothes and shoes. Dresses, blouses, slacks, jackets, suits. Enough, Nick guessed, to easily outfit ten or twenty normal women. In one corner of the massive closet was a large heap of men's clothes. He glanced at it. Expensive designer suits, some cashmere sweaters, dress shirts, ties, heaped in a pile. Clothes, obviously, that Dr. Taylor had not had an opportunity to remove. He had little doubt that if he eventually got them they would all bear some indicia of Livie's wrath.

In the bedroom, there were dozens of pictures of Jessica and dozens more of Livie on dressers, bookcases and the walls. Not surprisingly, there was not a single picture of Daniel. There was also a huge oil painting of Livie on the wall above the headboard of the king-sized bed. She looked stunningly beautiful dressed in a long spaghetti strapped black evening gown and wearing long black gloves. A diamond necklace circled her neck and dipped into her decolletage. She had that incredibly seductive half-smile Nick had come to know...and to fear.

He walked to the dresser and began opening drawers. Drawer after drawer of elegant lingerie revealed themselves. He stuck his hand underneath the lingerie in each drawer wondering if perhaps she hid a journal or diary under the silk and lace. But there was nothing. Likewise, he looked through each drawer of the massive roll-top desk. One drawer served as a file cabinet. He quickly thumbed through the files. "Electric" "Credit Cards" "Medical"...each was labeled. Finally, he came to a thick manila file labeled "Divorce." His heart began beating faster as he noted its location between "Medical" and "Checking Account" and pulled it out. Would he find notes in there about her plan to falsely accuse Daniel? Would there be anything to document an overt conspiracy between Livie and Dr. Cox? He flipped rapidly through the pages trying to gain as much information in as little time as possible. He glanced at his watch. He figured he had five minutes left before she returned.

As he flipped through, he suddenly stopped when the name, "Dr. Miranda Cox," on the top of the stationery jumped out at him. But it was only a bill for her services. He was about to keep flipping through the file when he noted something odd about the bill. There was a billing for the day when he and Livie had both visited her. There was also a billing for the previous day, Wednesday, when Livie had initially taken Jessica to Dr. Cox and when Dr. Cox had done the video of Jessica.

But, curiously, there was also a billing for an evaluation done the prior day, Tuesday. The statement indicated that Dr. Cox had met with Livie and Jessica for two and a quarter hours on Tuesday. She had billed Livie one hundred sixty-five dollars an hour...three hundred seventy-one dollars and twenty-five cents for Tuesday. There were also numerous bills from Dr. Cox to Livie dated at least six months before Livie had even been in to see Nick.

"Shit," Nick muttered. Neither Livie nor Dr. Cox had mentioned anything about Livie having previously been Dr. Cox's patient. Nor had either said anything about meeting with Jessica for over two hours the day before the video was made. In fact, if Dr. Cox hadn't come out in her affidavit and said directly that she first met with Livie and Jessica on Wednesday she had certainly implied it. There had been absolutely no reference to a prior patient relationship or a prior visit with Jessica. Why hide it if it hadn't been sinister?

Nick added two and two together. Unfortunately, it added up to four. *They met on Tuesday,* he silently told himself. *They decided Dan Taylor was a pedophile. They worked on poor Jessica for two hours, probably made a dry run on the video but were unhappy with it, and they came back the next day and kept working on it until little Jessica finally performed to their satisfaction.* He briefly wondered if Livie had used her seductive powers on Dr. Cox too. There was little doubt in Nick's mind as to Dr. Cox's orientation and even less doubt about Livie's ability to use sex to get what she wanted, no matter the sex of her intended victim. "Jesus Christ," he said aloud, "what the hell kind of people am I dealing with?"

He heard the front door open followed by Livie's voice, "Nicky?"

"Shit," he whispered as he stuck Dr. Cox's bills back in the file and the file back in the drawer between "Medical" and "Checking Account." He closed the drawer quietly and rose and walked towards the bedroom door. As he approached the door Livie entered.

She smiled. "Well, when I told you to make yourself at home, you did, didn't you?"

"Umm," he stammered, "I was looking for a bathroom."

"Well, you passed two or three on your way here," she smiled. "Come on. Admit it. You wanted to see my bedroom." She giggled and grabbed him around the waist and pressed herself to him. "Oh God, I've missed you so much. I've got something important to tell you later." She laid down on the bed. "Make love to me," she said.

"We have to talk. Now. About some serious matters."

Offended at his rejection of her offer, she gave him an angry glare and stood up. "Well. Okay. All right. I'm sorry if I offended you." She walked back out to the living room and he followed. She took a seat on the couch across the coffee table from him.

"Livie," he began, "why didn't you tell me you saw Dr. Cox on Tuesday? And why didn't you mention that you were already her patient?"

She looked startled for a moment. He could see her calculating. *Do I deny it?...or act like it's no big deal.* She chose the latter.

"Oh, I didn't tell you?" she answered. "I guess it just slipped my mind...in all the trauma you know. Why?"

"Why didn't Dr. Cox tell me?" he pressed on.

"I don't know. Ask Miranda."

"Miranda?" Nick asked wondering if there was some truth to his suspicions about the two of them.

"Yes, Miranda. Dr. Cox. What's this all about? What's the big deal?"

"The big deal? The big deal is I filed an affidavit in court... *Miranda's* affidavit...which, if it wasn't perjury, was certainly less than complete and honest. She never mentioned anything about you being her patient or about meeting with you and Jessica on Tuesday. Meeting for over two hours..."

"It wasn't that long..." she protested.

"Two and a quarter hours to be precise." Nick was almost shouting now. "What happened on Tuesday, Livie? Jessica didn't perform well enough? Didn't say the right things? Didn't cry on cue? You had to bring her back Wednesday for take two? Did you make *Miranda* an offer she couldn't refuse?"

Livie sat back against the cushion of the couch as if she had been physically struck. He could literally see the breath whoosh out of her. "I don't think I like your attitude," she replied when she overcame her shock. "What's wrong with you? What the hell are you suggesting?"

"Well, here's something else you won't like," he said as he grabbed the envelope and removed Dr. James' report. He angrily tossed it over the coffee table at her.

"That is Dr. James' initial report. I'll leave that copy for you. But let me put it in a nutshell for you. He doesn't believe you or *Miranda*. Not a word. He believes Jessica was coached to say those things about Daniel..." Before he could finish, Livie sprang up from the couch. She began shrieking and gesturing as if a swarm of bees had suddenly materialized within her dress. Most of what she was saying was unintelligible but he could clearly discern an occasional "bastard" and "liars" and "They got to him." She suddenly reached down and picked a ceramic elephant off the coffee table and hurled it against the massive stone fireplace. The elephant shattered into a thousand pieces. Though Nick lacked prior experience with the dangers of ceramic elephant shrapnel, instinctively he put his arm over his eyes.

She collapsed onto the couch and heaved and sobbed without another word for five minutes. Nick watched her silently. Two weeks ago, he could have been overcome with empathy for her. He would have comforted her. She would have responded to his comforts. It would have led to...well, he didn't want to think about where it would have led. Today watching her heave and sob uncontrollably he felt only one emotion: contempt. Eventually, her sobbing diminished and she sat upright. There was a look on her face, not of shame or guilt, but of righteous indignation.

"Well," she began slowly, calmly, "I think we have a real problem on our hands, don't we?"

"Yes, I agree," he answered. "Dr. James' report is going to be devastating to your case."

"I'm not referring to that right now. I mean WE have a problem. You and me." She paused a minute, wiped the last of her tears, then continued. "You don't believe me, do you? You believe him. You think I put her up to it, don't you?"

"It really doesn't matter what I believe..."

"Oh, it does," she interrupted him. "You think I'm weak, frivolous, don't you? Spoiled little rich girl. Well, you'll see. I'm not weak, I'm not frivolous. I know what I have to do. Maybe I'm not perfect. Maybe I have some problems. But that is my baby girl. And whether you or Dr. James or the judge, believe it or not, I love her. More than anything in the world. And I will NOT let that bastard abuse my baby girl." She paused then stood up, "Look at me, Nick!"

Nick refused and glanced away. "LOOK AT ME!" she screamed.

Startled, Nick looked directly into her eyes. "IT IS NOT GOING TO HAPPEN. I already told you that. It simply is not going to happen, EVER. I did not get Jessica to say those things. I did not get Miranda to say those things. That bastard is molesting her and he's going to get the opportunity to do it again over my dead body..." she paused, then looked directly into Nick's eyes and added with chilling sincerity, "...and Jessica's."

It was Nick's turn to fall backward onto the cushions as if the wind had been knocked out of him. He was scared. Scared to death. There was the intense rage and fear of a cornered animal in her eyes. He had no doubt that what she just said was not hyperbole. She meant every word of it. And equally, there was no doubt in his mind that she was capable of turning her paranoid fantasies into reality. *Oh Christ,* he thought, *what's wrong with me? I couldn't have mishandled this thing any worse had I tried. I must have forgotten everything I've learned about psychosis over the past weeks. She isn't lying. She believes everything she said, even if she made it up She believes her husband is molesting her three-year-old daughter. She's made herself believe it. She believes Dr. James is a part of a huge vast conspiracy, a conspiracy that apparently now includes me, to take Jessica from her loving mother and deliver her to a child molester. She believes, if necessary, in killing Jessica, to save her. I leave here now and she's going to pick up Jessica from the babysitter, come back here and kill both herself and Jessica. And in her sick mind, she'll be thinking she's being a good mother. A little girl's life is in my hands,* he realized, *not to mention the life of a desperately sick woman.*

He breathed deeply and slowly and forced himself to regain his composure. He began slowly. "Livie, look...I'm sorry... so sorry...I...I just got overwhelmed by this report...I lost my head...I'm so sorry for not believing you, can you forgive me? You're probably right. James was probably paid off. I bet Martha bribed him. She tried to bribe me. Did I tell you that?" He noticed a change in her demeanor. As he continued talking, her eyes morphed from the fear and rage of a wild animal to excitement and anticipation.

"Do you think so?" she asked.

"I'd bet on it," he continued "But, Martha and Daniel... they're not professionals at this kind of thing. They probably screwed up. I'll bet my last dollar they left a paper trail showing the bribe to Dr. James. I can subpoena every check they've written. I'll subpoena Dr. James' books. I know how these things work. We'll find it. I promise we will."

"Oh my God, Nicky! Yes," she said as she walked around the coffee table over to him and sat next to him. She leaned her head against him and put her hand on his knee.

"And when we do," he added, "by God, you'll get sole custody..."

"Yes!"

"And Jessica will never have to see them again."

"Yes!"

"Or ever be abused again!"

"Yes!"

"And you can love her forever."

She reached up with her other hand and turned his face towards her.

"No."

"No?"

"No, Nicky, not me. Us. We can love her forever."

Nick looked directly into her eyes and smiled. "Oh, yeah, I'm sorry. I meant 'we,' 'us,'" he repeated as she began unbuttoning his shirt and kissing his chest.

"And as far as Miranda is concerned, I promise Nicky, nothing happened. It's just...I thought maybe if I flirted with her a little, maybe, you know, she might be more on our side. But I swear to you, honey, nothing happened." She smiled seductively and added, "You, of all people, know I'm not like that."

"I understand," he replied "I didn't mean anything. I just lost my head for a minute. I'm sorry. I apologize. Can you forgive me?"

"Of course I do. I know the stress you're under. It's okay." She whispered into his ear as she removed his shirt, "now let me tell you my news."

CHAPTER 31

The Acura's air conditioner was spewing out ice cold air at full blast. But still, he had to wipe the sweat from his forehead at regular intervals. Not heat sweat, but nervous sweat. Scared to death sweat. Curiously his sweat seemed to increase in intensity as the interior temperature of the Acura plunged. Every few minutes his body would tremor as if he was in the throes of alcoholic detox.

"Get a grip," he instructed his body. But his body was in no mood for lectures and continued its sweating and shaking unabated. He pulled into the driveway and exited. He bent over and took huge gulps of the humid summer evening air and slowly regained a small modicum of control.

He walked up the front steps. The big door was open leaving only the old green and gold screen door guarding the entrance. He knocked several times before hearing the familiar voice. "Coming." A second later he saw Rosa trotting towards the screen. She was wearing denim cutoff shorts and a maroon SIU tee-shirt. The rusty gauze of the old screen filtered and diffused his view of her and the living room inside.

She recognized him and pushed open the screen. "Nick," she said, "what are..." she stopped when she saw the look on his face. "My God," she continued, "you look like you've seen a ghost. What's wrong?"

Nick followed her into the living room and sat down on the

tall wingback chair. Rosa sat on a couch across from him.

"What's wrong?" she repeated.

"Rosa..." he stammered as he spoke, "I don't know where to begin. I don't know what to do. She'll do it. I swear to God, she'll do it. What am I supposed to do? I don't..."

"My God," Rosa interjected, "you're scaring me. What's going on? What are you talking about? You need to calm down. Do you need something to drink?"

"Uh...yeah...sure," he mumbled, "thanks." Rosa got up and returned a minute later with two tall tumblers full of lemonade and ice. "Here," she said as she handed him one of the glasses.

He took it and wordlessly drained the entire glass, then fidgeted, wiped more sweat from his brow and said, "Um...I have to...use the bathroom."

"Sure," Rosa said nodding towards the hall. He was in the bathroom a good ten minutes. She could hear the water running and splashing. He emerged looking as if he had just gone swimming, his hair wet and glossy and slicked back. He was still perspiring. He sat back down and began slowly.

Rosa listened intently but without surprise as he told her of the contents of Dr. James' report. Her interest and concern peaked as he told her of driving out to Livie's house with a copy of the report.

"You went to her house? Alone?" she asked accusingly.

"Yeah. I had to resolve this thing. I intended to tell her I was going to withdraw..."

"But you didn't?"

"No."

"I can imagine how she convinced you not to," she stated, without attempting to disguise the disdain in her voice.

"No...Rosa...please...it's not like that. Turns out Livie had been seeing Cox for months before she even came in to see me. And she met with Cox the day before the video was made. She never told me any of that. I bet they had this plan to accuse Taylor before we even filed the divorce. I think they worked on Jessica until they got her to say what they wanted. And then...I don't know...you know Cox is gay...and Livie admitted coming on to her...I don't know how far they went. But everything, everything's a lie with that woman. There's nothing she's not capable of doing to get her way. Then when I told her what Dr. James' report said she jumped up off the couch and was wailing and shrieking like one of those foreign women on the news. You know, you've seen the news clip when her whole family's just been blown up by terrorists or a bomb or something and she's shrieking and wailing and you can't understand a word she's saying. Livie was screaming about Dr. James being paid off and how they got to him and none of it made any sense. I've never seen anything like it."

"Yeah, well, so she's a histrionic too. So what?"

"When she calmed down she said I'd turned on her too but that Daniel was a pervert and he had been molesting Jessica and she hadn't made it up and then...Jesus..."

"What?"

"She said with this icy certainty...this calmness...she said... he'd get the opportunity to molest Jessica again over her dead body...and Jessica's."

"Oh, Christ. You think she's capable of it?"

"Rosa, I KNOW she's capable of it."

"Did you call the cops?"

"Why? What would I tell them? They'd laugh at me. And can I tell anyone anything? I'm her lawyer. What about attorney-client privilege? Jesus, what the hell do I do?"

"My God, you need to do something. She could be doing it right now."

"No. She won't. Not yet."

"How can you be sure?"

"Because...because when she said that and I saw the look in her eyes and I knew, absolutely knew, she was capable of it, I...I realized what I'd done. I pushed this sick woman over the edge.

It's not about Jessica, it's about her. Everything's about her. She's incapable of letting Daniel win. She'd rather have Jessica dead than with him. That's part of her sickness. So, I told her, I told her I was sorry and she was right, Dr. James was probably bribed. And I told her we...she and I...we'd uncover the conspiracy together and...and we'd make sure she got custody and that he'd never see Jessica again."

"Did it work?"

"Yeah. She calmed right down and said that was great and she thanked me..."

"So, Jessica's safe, for now?"

"Well, yeah, I think. Unless she realizes I was just pacifying her and it's all bullshit and she is going to lose Jessica."

Nick looked into Rosa's eyes. He could see her mind going a thousand miles an hour analyzing, synthesizing, calculating, proposing, modifying, rejecting, or accepting possible courses of action; coming up with solutions, while Nick's mind was frozen; no more capable of coming up with rational solutions to the situation than of solving the mystery of black holes. *It's now or never,* Nick thought as he watched Rosa thinking so hard it made his head hurt.

"There's more," he interjected.

"More what?"

"When she thanked me...she came over and...she told me she loved me and she kissed me and...I didn't know what to do."

"What did you do?" she asked.

"I...I played along. I told you I didn't know what else to do. If she hadn't believed me...truly, Jessica could be dead right now."

Rosa stopped analyzing and calculating. A pained expression came across her face. "How far did you play along?" she asked.

"Please, don't ask. I just...I just didn't know what else to do."

Rosa stared at him. His eyes answered the question he had refused to. "Excuse me," she said as she rose. "I think I have to go to the bathroom too," she added as she ran to the bathroom and slammed the door.

***

Nick sat silently on the old chair while Rosa was in the bathroom. He could hear the faint but unmistakable sound of retching coming from the bathroom. The hydration from the lemonade that Rosa had given him had caused him to start sweating profusely again. In a few minutes, Rosa emerged from the bathroom, her face ashen and gray.

"Rosa, please I'm so..." Nick began but she stopped him before he could proceed further.

"Nick," she began in an emotionless tone, "I'm going to speak to you as a lawyer, as your partner, and give you my professional advice on how you should proceed. Then, please, I think you should leave. Okay?"

Nick looked down to avoid eye contact with her. "All right. Go ahead. Then I'll leave, but I have to tell you one other thing before I go."

"Fine," she replied. Rosa spent five minutes outlining the precise steps she believed Nick should take. She spoke coolly and calmly and displayed no sign of the emotions swirling within her. When she finished she asked, "All right, did you understand all that? Do you need me to go over it again?"

"No," he answered, "I understand and I agree. You're right. I'll proceed exactly as you've just said."

"Fine," she replied. "Now I'd like to go to bed, so if you could please tell me the one other thing you have to tell me."

Nick looked down at the floor. "Okay," he began. But when he finished Rosa did not go to bed. She went back to the bathroom and he could hear her retching again as he let himself out and closed the door.

CHAPTER 32

The telephone conference the next morning with Judge Swanson and Cat Jagger was short. Nick gave one-word replies to the questions being hurled at him by both women. It took all his willpower not to scream into the phone, "Back off! She's fucking crazy! This has to be handled delicately. Push her too far and she'll kill Jessica. Then our God damn custody trial will be real short!" Judge Swanson advised that she had contacted the chief judge to send another judge to handle her regular call on the following Thursday and Friday. Next Thursday morning at nine they would begin a two-day temporary custody hearing. No delays. No continuances. In Judge Swanson's words, "I don't care if an attorney or a party or a witness breaks a leg on the way to court. This hearing will not be delayed. Understood?" Next week an order would be entered and Nick had no doubt what it would be. Dr. Taylor would get custody. If Livie got visitation at all it would be supervised. She would be ordered to undergo immediate psychiatric treatment if she ever wanted unsupervised visitation. And that, Rosa had explained to him was the perfect result. The result that would guarantee that Jessica would be protected. The trick would be to keep Livie convinced that she was going to win until the very end. Until the bailiff took Jessica from her mother's arms and handed her to Dr. Taylor.

By necessity, that would mean that Nick would intentionally be lying to his client, repeatedly, over the next several days. He would tell her he had uncovered evidence of bribery. That it would be devastating. That he would blow their case out of the water and that there was no doubt that she would get custody. Rosa had reminded Nick that attorney-client privilege did not bar an attorney from reporting a client's stated intent to commit a crime. Livie's threat to kill Jessica if she was going to lose custody was not protected by privilege. He could report it to the authorities. But as even Nick had realized, it was far too tenuous to allow the police to intervene at this point. How many people have said "over my (or his or her) dead body" in the passions of an ugly divorce? You had to be there. You had to see the look in her eyes, hear the icy coldness of her declaration, know her psychiatric history to truly know that she had been deadly serious and deadly capable of carrying it out.

Rosa had advised Nick that he should have an affidavit prepared, signed and notarized detailing what he knew and in particular Livie's threat that Dr. Taylor would get custody over her and Jessica's dead bodies. Right before the trial was to commence, he should advise Judge Swanson and Cat Jagger in chambers of what he knew and that Livie was deadly serious when she made the threat. Nick would make sure that Jessica was there, physically present in the courthouse, ostensibly to be interviewed by Judge Swanson, so that custody could immediately be turned over to Dr. Taylor.

Then Jessica would be safe. He didn't even want to think what would come thereafter. Livie would probably sue him, report him to the disciplinary committee, maybe even become physically threatening to him. But what choice did he have? Lives were at stake.

***

On Monday afternoon, Nick returned from court frazzled and worn out. He walked into his office and deposited his briefcase and suitcoat and glanced at his phone messages. Four from Livie Taylor. No doubt she wanted an update on how he was doing in cracking the conspiracy. He wanted to talk to Rosa again but knew that would not be possible. When they crossed paths in the office, she avoided all eye contact with him. He dialed Livie's number.

"Oh, honey," she answered, "thank God it's you."

"I was in court all day. What's up?" he responded.

"Have you got the evidence that Dr. James was bribed?" she asked.

"Well," Nick stammered, "we've made excellent progress. We'll have it by Thursday."

"Are you sure?" she asked.

"Yes, Livie. Very sure. Quite sure," he replied.

"That's not good enough," she responded.

Nick, terrified of what the consequences could be if she thought she might lose custody added, "Livie, it's there. Don't worry, please. Everything will be okay. I promise you. Are you okay?"

In reply, he heard nothing but tears for the next minute. Every ten seconds or so he would interject, "Can you tell me what's going on?"

Her sobbing finally ebbed to the point where she could speak. "Oh God, Nicky, it's worse than I thought."

"What is?"

"He is."

"Daniel?"

"Yes," she practically screamed. "Who else?"

"Livie," Nick urged, "calm down and just tell me what's happened."

"Calm down!" she screeched. "How can I calm down? You know what I just found?"

"No, what?"

"Do you remember Daniel saying his laptop was at the house?"

"Yeah, sure. Cat Jagger's pestered me about it for weeks. She keeps reminding me that if you find it, it's locked and everything in it is confidential."

"Well, he wasn't lying. It was in the closet in his study and it was on this high shelf, intentionally hidden in this box marked 'medical records' hidden behind these other boxes…"

"What was?"

"His laptop and an envelope with a bunch of computer CD's in it and some pictures."

"Yeah, so?"

She began crying again. Nick waited patiently for thirty seconds until she resumed speaking. "Child pornography. Oh God, some of them were younger than Jessica. It's so sick. I threw up. And the CD's are full of this child porn too. It's so awful. I can't describe it."

A thousand thoughts flashed through Nick's mind. *I have to act outraged. I have to continue to make her think I believe her; that she'll get custody.* But there was no doubt in his mind as to what was going on. She'd had Daniel's laptop hidden away all along. Now she figured it was time for a little insurance. Just to make absolutely sure she wouldn't lose. So she downloads some child porn onto Daniel's computer and prints some of it. *Jesus Christ,* he thought, *is there anything this woman was incapable of?*

"I thought the case was locked," Nick replied.

"What?"

"Cat Jagger said the briefcase the laptop was in was locked. How did you see this stuff?"

"The laptop and CD's were in the locked briefcase. The pictures were just in an envelope in the box. When I saw the pictures, I broke the lock on the briefcase."

"He left child porn lying around in an envelope in a box?"

"Yes. Why? What are these questions about?"

"Nothing, Livie. I'm just trying to figure this out. It seems awfully reckless. Were there pictures of Jessica?" he asked, already knowing what the answer would be.

"No!" she screamed indignantly then added as an afterthought, "...but...so what...it still proves he's a sick bastard."

"Oh...yeah sure...I just wondered. Well, this just about puts the last nail in the coffin, doesn't it?"

"Oh God, I'd hoped you'd say that. Does it? Does it really?"

"Of course. It proves he's a pedophile. Get it to me right now. I'll call the state's attorney. He'll go to prison."

There was silence for a moment. He could almost picture her thinking about the consequences of her meal ticket sitting in prison. Finally, she replied, "The state's attorney? Is that necessary?"

"It's a crime to possess child porn. He should go to prison."

"But...but..." she stammered, "wouldn't it be better if we just let his lawyer know we had it and that we'll use it in court if we have to? If he goes to jail, I won't get any child support or alimony."

"Oh...yeah," Nick said, playing along, "okay...yes...I see your point. Right. He's not much good to you in prison, is he? We just want him to be kept away from Jessica but we still want him to be able to work...yes...I see...okay. We'll do it like you said. Get it to me. All of it. Then I'll dump it on Cat Jagger in court and let her know what her client's facing unless he gives up all rights to Jessica."

"Oh, yes," she exclaimed. "Oh, Nicky, that's perfect! Perfect. I'll bring it right down. Love you!"

"Right," he replied.

"Oh...Nicky...one other thing?"

"What's that?"

"Well...what if...I mean, just suppose they say...you know they're capable of saying anything...what if they say something ridiculous like I planted that stuff on his computer?"

Nick smiled. *God damn,* he thought, *you are good. Want to make sure you cover all the bases, don't you?*

"Well," he replied, "that's just ridiculous. What judge is going to believe that you...a mother...planted child pornography on your husband's computer? Come on...how would you even find those kinds of websites?"

"Are you sure the judge will think that way? I know she doesn't like me. Is there something we should do to make sure they don't get by with that?"

"Like what?"

"Well...I mean...just suppose we say...you know, just to be sure...that I delivered the laptop to you the first day I came in to see you and it's been in your office ever since? You know, we could say you hadn't looked at it until now."

He knew he needed to agree with her to assuage any doubts she might have but he also knew he needed to make it look like he needed convincing. "Oh, jeez, I don't know, that would mean me lying in court."

"Oh, honey, I know. I wouldn't ask but...but..." she dissolved into tears again, slowly regained her composure then continued. "Oh God...I'm so sorry to even ask. But I know them. I know they'll accuse me. And the judge, she doesn't believe anything I say. We have to make sure. Our future's at stake." Not certain an appeal to Nick's altruism was sufficient, she resorted to bribery. "I'd never ever forget it, if you could do this for me, Nicky."

"Jeez...it's a lot to ask. What about the pictures already printed out? How could I have not seen them before now?"

"I've thought of that..."

I'll bet you have, Nick thought.

"...and we'll just say you printed them out from the CD's... just in case the C.D.'s got damaged or something. What do you think?

"Well...yeah...maybe that would make sense..."

"Oh yes!" she exclaimed.

"But you'd have to swear to me...on your life..."

"What?"

"That this is between us. I could get disbarred. We both take this to our graves. Right?"

"Oh God, honey, of course. Of course, I swear. I swear on my life."

"Okay. All right. Get me that stuff."

"I'm on my way," she answered.

"Good," he replied.

"Nicky?"

"Yes?"

"I love you so much."

"I'm a lucky guy," he answered before hanging up.

***

He wanted, needed, to talk to Rosa about Livie's latest revelation but knew that was not possible. *I'm on my own on this one,* he told himself. Although not religious, he silently prayed, *Dear God, let this turn out okay. Please don't let anyone die because of my mistakes. Do anything you want to me after this is done, but please don't let anyone die because of me.*

He glanced at his watch; four-fifteen. If Stu caught him leaving at this hour, he'd catch hell, but so what? He was exhausted and frazzled. Today was Tuesday. He would figure out what to do tonight, then somehow get through tomorrow. Thursday they would go to court and he would betray his own client, maybe even cause her to go to jail. He'd get suspended or disbarred, he had little doubt of that. Sued too. But even knowing what was in store for him he could still manage a slight smile. It would be over, one way or another. And that thought was enough to put a smile on his face regardless of the consequences.

CHAPTER 33

He managed to sneak out of the office without being seen by Stu. He got home at four-thirty. Felix glanced up from the couch and acknowledged his homecoming but was otherwise uninterested until Nick headed for the kitchen. He was surprised that he was famished at such an early hour, but tension always seemed to give him a nervous appetite. He could tell from the tightness of his khakis that he'd put on more than a few pounds since Livie Taylor had come into his life. And all of it, every last ounce, had seemingly chosen his waistline as the place to congregate. Felix did figure eights through and around his legs as he bent over and searched the refrigerator. Nothing looked all that appetizing, but he didn't have the energy to go out. He finally mixed some Velveeta, a half-rotted piece of a green pepper, some salsa and a little onion with his last three eggs into an unappetizing looking omelet. He knew he'd have trouble sleeping tonight so he didn't make any coffee. He gulped down a forkful of the eggs with some orange juice. His first bite told him that the green pepper had looked as bad as it did because it likely had been culturing a cure for cancer on it. He picked out each piece of green pepper from the omelet and proceeded to finish the omelet and the orange juice.

God, he thought, *how wonderful it would have been on a night like this to come home to Rosa. To have a real meal with her. To talk about my day. To share my worries, my concerns. To make love. You reach a certain age and you think you're pretty sophisticated, pretty wise in the ways of the world. And then something like the last couple months happens and you realize you don't know shit. I guess what they say is true...you stop learning when you stop breathing. If only,* he thought, *the lessons didn't come at such a high tuition.* And the more he thought about it, the more he worried that he had not yet finished paying for this particular lesson.

The phone call at eleven thirty-two woke him up. He had fallen asleep once again in his recliner, Felix curled contentedly on his lap, the remote lying on the floor where it had fallen from his hand. He glanced up at the flickering image on his T.V. as he reached for the phone. A naked couple was lovelessly panto-miming making love on some Cinemax movie. He groped for the remote and rudely terminated the couples "loveless making," then grabbed his cell.

"Hello."

"Hi, honey, it's me," Livie began. "I'm sorry it's so late. I didn't wake you, did I? I couldn't sleep."

"No...no..." Nick lied, "I wasn't asleep yet."

"What's up?"

"Oh, Nicky," she continued, "I'm just so scared. Our whole future...our family's future...depends on what happens Thursday. I'm such a wreck. Could you come out here?"

"Now?"

"Please."

"We've talked about this," he demurred. "I can't. We can't. It's just too big a risk. We only have to get through Thursday and things will be different...everything will be different."

"Are you sure?" she pleaded. "Are you absolutely certain?"

"Livie," he replied, "I have never been more certain of any-thing in my life."

CHAPTER 34

On Thursday morning, Nick escorted Livinia Taylor to the third floor of the Martin County Courthouse. As they exited the elevator, he glanced at the people seated in the chairs lining the walls. Miranda Cox was seated a few chairs away in her brown pantsuit uniform. He smiled at her, but she did not acknowledge his greeting. He also saw two very distinguished looking older gentlemen in suits. They were clearly not lawyers and did not otherwise fit in with the usual courthouse crowd. He quickly concluded that they were Dr. Bowman and Dr. James. Daniel Taylor and Martha Taylor were seated in chairs at the far end of the hallway. Nick found the jury room empty and deposited Livie there.

As he exited the jury room, he was nearly run over by Cat Jagger. She was headed, at breakneck speed, from the elevator to the judge's chambers. She was laden down like an overburdened pack mule with two huge briefcases. Her short stature caused the huge briefcases to skim, barely, above the floor.

"Nick," she said curtly as she strode past him at full speed. Nick followed behind her then sprinted past her and opened the door. She did not thank him. They sat in the chairs in the hallway of the judge's chambers without exchanging a word. After what seemed like an eternity, the door to Judge Swanson's office opened and she emerged. "Carla," she barked to one of the clerks, "get Judge Harrington on the phone and let him know I can't cover for him in Effingham next Tuesday." She glanced at Nick and Cat and continued giving orders. "Counsel, in chambers please. We have a lot to cover." Nick followed Cat into Judge Swanson's private office and closed the door.

"Before we get started," Judge Swanson cautioned, "I have a few things I'd like to make clear."

"Judge, if I may..." Nick attempted to interject.

"No, Counsel, you may not. Not until I'm done. September 19 will make twelve years on the bench for me. I've done hundreds of divorces, tried many custody cases, but I will have to say I have never...never...seen a case deteriorate so rapidly to such depths of vitriol. I am not commenting on or prejudging the truth or falsity of either side's allegations. Dr. Taylor says, in so many words, that his wife is a psychotic narcissist capable of murdering her own child. Mrs. Taylor says Dr. Taylor is sexually abusing his own daughter. Dr. Taylor responds that Mrs. Taylor is herself guilty of horrific abuse in falsely planting these charges into an innocent little girl's mind. I can only say two things. First, whatever the truth or falsity of these allegations, God help Jessica Taylor. Second, God help any party or counsel or witness in this case if I conclude that someone has made allegations of this nature without good cause or for the purpose of harassment or strategy or...'getting even...' I will give counsel ten minutes to talk to their clients and witnesses and give them an opportunity to consider what I have just said. Each side will have an opportunity to dismiss the charges they have made without repercussions. But once we start...as I have stated... God help anyone who doesn't back up the dirt that's being hurled here. Do you both understand my position?"

"Yes, your Honor," Cat began, "and I can assure you, speaking for Dr. Taylor and our witnesses, we do understand the seriousness of the allegations that have been made and fully intend to prove each and every one of them as well as disprove these recent. revolting allegations that have been hurled at Dr. Taylor."

"Your Honor," Nick asked, "may I address a matter which

has just recently come to my attention and which I think might possibly alleviate the need for the next two days of trial?"

Judge Swanson, at the mention of the possibility of avoiding the upcoming trial, perked up. "You certainly may."

Nick reached down beside his chair, grabbed Dr. Taylor's laptop and placed it on the judge's desk. "Your Honor, for some time, Ms. Jagger has told me that her client, Dr. Taylor, was contending that Mrs. Taylor had Dr. Taylor's laptop computer. My client denied any knowledge of it. My client says that this week she was cleaning Dr. Taylor's office out at the former marital home when she discovered it hidden in a closet."

"Your Honor, where is this leading?..." Cat interrupted.

"Yes, Counsel," the Judge added, "get to the point."

"The point is, that supposedly Mrs. Taylor found Dr. Taylor's laptop hidden away."

"Judge," Cat said, "there's no law against hiding your computer. There are privileged medical records in there. This is all a little melodramatic..."

"Counsel..." the judge began.

"There is a law against child pornography," Nick continued.

He looked at both women. The color drained out of Cat's face as if a drain plug had been pulled. Judge Swanson, rarely at a loss for words, sat in open-mouthed astonishment.

"Judge, Ms. Jagger...if you can both just give me ten uninterrupted minutes to explain. I have to say I've struggled with this matter. I didn't know what to do. What I was supposed to do, ethically, and morally, but my partner, Rosa Thomas, helped me understand what I had to do."

The two women exchanged befuddled glances at each other, but, heeding his request, remained silent. Nick reached into his briefcase and retrieved some paperwork for Judge Swanson and an additional set for Cat.

"This is my affidavit detailing what I'm about to explain. When I first received Dr. James' report which cast severe doubt on the allegations of sexual abuse my client and Dr. Cox had made, I confronted my client with it. I told her the contents of Dr. James' report and she told me…"

"Counsel," Judge Swanson interrupted, "you're treading on thin ice. Are you about to reveal confidences of your client in breach of the attorney-client privilege? I must warn you that, if you do, no matter what your motivation, I'll be required to report your breach of ethics."

"I understand that, your Honor, but I've researched the issue and I believe a client's stated intent to commit a criminal act is not covered within the privilege…"

"I think that's true," Judge Swanson concurred.

"Anyway, when she heard Dr. James' report, my client advised me that Dr. Taylor would get custody of Jessica over her and Jessica's dead body."

Nick paused and looked at each of them. He could tell they were concerned but not necessarily shocked. Judge Swanson broke the silence, "Mr. Barnett, in the throes of a heated divorce people say things…"

"She was deadly serious, your Honor," he said then added after a brief pause, "and deadly capable of it. I know."

"How can you know?" Judge Swanson asked.

"Because," Nick answered, "when I gave her Dr. James' report she went into an absolutely psychotic rage. I have learned both through her psychiatric records and personal experience that she is very, very ill. I have gotten to know Mrs. Taylor very well…"

"Counsel, please. How well can you get to know a client?"

"Very well, your Honor," Nick interrupted. "Mrs. Taylor informed me during this same conversation last week that she is pregnant."

"Well," the judge replied, "that certainly doesn't help her defend against the adultery charge her husband has filed. But how does that go to you being able to know her so well?"

"Because," he answered, "she tells me I'm the father."

"Oh, fuck me!" Cat blurted out involuntarily before glancing at Judge Swanson and mumbling, "Sorry, your Honor!"

Judge Swanson gagged on the bottled water she was drinking. Her face turned ashen as she grabbed some tissue and dabbed at her mouth. Finally, she spoke.

"Counsel," Judge Swanson stated, "you have just acknowledged a very serious breach of the Cannons of Ethics. Do you understand the consequences of this admission?"

"I do."

"Then you understand that Ms. Jagger and I will both be required to report this conduct to the Attorney Disciplinary Committee for action including suspension or disbarment."

"You don't have to report me," Nick responded.

"I'm afraid we do," the judge retorted.

"Your Honor, I am filing here today a Motion to Withdraw as Mrs. Taylor's attorney. Also in this affidavit I've handed you is a full recitation of what I've just told you...and more. Also included is my letter to the Disciplinary Committee enclosing a copy of the affidavit. I'm reporting myself."

"Jesus Christ, Nick, I warned you about this woman," Cat responded.

"May I finish now, your Honor?" he asked, ignoring Cat's *I told you so.*

"You said there's more? You mentioned child pornography" she asked.

"Yes. Two days ago my client advised me that she had just so happened to find Dr. Taylor's laptop...like I said. She told me there were pictures and computer CD's full of child pornography. She brought it to me and I confirmed that there is..."

"Well," Cat interrupted, not being able to resist the urge to defend her client, "he's been out of the house since April. Who knows who's had access to it?"

"Cat, please," Nick urged, "let me finish. My client urged me to lie to the court. To swear that she had delivered the laptop to me in April before Dr. Taylor even left the house, just so no one could say she planted the stuff. I told her I would because I feared for Jessica's safety and hers and my unborn child if she thought she would lose custody. I have no doubt that Mrs. Taylor downloaded these images of child pornography within the last few days in an effort to portray Dr. Taylor as a pedophile.

In addition, your Honor, it has come to my attention that Mrs. Taylor brought Jessica to Dr. Cox's office on Tuesday the day before the video was made and Dr. Cox spent over two hours with Jessica on that day. It also turns out that Mrs. Taylor was previously a patient of Dr. Cox's. It appears likely that the two of them worked with Jessica that day to get her to accuse her own father. That was not revealed in her affidavit filed with this Court.

In summary, it is my belief that Dr. Taylor has been the victim of an intentional, false effort to portray him as a pedophile who is molesting his own child and is in possession of child porn. In addition, it's my belief that Jessica's safety would be in serious jeopardy if Mrs. Taylor knows she is going to lose custody. Everything I've just told you is in this affidavit," he concluded while holding the affidavit in his hand. "There."

Judge Swanson leaned back in her chair. "I want ten minutes to read your entire affidavit, Mr. Barnett. Then I want you and Ms. Jagger and Dr. Taylor back here in my chambers, on the record. In the interim, what was just discussed in this office stays in this office. Understood?"

"Perfectly," they both responded.

They exited Judge Swanson's private office. Cat Jagger made a beeline for the door to exit the judge's chambers, avoiding any eye contact with Nick.

Nick entered the jury room to check on Livie. She smiled. "What's going on, honey?" she asked. "Have you told Jagger about the computer yet?"

"No, not yet. We're just covering some legal b.s. with the judge. Evidence questions, you know. It'll just be a few more minutes. Then when I have Cat Jagger alone for a minute, I'll spring it on her."

"Oh, God, are you okay?"

"Me? Yeah, I'm fine. Where's Jessica?"

"She's with Maria."

"Maria?"

"My housekeeper. She takes care of Jessica sometimes too."

"They're both here though, in the courthouse, aren't they?"

"Yeah, sure. You told me the judge would want to talk to Jessica. They're in the library. You sure you're okay?"

He smiled and put his arm on her shoulder. "Yeah, fine. It'll all be over soon. I better get back."

"I love you," she said. She grabbed and placed his right hand on her abdomen then added, "We love you."

"Love you, too," he replied.

***

A few moments later the five of them, Cat Jagger, Dr. Taylor, Judge Swanson, the court reporter, Lori, and Nick were crowded in Judge Swanson's private office.

"Dr. Taylor," Judge Swanson began, "this is highly unusual to have only one party present, but I have been presented with a highly unusual situation."

Taylor glanced at Cat, obviously deeply concerned that the "unusual situation" was not welcome news.

"It has come to my attention just this morning," Judge Swanson continued, "that your wife has suborned perjury from her own attorney, that she was intending to offer manufactured and false evidence against you, in particular child pornography which was placed on your laptop computer."

"Good Lord," Taylor interjected.

"...further that she has communicated threats to kill Jessica if she loses custody..."

"Oh, Christ, no," Taylor blurted out, "I knew she was sick... but my God..."

"This information has come from your wife's attorney..."

Taylor stared at Nick in amazement.

"Mr. Barnett is withdrawing as of this moment as your wife's attorney. You should also be made aware that Mr. Barnett has acknowledged that he has been involved in a sexual relationship with your wife and she has advised him that she is pregnant with his child."

"God damn you," Taylor screamed. "I knew it, I knew it...I could see it in her eyes and the way she would touch you, you son of a...."

"DR. TAYLOR," Judge Swanson commanded, "control yourself or I will have the bailiff escort you out. What Mr. Barnett has acknowledged is a serious breach of rules governing attorney conduct and will be dealt with appropriately. I am more concerned about Jessica right now."

"I apologize, your Honor," Dr. Taylor said. "The strain has been unbearable and to hear all this..."

"I'm sorry," Nick interjected.

Dr. Taylor glared at Nick with more disbelief than rage. "You're sorry? Are you serious? You're telling me you're sorry? For ruining my life? For ruining Jessica's? Well, I'm sorry, too. I can't accept your apology, Mr. Barnett. You have no idea what you have done to me, and to Jessica. Who the hell gave you the right?"

"Dr. Taylor," Judge Swanson began, "I certainly understand your feelings, but my primary concern right now is Jessica. I have given this some thought. I intend to revoke all prior custody and visitation orders. I will, sua sponte, enter an order granting you full custody and reserving the question of visitation in Mrs. Taylor until she can be fully evaluated by Dr. James. She will be given twenty-one days to hire new counsel and we will go from there. Mr. Barnett?"

"Yes?"

"Where is Jessica?"

"She's in the library with a woman named Maria, the house-keeper."

"Fine, please take Judy, our bailiff, back there with you and have her bring Jessica here. I want to talk to her first, then we'll convene in open court and I will advise Mrs. Taylor of what has transpired and the orders that are being entered today. Judy can keep Jessica back here. I am also signing an order granting your Motion to Withdraw. It goes without saying that I would be removing you as Mrs. Taylor's counsel had you not acted to withdraw. As soon as you have Judy bring Jessica back here, you are released of all further association with this case, Mr. Barnett. Your actions, as you are no doubt aware, have been reprehensible and I will advise you here and now that I intend to write a personal letter to the appropriate authorities emphasizing the seriousness of your misconduct. You bear substantial responsibility that this case has deteriorated to the point it has and that Jessica was put at risk."

"I'm aware of that, your Honor," Nick replied, "and I am prepared to accept the consequences."

Nick found Judy in the hallway and walked back with her to the library. Maria and Jessica were seated at a table playing with a small collection of Duplos.

"Hi, Jessica, remember me?" Nick asked. Jessica cowered behind Maria. "She's a little shy with men," Maria explained through her thick Latino accent.

"I know," Nick replied. "Jessica, this is Judy. She has kids too. Right?"

"Oh, yeah," Judy added, "three".

"She needs to have you go with her to talk to another nice lady, okay?"

"Okay," Jessica finally replied meekly. She emerged from behind Maria and hesitantly took Judy's hand. They left the library.

"Well," Nick said to Maria, "I guess this thing is finally going to end."

"Si," Maria replied, crossing herself. "It has been such a strain on Senora Taylor. I worry about her. I maybe should not say this, but she has been drinking way too much."

"But surely she hasn't been drinking lately, has she? Not in her condition."

"What condition, Senor?" Maria asked.

"She hasn't told you?"

"About what?..."

Maria looked confused for a moment then suddenly realized what Nick was getting at. "Oh...oh...you mean you think Senora Taylor is pregnant?"

"Yes," he replied. "She showed me the pregnancy test thing. It was positive."

Maria backed away from Nick, comprehension, then apprehension in her eyes. "She tell you she pregnant?"

"Yes."

"And she tell you...you are the father?"

"Yes."

"Oh, Sweet Jesus in Heaven," she said crossing herself again. "Please, please Senor. I'm sorry I say anything. Please, you do not tell Senora Taylor? Please, it will mean my job."

"Don't worry, Maria. I won't say anything. But...what...you don't think she's pregnant?"

"I say too much already. Please do not ask me anything else," she begged.

Nick took a step towards her and grabbed her arms. "I need to know," he demanded. "I have a right to know."

The apprehension in Maria's face changed to fear. "Please, Senor"

"I won't tell a soul how I found out. Is she?"

"Senor, please...I'm just her maid..."

"Maria, please..."

"Well...it is not right to tell a man that if..." Maria stammered. "I don't know...how could I know?...But I know what I find in her bathroom trash can."

"She's having her period right now?" Nick asked.

"I just know what I find in the trash. Please, Senor, I told you, I'm just her maid."

"My God," Nick muttered, "she lied about that, too?" Nick let go of Maria but continued with his questions. "Maria, one more thing. This is very, very important. Do you know anything about this laptop of Dr. Taylor's that was just found?"

"Si," Maria replied, "I'm just so happy I find it and those awful pictures."

"What?" Nick asked, not sure he understood her.

"I'm just glad I find that computer with those awful pictures so Senora Taylor make sure she get custody. No man who have those pictures should have a child"

"You found them?"

"Si"

"When?"

"What...today is Thursday...Monday, I think..."

"Wait a minute," Nick interrupted, "are you saying Mrs. Taylor did not know where that computer was before last Monday?"

"I don't know Senor. But I find it, not her."

"And you found the pictures too?"

"Oh, si," she said as she crossed herself. "Oh...what pictures! You see them?"

"Yes, sure. Maria, please, this is very, very important. Are you telling me you don't think Mrs. Taylor ever had access to that computer, that she never saw those pictures before Monday?"

"I don't know. She ask me to clean out his study. I do. I find the pictures. I show her. That's all I know." She looked at Nick as if he had been out in the sun too long. "She was very upset. Screaming, crying when I show her."

"I gotta run," Nick blurted out and dashed to the jury room nearly knocking over Judge Swanson and the court reporter who were walking towards the courtroom.

"Judge, can I talk to you?" he asked.

"Counsel, we're convening in court right now," she replied.

"Please, can I just have a ten-minute delay? Please. I think maybe there were some mistakes."

"Mistakes?"

"Yes, Judge. I can't explain. I just need ten minutes with my client."

"Your client? Are you forgetting something? She's not your client anymore. I just signed an order granting your withdrawal. And, as I said, under the circumstances you have revealed this morning I would have ordered you removed as her counsel had you not withdrawn."

"Judge..." sweat was running down his forehead, "please... ten minutes..." He dashed ahead of the judge and opened the door to the jury room.

"She's already in the courtroom Mr. Barnett, I had Bill bring her in..."

"I have to talk to her...to you...there may have been some mistakes."

"Yes, there have been. Plenty of them," the judge replied, "and I don't want any more. If you do not control yourself I will call security to have you removed. Mr. Barnett, you are no longer part of this case. Likely you will not be an attorney for much longer. Do not come into that courtroom or I will have you arrested."

With that, she and Lori walked past him and entered the courtroom through the rear door. Nick stood in the hallway frozen, paralyzed. "All rise, Honorable Judge Leslie Jones Swanson presiding," he heard Bill announce. The door closed.

Nick stood in the hallway for another few minutes listening to the muffled sound of Judge Swanson's voice coming from the closed courtroom. Finally, he heard Livie shrieking and wailing...a sound he had heard before. A sound that would reverberate in his mind forever.

CHAPTER 35

Twenty-five minutes later Nick pulled into his office parking lot. He walked past Mona and grabbed the phone messages she handed to him without speaking a word.

"Nick?" Mona said.

He stopped and looked at her, "Yes?"

"Well?"

"Well what?"

"I just asked you. Didn't you hear me? The motions on Murphy? Should I file them?"

"What?"

"Murphy. The motions."

"Oh, yeah, sure. File 'em."

Mona gazed at him with concern. "Are you okay?"

"No, Mona. As a matter of fact, I'm not," he replied, then continued into his office. "Hold my calls," he added before shutting the door that separated their offices.

Nick took off his suit coat, hung it up, unbuttoned and rolled up his sleeves and loosened his tie. He sat down and leaned back. *My God,* he asked himself, *was it all true? Is Daniel Taylor really a child molester? Are Livie and Dr. Cox right? Was that child porn his? Or was it what I originally thought? Did she instruct Maria to clean out the office knowing she'd find the laptop and pictures? Why would she have asked me to lie to the court about having the computer if she hadn't set it all up? Or did she frame an already guilty man? What have I done? My God, what's the truth and what's a lie?*

His hands were still shaking as he began drafting a letter to Judge Swanson. If he told her everything, surely she would act on it, he thought. She'd have a hearing. Get to the bottom of it. She had been emphatic in expressing her intention to protect Jessica.

He was halfway through the third handwritten page when his office door burst open. Livie Taylor stood in front of him. Her face was purple with rage. Her streaked mascara and the undisguised vitriol evident in her face overwhelmed her beauty and made her appear as if she was some otherworldly demon, straight from the seventh level of Hades.

"Livie," Nick said.

His other office door leading to Mona's office opened. "Nick," Mona said, "she barged right in. I'm sorry. I told her..."

"Get the fuck out!" Livie screeched at Mona.

Mona, terrified, glanced at Nick. "It's okay. Leave us alone," he instructed.

Mona breathed an involuntary sigh of relief. "Okay. Buzz me if you need me."

"Sure."

Livie closed the other door behind her and walked up to Nick's desk. She was breathing slowly and heavily.

"Why?" she finally asked.

"Look, there's no point..."

"Oh, yes," she interrupted, "there is a point. I want to know. That's the fucking point. I want to know why my own lawyer betrayed me. Not only my lawyer but a man I gave myself to. A man I thought I loved. A man I thought loved me and Jessica. And," she added, touching her belly, "our baby. And the Supreme Court's going to want to know when you're disbarred. Your malpractice insurance company is going to want to know when I sue you...even that's too good for you. I should...I should...I guarantee you will never ever see this baby," she added patting her belly again. "How much did Martha pay you? What did it take for you to turn a little girl over to a pervert? A million? Two million?"

"No one paid me anything," Nick replied. "I did what I thought I had to do. I...I thought you planted that stuff on his computer...I thought you made it all up about him molesting her. Dr. James and Dr. Bowman thought so too. You told me you'd kill her if you lost custody. I thought you were going to kill yourself and Jessica when you lost custody. I had to do something. They've been so many lies. So many lies. I still don't know what the truth is. Are you pregnant? Did you put that stuff on his computer? My God, Livie."

She rose from her chair. "Here's the truth. I am pregnant with your child and Daniel Taylor is a child molester. You have killed my little girl...worse than that even...and here's something else I know for a fact: I will never ever let you forget what you've done to me. I swear to God, Nick Barnett, every single day the rest of your life, you'll think about me and you'll regret the day I walked into your office." With that, she turned, stormed out of his office and slammed the door.

"I already do," Nick said aloud to his empty office.

As Livie exited Nick's office she passed Stu in the hallway. Stu smiled, nodded and added, "Mrs. Taylor." Livie stopped, looked Stu in the eyes then replied, "Fuck you and fuck your God damn law firm," before barging out the front door.

A moment later Stuart Ford stood in front of Nick in Nick's office. "Nick," he stammered, "what the hell? Mrs. Taylor just told me and the firm to fuck off. What's going on?"

Nick paused in the writing of his letter to Judge Swanson and looked up at Stu. "I'll be gone by Saturday," he said.

"Gone? Gone where?"

"I don't know yet. Just gone from here."

Stu sat down. "Tell me. What's going on?"

Nick put his pen down and leaned back in his chair "You want to know what's going on? Okay, here's the Reader's Digest condensed version. You'll have to wait for my disbarment opinion to get the unedited version. I thought she was going to kill herself and Jessica if she lost custody. I thought she had manufactured all this crap about her husband molesting Jessica. I thought she planted false evidence on his laptop to frame him. She asked me to lie about it, to commit perjury. She said she was pregnant. I couldn't let her get custody of Jessica. So I told the judge and Cat Jagger everything..."

"Jesus," Stu interrupted, "what about the privilege?"

Nick continued, ignoring Stu's interruption "...so they gave Jessica to Dr. Taylor and Livie was denied visitation. Only now, now I'm not so sure she planted that evidence at all and...I don't think she's pregnant and I don't know. There have been so many lies. I don't know anything anymore...maybe he was molesting her...maybe she is pregnant."

"Oh, for Christ's sake, Nick. God damn. You fucked up big time. Why the hell didn't you talk to me? Jesus, we'll get sued. There's going to be consequences. Real consequences and..."

"I'm not through."

"What?"

"If she is pregnant..."

"What about it?"

"I'm the father."

Nick watched Stu as the little color left in his face drained. Stu pointed his finger, shaking with rage, at Nick. He tried to talk but, momentarily, was unable to. His jaw moved up and down but no sound emanated from it. His face and his bald head turned scarlet red.

Finally, Stu was able to succinctly verbalize the myriad thoughts swirling in his head, "Get the fuck out of this office... and never come back."

***

Nick glanced at his watch, eight twenty-three p.m. He was the only one in the office and that's just how he wanted it. He'd promised he'd have his office cleared out by Saturday. It was Friday night and he was filling the last of the cardboard boxes. He wanted to clean his office out in the evening, alone. There would be no explanations to offer, no tears to shed, if, in fact, his leaving the office and the practice of law would have merited tears from anyone.

Stu and Larry had both promised Nick that there would be hell to pay. That he would have to sue them to get a nickel for his partnership equity and that if Livie Taylor sued the firm or them for what Nick had done, they would counter-sue Nick. Nick assured them first, that they could have their partnership and that he would not sue them, and second, that Livie Taylor most certainly would sue them. His assurances did not improve their moods any.

As he was packing the last of the boxes he heard a car pull into the office lot then heard the back door of the office open. He stepped into the hall and saw Rosa, dressed in jeans and a tee-shirt, and carrying a small box.

"Hi," he said.

She returned his "hi" and entered her own office. He followed. She was placing a few of her personal things from her desk in the box.

"Rosa," he said, "you don't have to. Haven't you heard?"

"Don't have to what?" she asked without stopping her packing. "And heard what?"

"You don't have to quit. You don't have to leave. I've already resigned from the firm. I won't even be a lawyer much longer. I'm going to surrender my license. I'll be gone tomorrow. You don't have to leave."

"You think I'm leaving...because of you?"

"Well...I don't know...I just thought..."

Rosa stopped her packing and walked to the front of her

desk and sat down on it to face him. Nick sat facing her in a client chair. "Remember my mom's little sister, my Aunt Edna... you met her at the visitation. Short, gray hair, stocky. Married to that obnoxious little man...Henry..."

"Not really..."

"Well, they live in Orlando. Henry's a big wig with Disney. Edna's my mom's only sister. They lost their brother in a car wreck when he was seventeen. Anyway, my mom's been lost since my dad died. She wants to move there to be close to Edna. I'm taking a sabbatical. I'm going down there with her. Help her get situated. I may be gone a month or two or three or maybe I'll never come back. I don't know. I know I need some time off right now. I wouldn't be any good to my clients right now anyway. I hate leaving Stu and Larry in such a mess, but I don't have a choice. When I come back, maybe I should say if I come back, I'll figure out what comes next. But there's a silver lining to every cloud, isn't there? I always wanted to go to Disney World, since I was a little kid. But my dad thought it was frivolous. We used to tour civil war battlefields for vacations. I could tell you anything you want to know about Bull Run." She chuckled slightly as she reminisced. "So, anyway, Henry has promised to give us the V.I.P. tour of the whole place. Ever been there?"

"Yeah, I have. Matter of fact, Sheila and Natalie and I went there once, stayed at a resort called 'The Beach Club'...it was nice...we had a good time." As he continued to reminisce, his eyes misted, "...the pool...the pool has a real sand bottom...can you believe it...real sand...Natalie was only about four...it was a long time ago...a long time..." The tears accelerated as he looked into Rosa's eyes. "Oh God, Rosa, I'm sorry. I'm so awfully sorry."

Rosa averted his eyes until his tears stopped. "Here, I was going to leave this on your desk," she said handing him an envelope. "You might want it. I don't."

"What is it?"

"It's a letter from Livie Taylor to me. She left it with Betty for me. I only read the first paragraph...that was enough...too pornographic for my tastes."

Now it was Rosa's turn to have her eyes mist over. "By the way, did you really tell her she was...let's see how did she put it? Oh yeah 'the best lover, by far, you'd ever had'...I...I was just wondering because I thought what we had was kinda special. I just thought maybe, for future reference, I should know what I was doing wrong."

"For God's sake," Nick moaned, "you didn't do anything wrong. Don't talk like that. I said I'm sorry. And, look, for what it's worth, I'm pretty sure she lied about being pregnant."

"Yeah, you did apologize. Everyone knows you're sorry. Trouble is, sorry doesn't do anything. Sorry doesn't change anything. And if she's not pregnant by you, it's not for lack of trying, is it Nick?"

Nick did not reply.

Rosa continued. "Who knows anything anymore? Is she pregnant? Did she plant that stuff on his computer? Is he molesting the little girl? What's the truth and what's a lie? I guess that's why we have an adversary system, Nick. Maybe you should have trusted more in the system. You do your job and Cat Jagger does hers and you hope the system figures it out right."

"I thought I was doing the right thing."

"Did you? Does that apply to you fucking her too?"

Nick flinched at the remark but again remained silent.

"So," she added as she finished packing her box, "what are your plans?"

"I'm not sure. I'm thinking of going to Champaign. My cousin is sales manager for the Honda dealer there. He always told me if I ever got sick of being a parasite on society, I should try selling cars. I don't know shit about cars but I may take him up on his offer. I'd like to try dealing with people during a happy time in their lives. Besides, I need to start making some money. Sheila's already let me know there's no way in hell she'll agree to reduce child support." He smiled slightly then added, "and God knows I can't afford a lawyer to fight her."

"What about Natalie?"

"It's going to be tough on her. I already told her most of what's happened. I didn't want her to hear it through the grapevine. She's hurt. Embarrassed. I think she just needs some time. Maybe if I go to Champaign I can convince her to go to college there in a few years. It might give us some time together to heal."

"I hope so," Rosa added.

"Yeah, well I better let you go," he extended his hand.

She took it and shook it lightly then added, "Nick?"

"Yes?"

"Remember Mr. Cole?"

"Who?"

"The client that was on the phone with me when we...you know...had our little accident...when we tumbled off the bed."

"Oh yeah, sure."

"You know, the next time I talked to him I started to stammer an apology and he interrupted me and...and he said 'Don't apologize. I heard you and your boyfriend laughing. I figured out what was going on. I was in love once, too.' And, you know, it made me think...when we were lying there on the floor naked, laughing hysterically, I really felt it. Like I never had before. I never felt closer to another human being in my life. Like we were sharing something that in the history of the universe only the two of us, you and me, could have ever shared. And I thought, at that moment, that I really knew you and I thought that I loved you."

"I thought I loved you too, Rosa," Nick replied.

She picked up her box and walked to the door. She reached the door, paused and turned to face him. "Turn the lights out and lock up when you leave, please."

"Sure."

She started to turn to leave, then stopped and turned back to face him, "You know what?"

"What?"

"I was wrong," she said before turning back around and leaving.

He leaned against her desk. In a minute he heard her car start. "I wasn't," he said aloud to no one. "I wasn't," he repeated quietly.

EPILOGUE

Jessica Taylor, 18, sat in the college psychologist's office crying softly. Dr. Sanders, 62, PhD., mother of four and grandmother of nine, smiled warmly and inquired, "What brings you here, Jessica? What can I do to help?"

Jessica replied, "I don't know if you or anyone can help me."

"I'd like to try. What is it about?"

"It's …everything…my entire childhood. My parents. My entire life. Where do I begin?"

"Begin at the beginning. And know you're safe here."

Through her tears, Jessica answered "Thank you Dr. Sanders. Okay…" And she began.